PRE-ACTION DISCOVERY

AUSTRALIA AND NEW ZEALAND
The Law Book Company Ltd.
Sydney : Melbourne : Perth

CANADA AND U.S.A.
The Carswell Company Ltd.
Agincourt, Ontario

INDIA
N.M. Tripathi Private Ltd.
Bombay
and
Eastern Law House Private Ltd.
Calcutta and Delhi
M.P.P. House
Bangalore

ISRAEL
Steimatzky's Agency Ltd.
Jerusalem : Tel Aviv : Haifa

PAKISTAN
Pakistan Law House
Karachi

PRE-ACTION DISCOVERY

D.G. FLETCHER ROGERS
Barrister with Walker Martineau Stringer Saul
Associate Chartered Institute of Patent Agents

LONDON   SWEET & MAXWELL   1991

Published in 1991 by
Sweet & Maxwell Limited
183, Marsh Wall, London
Computerset by Promenade Graphics Limited
Cheltenham
Printed in Great Britain by
Butler and Tanner Limited, Frome, Somerset

British Library Cataloguing in Publication Data
Rogers, David Fletcher
Pre-action discovery
1. England. Civil Law. Cases. Documents.
Discovery and inspection. Law
I. Title
344.20772

ISBN 0–421–40180–X

To the Team

Ellis Evans
Jurgen Geib
Rosalyn Pulfer
Roy Pollard

Preface

In recent years the custom of commencing a civil action by writ or summons has changed so that in certain, though comparatively few circumstances, actions are started before issue of a writ, and indeed start with an action relating to the evidence which is ancillary to the substantive action as well as for restraining movement of assets. There are several reasons for this approach—it may be cheaper in an accident case if the injured party can see the medical evidence first to assess the strength of his claim, for indeed he might decide he has not got one. Thus a "fishing expedition" is given statutory respectability.

The modern actions of this nature have an ancient common law lineage so that the ancient action for discovery, thought to have died with the passing of the Judicature Act 1873, has been revived by the *Norwich Pharmacal* decision. The Anton Piller order is founded on a precedent of 1821 which itself derives from an old authority, and as for the Mareva order or injunction, this was in use during the Roman occupation by the merchants of London and also in Tudor times.

Whilst some of the old forms have attracted the names of the new authorities which resurrected them, the right to prevent a person taking himself and his assets out of the jurisdiction has maintained its old name of *ne exeat regno*. That our legal system permits old remedies to be revised to suit the issues of today is a compliment to it, as well as to the ingenuity and skill of counsel.

The "new" law as dealt with in this work has largely come into use in the last 16 years. It has been quickly developed. This process has not been without its problems—the comparatively few reports on Marevas and Anton Pillers give about a dozen instances where the court has criticised and penalised the lawyers.

Scott J. in *Manor Electronics* v. *Dickson* suggests that these matters (in this case an Anton Piller order) should be left to specialists, but this cannot be right. A deserted wife from the counties should not need to engage a City firm with specialist counsel to stop her husband making away with the family savings. Such matters should be, and in many cases will be, within the competence of local solicitors with a matrimonial practice who can brief counsel from a provincial Bar. Indeed matrimonial practitioners are so used to dealing with *ex parte* injunctions concerning domestic disputes that this aspect of the law is only dealt with here in respect of Anton Piller and Mareva orders.

I have found of great help *The Mareva Injunction and Anton Piller Order* by Richard Ough, a Barrister of Leeds and *Due Process of the Law* by Lord Denning. Some of the written work is by two members of the Bar, Mrs. Helen and Miss Karen (Mary Anne) Fletcher Rogers, and one is indeed grateful for their help and guidance. I am also very grateful to all the staff of Sweet & Maxwell who have been so patient and helpful. Any mistakes in this book are entirely my own.

Some of the precedents in this work have been provided by the Chancery Division of the Royal Court of Justice, the others have been used in cases.

I am grateful to Stephen Aldred of Clifford Chance for letting me have on "permanent loan" some important books, also to Ms Stephanie Cheung of Cheung, Tong & Rosa, Solicitors in Hong Kong for information on this subject in which she is peculiarly skilled. The Company Secretary and Director of Kodak Ltd. has also kindly allowed me to use her department's law library for which one is grateful, and Ms C. Winterton of Gray's Inn Library has gone out of her way to be helpful in digging out some of the more obscure authorities.

Importantly, one must remember with thanks and gratitude Mrs. Maureen Phillips and Mrs Tina Fountain who have turned my scrawl into typeface via the word processor.

Lastly, I am glad to recall the help and encouragement of the partners of Walker Martineau Stringer Saul, London.

D.G. Fletcher Rogers
July 1990

CONTENTS

TABLE OF CASES

All page references in bold refer to where the case is set out more fully in the Appendix

TABLE OF STATUTES

TABLE OF RULES

1 INTRODUCTION

General

Discovery is the name given to the process in litigation whereby the parties disclose to each other evidence which is in their possession or under their control. The evidence, such as documents or other material, must be relevant to the issues in the action, and is required to be produced as a matter of law, save for those items which are privileged from disclosure. Failure to disclose, following an order of the court, is contempt of court.

Discoverable items
Discovery includes any relevant documents but in addition can include other things such as parts of machinery, chemicals, computer programs and their output. Tape recordings of evidence or other such information are documents.[1] The process of discovery will be, from time to time, referred to as "discovery of documents," but this term is used to include discovery of anything which is, in law, discoverable.

In the usual litigation process, discovery follows a well-established pattern, and there is generally no difficulty with each party disclosing the necessary documents. In the normal course of events, discovery is taken after the action has commenced and the pleadings exchanged. However, this process of discovery has been found to be inadequate in certain circumstances, and this has impeded litigation to such a marked degree that both the legislature and the courts have found it necessary to evolve procedures whereby discovery may be obtained prior to a substantive action being commenced.

Orders of a discovery nature
In addition to discovery in the sense of requiring evidence to be produced, orders of a discovery nature can be obtained. These are, for example, orders requiring that property or goods be delivered up, and that persons having them in their possession be restrained from dealing with them; assets may be frozen, or placed under a preservation order. Such orders are obtained by the injunction process and are available before or after the substantive action which concerns them has commenced. There are thus two

Two types of discovery cases
types of case for discovery: cases to obtain evidence, and injunctive cases requiring things to be done or goods to be delivered up.

The word "cases" is used to describe what in reality are actions against someone, but actions relating to property or evidence which are ancillary to substantive actions. All these cases may take place before the substantive action to which they relate has commenced, or, in some instances during the course of such action. The most common situations which give rise to the necessity for these procedures are listed below.

Orders relating to cases concerning property The potential plaintiff may be unable to conduct his action properly without

[1] *Grant* v. *Southwestern and County Properties* [1975] Ch. 185.

Preservation of property   the property being inspected or photographed. Also, there may be circumstances where the property might be altered or destroyed before the action commences. In these circumstances, orders can be made for the preservation of the property.

Early sight of documents   **Orders concerning documents in death or injury**   In many death or injury cases, a person wishing to bring a claim needs to obtain sight of relevant documents early on, to be in a position to assess the strength of any claim.

Innocent involvement   **Orders concerning documents in cases other than death or injury**   These may arise when a person has reason to believe that another person or body such as a public authority has information which, if available to the first-mentioned person, will enable him to bring a claim against another. As a general rule of law, no independent action for discovery will lie against a person against whom no cause of action can be alleged, or who is in the position of a mere witness in the strict sense. There are exceptions to the general rule, and an action lies in cases where the person against whom discovery is sought has himself been involved, albeit innocently, in facilitating the wrongdoing.

Counterfeit goods   **Orders concerning cases in which the evidence might be destroyed or hidden**   These arise most commonly in actions concerning counterfeit goods, but they are also used in many other instances; for example, matrimonial disputes concerning financial matters.

The above matters relate to evidence. In addition, there are two orders available which supplement the pre-action discovery orders.

Mareva injunction   **Orders relating to preservation of assets**   A defendant who is likely to destroy evidence is also likely to dispose of assets and thus defeat the remedy granted to a successful plaintiff when claiming damages. An order freezing the defendant's assets is of great value in such a case and may be granted. However, the burden of proving the necessity or appropriateness of such an order, known as a Mareva injunction, is relatively high.

Order of arrest   **Orders relating to restraint on persons**   Defendants who are likely to destroy evidence might also be prepared to abscond from the jurisdiction to avoid a plaintiff succeeding in his claim, and an order of arrest can be obtained for a short time pending suitable undertakings being given. The order can also extend to a requirement for the surrender of a defendant's passport. These orders require the plaintiff to prove the necessity or appropriateness of the order and the burden of proof is very high. The order of arrest is obtained by a writ known as *Ne exeat regno*.

Application

In pre-action discovery cases, applications may be made *inter partes* or *ex parte* according to the circumstances of each case.

Inter partes: orders including injunction   These will arise when there is no risk of the subject-matter of the action being destroyed and there is time to warn and, indeed, include in the action, the person having possession of evidence. The action will be necessary in order to establish whether there is a substantive case.

Risk of loss or destruction

Ex parte: orders including injunction   These will arise where there is risk of the subject-matter or assets being destroyed or lost if the person against whom one is proceeding has forewarning of what is likely to happen. The *ex parte* order is one which, but for the above risk, would otherwise be applied for *inter partes*. In addition, an *ex parte* order may be sought in cases of emergency, when it is not practicable, owing to the circumstances of the case, to give notice to the other side.

"Fishing expedition"

In *inter partes* and *ex parte* applications, as dealt with in this work, the orders sought will be of an interlocutory nature save in the case of those orders which are sought to ascertain whether a substantive action should follow. As this is a form of "fishing expedition," application for such orders must be supported by very persuasive evidence. Thus pre-action discovery arises in cases when an order relating to evidence is required before the commencement of the substantive action, examples being where it is necessary to obtain medical records to assess the strength of a personal injury case, and if that case is strong, whom one should pursue; or, to obtain evidence from a third party to ascertain the nature and status of a defendant.

Preservation order   This order may be sought to prevent the destruction of evidence or property which is the subject-matter of a later action, or to prevent disposal of assets which, if it occurred, would prevent a successful plaintiff enjoying the benefit from the main action.

It will be noted that each of the matters mentioned has the common characteristic that the order or remedies sought precede the commencement of a substantive action. It is the substantive action which gives rise to the need for these actions.

History of the action for discovery

The action for discovery goes back to the time of Henry VI[2] and this system was regularly used until just over a century ago. Today it gives a remedy after almost a century of disuse. The courts of equity, that is the chancery and exchequer courts, had evolved the action for discovery of deeds and documents by which a person could be compelled to produce relevant documents in his possession. The common law courts did not have, save in a limited sense, a discovery process. If discovery was necessary, cases at common law were adjourned until parties had obtained their bill of discovery, that is, an order for discovery in a court of equity.

Bill of discovery

By the Evidence Act of 1851 and the Common Law Procedure Act of 1854, powers were conferred on all the courts,

[2] (Sp.Eq.Jur. 1 678).

both common law and equity, to order discovery, and thus it seemed that the action for discovery was no longer required. The underlying purpose of these two Acts, as well as the Judicature Acts which followed, is now effected by the Rules of the Supreme Court and the Supreme Court Act 1981 which generally govern the process of discovery in all divisions of the High Court.

The Judicature Act 1873

Regulation of discovery

Action for discovery obsolete

This Act further enlarged and regulated the practice of discovery in the High Court, and rules and orders concerning discovery made thereby. Where no provision is made under the Act, its predecessors and following Acts or under the Rules of Court, the old law in substance remains, although the procedures have changed. The effect of the 1873 Act was to eliminate in most cases the necessity for the action for the bill of discovery, for general discovery could be obtained, as is the practice today, by following the system laid down in the Rules of the Supreme Court.[3] Since every division of the High Court of Justice possessed equal powers to compel discovery in proceedings before it, the action for discovery appeared not to be required. Between 1873 and 1972 there were only six reported cases for pre-action discovery against non-parties.[4] However, the action still exists and has recently become of importance.

The Judicature Act 1925

Continuation of former practices

The Judicature Act 1925 was both a consolidating statute and a reformatory one which repealed the Judicature Acts of 1873 and 1875. It contained an express provision in section 103 for the continuation of the former practice and procedures.

Old cases not binding

The Supreme Court Act 1981 uses the English language more in keeping with its time, but one of its purposes is to consolidate the 1925 Act with other amendments. Though many of the provisions of the SCA 1981 are of the same effect as that of the 1925 Act, the wording is different and there will be room for argument on occasions that some of the pre-1981 authorities, which relate to interpretation of wording, are no longer binding on the court. As the Act provides for the administration of civil justice, there is continuity of practice, and it is the intention that the SCA 1981 is better suited to the final years of this century than its predecessors.

Jackson* v. *Litchfield

The SCA 1981 is still governed by the law as pronounced in *Jackson* v. *Litchfield*:[5]

"In all cases at common law, which are not provided for by the Judicature Acts[6] the proceedings are to be as they were before these Acts, and in all cases within the Judicature Acts, where no special steps in proceedings are provided, the

---

[3] See *The Supreme Court Practice 1991.*
[4] *Orr* v. *Diaper* [1876] 4 Ch.D. 92; *Reiner* v. *Salisbury* [1876] 2 Ch.D. 378; *Dreyfus* v. *Peruvian Guano Co.* [1889] 41 Ch.D. 151; *Ainsworth* v. *Starkie* [1876] W.N. 8; and two overseas authorities, *Post* v. *Toledo Cincinnati & St. Louis Railroad Co.* [1887] 11 N.E. 540; and *Colonial Government* v. *Tatham* [1902] 23 N.L.R. 153.
[5] [1882] 8 Q.B.D. 474.
[6] The court had in mind the Judicature Acts of 1873 and 1875.

proceedings are to be as nearly like as they can be to analogous proceedings before these Acts."[7]

The effect of this authority is that the statutory forms of administration will govern a particular process, but if there is a situation for which no provision is made, then one falls back on the law as it was prior to the Judicature Act 1873, but adapts the situation so as to comply with the present-day practice of the court.

Lyell v. Kennedy   Regard should be had to *Lyell* v. *Kennedy*[8] to ascertain the powers exercised by the old equity courts and the principles which they applied in relation to discovery generally, and also how it was affected by the Judicature Acts 1873 and 1875. These powers have been carried on and in some measure increased through sections 33 to 35 of the SCA 1981.

[7] *Per* Brett L.J. at p. 477.
[8] [1883] 8 App.Cas. 217.

2 ORDERS PRECEDING PROPERTY ACTIONS

Supreme Court Act 1981, s.33(1)

Section 33(1) of the Supreme Court Act 1981 (SCA 1981) provides:

"(1) On the application of any person in accordance with rules of court, the High Court shall, in such circumstances as may be specified in the rules, have power to make an order providing for any one or more of the following matters, that is to say—

(a) the inspection, photographing, preservation, custody and detention of property which appears to the court to be property which may become the subject-matter of subsequent proceedings in the High Court, or as to which any question may arise in any such proceedings; and

(b) the taking of samples of any such property as is mentioned in paragraph (a), and the carrying out of any experiment on or with any such property."

Person interested or affected **"Any person"** This means a person who has an interest in the property whether as owner or claimant, or is acting on behalf of such a person, and in addition can mean a person who is in some way affected by the property, an example being a landowner who has the right of support from a wall or building which does not belong to him. The category of persons who may apply is limited only in the sense that there must be some connection between them and the property which is the subject of the application for an order.

"Rules of court" This refers to the Rules of the Supreme Court 1965 (as amended).

Subject-matter of proceedings **"Property"** This includes any land, chattel or other corporeal property of any description. The property must be such as may become the subject-matter of subsequent proceedings, or concern any question which may arise in the proceedings.

Examinable items **"Inspection"** This may include the examination of parts of machinery, or moulds for appropriate parts in a trademark infringement or passing off action, so as to ascertain if they have the plaintiff's marks thereon, as well as relevant commercial retail items such as stock in trade. Inspection does not include methods of manufacture as this is not property.[1] Inspection also includes examining electronic tapes and the like using the appropriate

---

[1] *Tudor Accumulator Co.* v. *China Mutual Co.* (1930) W.N. 201.

machinery, such as computer software and output.[2] Microfilms of records are "books" for this purpose under the Bankers' Books Evidence Act 1879.[3] Inspection can refer to the condition of things; for example, a wall which is due to be demolished, and the necessity for inspection may arise in cases of trespass.[4] The inspection can be by a surveyor or other experts.[5]

"Photographing"   An order to permit photographing is suitable in those cases where property, such as a wall, is due to be destroyed or is likely to deteriorate, or is in the possession of an opponent or third party,[6] and the state of it needs to be recorded.

"Preservation, custody and detention"   An example is afforded in the case where parts for machinery must be preserved as evidence for an action and there is serious risk, if they are not taken into custody or a preservation order is not granted, that they will be destroyed or otherwise disposed of. The order,
Covers any property however, can comprise any property, not just that which is likely to be destroyed, lost or otherwise disposed of. Thus, in an action to recover jewellery where the defendant alleged that the jewellery had been deposited with him by a third party to secure a debt, the court ordered the jewellery to be delivered to the court for preservation.[7] An order for preventing a wall from being demolished would be by way of injunction under section 37(1) and (2) SCA 1981 and is not in the nature of pre-action discovery or preservation of evidence.

"Subsequent proceedings"   Under this section, the proceedings in respect of the property will not have commenced.

"Taking of samples"   If the court considers it necessary or expedient for the purpose of obtaining full information or evidence, the court may, on the application of a party to the case (*i.e.* plaintiff, defendant or other party) and on such terms as it thinks fit, order, authorise or require any sample to be taken of any property which is the subject-matter of the case or upon which any question may arise. An order for samples may be given
Comparison or analysis of products if it is necessary to compare the defendants' products with another's in order to compare their quality. Similarly, an order may be made for experiments to be made on samples, such as the analysis of a product to ascertain its composition.
Applies to all classes of action Section 33(1) of the SCA 1981 (which is derived from section 21(1) of the Administration of Justice Act 1969 and 1970) applies to all classes of action. It is of importance in situations whereby the plaintiff's case cannot be properly conducted without an order in respect of all or any of the matters referred to therein, being granted in respect of property. It is particularly important in circumstances where the property might be altered before action is commenced or the trial concerning it takes place.
The effect of this provision, in addition to ensuring that

[2] *Grant* v. *Southwestern and County Properties* [1975] Ch. 185 at p. 198.
[3] *Barker* v. *Wilson* [1980] 1 W.L.R. 884.
[4] *Wales Co.* v. *Brancher* [1864] 12 W.R. 570 at p. 595.
[5] *Colls* v. *Home and Colonial Stores Ltd.* [1904] A.C. 179.
[6] *Lewis* v. *Earl of Londesborough* [1893] 2 Q.B. 191.
[7] *Velati* v. *Braham* (1897) 46 L.J.C.P. 415.

Acceleration of legal process

certain things are done (such as tests concerning the property under an order) can be to speed up the litigation process by permitting the parties to obtain information well before trial, which may in turn lead to early settlement of the action. It also helps a party when litigating against an opponent who practises or is likely to practise delaying tactics, though delay can still, nevertheless, be lengthy. In a case[8] in the Chancery Division in which the plaintiff sought delivery up and inspection by way of experiment on parts, it took a year to achieve this with first a request by letter, followed by summons to the Master and appeal to the judge before the defendant produced the parts. The defendant lost in both hearings. Whilst the application was not under section 33(1), if it had been, the delay could have been the same or even longer.

Section 33(1) of the SCA 1981 only applies to pre-action inspection and other matters relating to property.[9] The High Court has power under Order 29, rules 2 and 3 to make similar orders in relation to property which is the subject of existing proceedings.

Application for an order

Applications for orders in relation to property are made by originating summons.[10] Order 29, rule 7A provides:

Order 29, r. 7A

"(1) An application for an order under section 33(1) of the Act in respect of property which may become the subject-matter of subsequent proceedings in the High Court or as to which any question may arise in any such proceedings shall be made by originating summons and the person against whom the order is sought shall be made defendant to the summons.

(2) An application after the commencement of proceedings for an order under section 34(3) of the Act in respect of property which is not the property of, or in the possession of, any party to the proceedings shall be made by summons, which must be served on the person against whom the order is sought and on every party to the proceedings other than the applicant.

(3) A summons under paragraph (a) or (b) shall be supported by affidavit which must specify or describe the property in respect of which the order is sought and show, if practicable, by reference to any pleading served or intended to be served in the proceedings or subsequent proceedings, that it is property which is or may become the subject-matter of the proceedings or as to which any question arises or may arise in the proceedings.

(4) A copy of the supporting affidavit shall be served with the summons on every person on whom the summons is required to be served.

(5) An order made under the said section 33(1) or 34(3) may

---

[8] *Dunlop* v. *Staravia (No. 2)* (1988) (unrep.).
[9] SCA 1981, s.33(1) in its application to the Crown is limited to property involved in an action for death or personal injuries: SCA 1981, s.35/4.
[10] O. 29, r. 7A(1).

be made conditional on the applicant's giving security for the costs of the person against whom it is made or on such other terms, if any, as the Court thinks just.

(6) No such order shall be made if it appears to the Court:

  (a) that compliance with the order, if made, would result in the disclosure of information relating to a secret process, discovery or invention not in issue in the proceedings; and

  (b) that the application would have been refused on that ground if:

    (i) in the case of a summons under paragraph (1) the subsequent proceedings had already been begun; or

    (ii) in the case of a summons under paragraph (2) the person against whom the order is sought were a party to the proceedings."

"Shall be made defendant"   The person against whom the order is sought in respect of any of the matters set out in section 33(1)(*a*) and (*b*) SCA 1981 is, or will become, a defendant to the originating summons. If the property belongs to, or is in the possession of, someone who is not a defendant, an order can only be obtained under section 34(3), SCA 1981 after the commencement of proceedings. If the property is in the possession of a bailee of the defendant, the order against the defendant will instruct him to bring about the accomplishment of the order. If a third party is holding the property as security, he will have an interest in it and can be made a defendant. The summons is served in the usual way.

Must be potential defendant

An order under section 33(1), SCA 1981 is sought before the commencement of proceedings. The summons should state that the application is made pursuant to Order 29, rule 7A(1) and it should specify the property in respect of which the order is sought, together with the particular relief claimed.

"Secret process, discovery or invention"   Facts concerning the property may exist in a research establishment which contains secret information and the like. If such information is not the subject of the contemplated action, no order concerning inspection of the property will be granted if this would result in disclosure of the secret information. However, the court will be loath to refuse an order which otherwise should be granted, and will need to be satisfied that the effect of carrying out the order will be to disclose secret information which is not the subject of the contemplated proceedings. In many cases the defendant will be able to arrange his business so that the order can safely be carried out. It is for the defendant to prove to the court that the order should not be made in any particular case.

Secret information

Affidavit

The originating summons must be supported by an affidavit. This must specify or sufficiently describe the property, the subject of the proposed order, and must also show how the property may become the subject-matter of the subsequent proceedings, or how it relates to any question which may arise in

Affidavit in support

Facts justifying order

the proceedings.[11] This may be done by reference in the affidavit to what is set out in any pleadings intended to be served. The affidavit must also show that the plaintiff has a claim concerning that property and should set out the facts which justify an order for inspection, photographs, preservation, detention, the taking of samples or the carrying out of any experiments on such property. A copy of the affidavit shall be served on every person on whom the summons is required to be served.[12]

Authority to enter land

Order 29, rules 2 and 3 provide that the court may authorise any person to enter upon land or building in the possession of any party to the cause or matter for the purpose of enabling any order for detention, custody or preservation of property to be carried out, or in the case where an order issued for the purpose of obtaining full information, or authorising a sample to be taken, or an experiment made, or a report given of the property which is the subject-matter of the action or concerning which a question may arise. The rules do not provide for similar orders in respect of the remaining elements of section 33(1) but the court has the power to grant similar orders under its inherent jurisdiction.

Service of affidavit

In a case begun by originating summons (not being an *ex parte* summons) the plaintiff must, before the expiration of 14 days after the defendant has acknowledged service, (or if there is more than one defendant, after at least one has acknowledged service) file the affidavit in support with the court which issued the summons. Copies of the affidavit evidence as filed must be served on each defendant before the expiration of 14 days after the service of the originating summons has been acknowledged by each defendant. A defendant, having acknowledged service,

Affidavit in rebuttal

may, if he wishes, file affidavit evidence in rebuttal of the plaintiff's case.[13] Such affidavit evidence could deny the facts of the plaintiff's case in whole or in part, or set out reasons why the order, as sought, should not be granted. As an example, if the plaintiff has made an application under section 33(1), SCA 1981, a defendant can plead that in the circumstances of the case it would not be right to grant the order, as to do so would bring about disclosure of a secret matter not relevant to his case.

Ex parte application

If the matter is commenced *ex parte*, the affidavit must be filed not less than four clear days before the date fixed for the hearing.

Method of application

Application to the Chancery Division may be made:

    (a) by petition of course; or
    (b) motion of course; or
    (c) by summons in chambers.

Applications are normally heard by a judge in chambers. Orders in the Queen's Bench for injunction are made by a judge and for other matters by a Master. The procedure is similar in both divisions.

If the application is other than by summons in matters concerning orders under section 33(1), SCA 1981, the Torts (Interference with Goods) Act 1977, Anton Piller orders and

---

[11] O. 29, r. 7A(3).
[12] O. 29, r. 7A(4).
[13] O. 28, rr. 1 and 1A.

Mareva injunctions, leave can be sought *ex parte* in most cases to issue and serve a writ, notice of a writ or originating summons, and with such, the order of the court following the *ex parte* hearing.

Contents of affidavit

An affidavit with an *ex parte* application should contain a clear and concise statement of:

(a) the facts giving rise to the request for an order in the proceedings or proposed proceedings;

(b) the reasons giving rise to a claim for interlocutory relief and the evidence to support them;

(c) if there has been no notice of the matter to the defendant, the reasons for not so doing, such as that the defendant might destroy evidence. If notice has been given, even though it may not have reached him yet owing to the urgency with which the case is being pressed, details of what it contains should be in the affidavit. These facts should show why an *ex parte* application is justified;

(d) if the defendant can give or may give an answer to the claim in the substantive action, or for interlocutory relief, then answers, if known, should be given. The affidavit should be to the point, only illustrating the claims set out in the writ or originating summons;

(e) any facts known to the applicant which might lead to the court refusing *ex parte* relief, for example, where interlocutory relief is sought belatedly, or where the property is the subject of a previous application in other proceedings in which application was refused;

(f) the affidavit should specify the precise relief sought.

Specification of precise relief

Draft minute of order   Applicants should lodge with the papers a draft minute of the order being sought. This minute will specify the precise relief which the court is asked to grant, and is thus a draft of what could reasonably be expected to be issued by the court if the order is granted.

Undertakings   If *ex parte* relief is being sought, undertakings will be required of the applicant, on the basis that if after the order is granted it transpires that it should not have been, the defendant might well have suffered and require damages in compensation.

Required undertakings

The undertakings which should be included in the draft minute of the order will vary from case to case, but the following will usually be required:

(a) an undertaking to indemnify the defendant for any damage he might suffer as a result of the order being improperly granted;

(b) notification to the defendant of the terms of the order forthwith;

(c) where proceedings have not been issued, to issue the same forthwith; and

(d) if a draft affidavit has not been sworn, or where facts have been placed before the court orally, to bring about the serving of the affidavit, or procure the making of and service of the affidavit which will verify the facts put before the court.

The court will usually only grant an order providing there is provision for the defendant to apply to have it discharged or varied, and the costs being reserved.

Torts (Interference with Goods) Act 1977, s.4

Delivery up of goods In addition to an application under section 33(1) SCA 1981, application may also be made for delivery up of goods pursuant to section 4 of the Torts (Interference with Goods) Act 1977 which provides:

> "(1) In this section 'proceedings' means proceedings for wrongful interference.
> (2) On the application of any person in accordance with rules of court, the High Court shall, in such circumstances as may be specified in the Rules, have power to make an order providing for the delivery up of any goods which are or may become the subject-matter of subsequent proceedings in the court, or as to which any question may arise in proceedings.
> (3) Delivery shall be, as the order may provide, to the claimant or to a person appointed by the court for the purpose, and shall be on such terms and conditions as may be specified in the order."

This Act, which replaces the old tort of detinue, provides for disputes concerning property, and orders will usually be granted only after the action has commenced. However, a party to the proceedings may apply for an order *ex parte* if the facts of the matter justify such an application.[14]

Change of division **"High Court"**   This means any division of the High Court. Application in the Queen's Bench Division should be made to a Master. If application is made *ex parte*, it will be to the Practice Master in the Queen's Bench Division, who may be reluctant to make an order, especially if the plaintiff wants delivery of the property to himself. In such a case it is possible to proceed in the Chancery Division by application to a judge.

Delivery to solicitor or receiver **"Delivery up"**   While the power to order delivery up is analogous to the detention, custody and preservation of property under Order 29, rule 2, it is limited to applications relating to wrongful interference with goods. Delivery up is made to the plaintiff's solicitor or a receiver appointed by the High Court, if the court is satisfied that the plaintiff's solicitor cannot arrange safe custody. The court has power to order delivery up to the plaintiff personally, but will be reluctant to do so.

Items not included No order will be made for delivery up of the defendant's clothes, bedding, furnishings, tools of trade, farm implements and livestock or any machines including motor vehicles, or other goods such as materials or stock in trade which it is likely he uses for the purpose of his lawful business. The court will not, however, omit from the order valuable furnishings or *objets d'art* which have been purchased to defeat a judgment.

---

[14] See above, pp. 8, 10.

Invitation to enter or seize   The order should not authorise the plaintiff to enter the defendant's premises or to seize his property, but will order the defendant to invite the plaintiff to do these acts. Failure by the defendant to issue such an invitation constitutes a contempt of court. Provision will be made in the order for the defendant to apply to have the order stayed, varied or discharged.[15]

Discretion of court   The court in the exercise of its powers has a complete discretion, which is not limited to cases where there is a danger or risk that the goods will be disposed of, or lost, or destroyed, or will otherwise be unaccounted. If the goods are not readily available on the open market and damages would not compensate the plaintiff in his business without the particular goods, the court is more likely to favour the plaintiff's needs for the goods, as opposed to the defendant's grounds for withholding them.[16]

"Rules"   This means the rules of the Supreme Court and in particular Order 29, rules 2 and 2A.

Application for an order

An application under the 1977 Act is made under Order 29, rule 2A. The applicant (being the plaintiff) may, if the case is one of urgency, make the application *ex parte* and must be supported by affidavit before issue of the writ or summons, but otherwise the application is made by notice or summons.[17]

Order 29, rules 2 and 2A provides:

Detention, custody or preservation of property   "2(1) On the application of any party to a cause or matter the court may make an order for the detention, custody or preservation of any property which is the subject-matter of the cause or matter, or as to which any question may arise therein, or for the inspection of any such property in the possession of a party to the cause or matter.

(2) For the purpose of enabling any order under paragraph (1) to be carried out, the court may by the order authorise any person to enter upon any land or building in the possession of any party to the cause or matter.

(3) Where the right of any party to a specific fund is in dispute in a cause or matter, the court may, on the application of a party to the cause or matter, order the fund to be paid into court or otherwise secured.

(4) An order under this rule may be made on such terms, if any, as the court thinks just.

(5) An application for an order under this rule must be made by summons or by notice under Order 25, rule 7.

(6) Unless the court otherwise directs, an appliction by a defendant for such an order may not be made before he acknowledges service of the writ or originating summons by which the cause or matter was begun.

2A(1) Without prejudice to rule 2, the court may on the application of any party to a cause or matter, make an order under section 4 of the Torts (Interference with Goods) Act

---

[15] *C.B.S. United Kingdom Ltd.* v. *Lambert* [1983] Ch. 37.
[16] *Howard E. Perry & Co.* v. *British Railways Board* [1980] I.C.R. 743; *Z* v. *A-Z and AA-LL* [1982] Q.B. 558.
[17] O. 29, r. 1(2).

Delivery up of goods

1977 for the delivery up of any goods which are the subject-matter of the cause or matter or as to which any question may arise therein.

(2) Paragraphs (2) and (3) of rule 1 shall have effect in relation to an application for such an order as they have effect in relation to an application for the grant of an injunction."

The elements of Order 29, rules 2 and 2A are considered below:

Dispute necessary

"Any party" Whilst any party to an action can make application for an order if there are co-defendants, one cannot obtain an order against another if there is no dispute between them[18] solely for the purpose of allowing an existing party to inspect photographs or property in the non-party's possession; but it may be proper to join a non-party for such purpose under the principle of *Norwich Pharmacal*.[19] In the event that a non-party is required to produce documents under *subpoena duces tecum* the interests of justice may not be served by a party having to wait until trial for this production.[20] It is to be noted that this is a Northern Ireland Authority and the rules are not quite the same as for England, though it is submitted that the underlying principle applies to English law.

Narrow application

"Application of any party to a cause or matter" The order is narrower than section 4 of the Act; the Act refers to "any goods which are or may become the subject-matter of subsequent proceedings," while the rule apparently only applies if the proceedings are in being. Rule 2A which relates specifically to section 4 does not enlarge the rule. In practice this need make no difference as the court has power to make interlocutory and *ex parte* orders, which can take place before the substantive action has commenced.

Bank account

"Detention, custody or preservation" The rule extends to any case where the court finds as between plaintiff and defendant that there is something which ought to be done for the securing of the property.[21] If sums are identifiable as being the fruits of the first defendant's alleged criminal activity, and are in the bank account of the second defendant, the court has power to restrain, by order, the second defendant from dealing with any sum in his account which has accrued from a specific date. This not only preserves evidence but also enables the proceeds, in due course, to be returned to the rightful owner.[22] The court has power to make a similar order in respect of goods which are the subject matter of Arbitration[23] and in an appropriate case can order a party to pay the amount in dispute into court and if that party

---

[18] *Shaw* v. *Smith* [1986] 18 Q.B.D. 193.
[19] *Norwich Pharmacal Co.* v. *Customs and Excise Commissioners* [1973]; *Doris Leci* v. *Findlay, The Times,* July 4, 1989.
[20] *O'Sullivan* v. *Herdmans Ltd.* [1987] 1 W.L.R. 1047.
[21] *Chaplin* v. *Barnett* [1912] 28 T.L.R. 256.
[22] *West Mercia Constabulary* v. *Wagener* [1982] 1 W.L.R. 127. See also under "Preservation, custody and detention," p. 7.
[23] Arbitration Act 1950, s.12(6).

fails to do so, then the court can stay the claims of such person in the arbitration.[24]

"Property"   must be *bona fide* the subject-matter of the action.[25]

"Specific fund"   If the property which is likely to become the subject of proceedings is a special or specific fund and that is the matter in dispute, the court may, on the application of a party to the dispute, order the fund to be paid into court or otherwise secured.[26]

ayment into court

Injunctive relief

Rule 2A(2) provides that paras. 2 and 3 of Order 29, rule 1 shall apply to an application for an order under rule 2A. Order 29, rule 1 provides:

Application for injunction

"(1) An application for the grant of an injunction may be made by any party to a cause or matter before or after the trial of the cause or matter, whether or not a claim for the injunction was included in that party's writ, originating summons, counterclaim or third party notice, as the case may be.
(2) Where the applicant is the plaintiff and the case is one of urgency, such application may be made *ex parte* on affidavit but, except as aforesaid, such application must be made by motion or summons.
(3) The plaintiff may not make such an application before the issue of the writ or originating summons by which the cause or matter is to be begun except where the case is one of urgency, and in that case the injunction applied for may be granted on terms providing for the issue of the writ or summons and such other terms, if any, as the court thinks fit."

Urgency

This rule sets out in general terms that an injunction may be granted before or after the issue of process. Also *ex parte* applications may be sought but only in cases of urgency. In practice, the courts have adopted "urgency" as having a wider meaning than "immediate," but also it includes cases where, if the *ex parte* relief sought is not granted prior to trial of the action, evidence vital to the success of the action may be destroyed or lost. The same applies to preservation orders. Orders for delivery up under section 4 of the Torts (Interference with Goods) Act 1977 are normally made after the commencement of proceedings, but rule 1(2) makes provision for *ex parte* orders to be made.[27]

An applicant for an order, whether after commencement of proceedings or before, is required to make an affidavit in support which must:

Affidavit in support

(a) identify as clearly as possible the goods or classes of goods which are to be the subject of the proposed order;

---

[24] *Richco International* v. *Industrial Food Co. SAL*, *The Fayrouz III* [1989] 1 All E.R. 613.
[25] See above, p. 6.
[26] O. 29, r. 2(3).
[27] For application for *ex parte* orders, see p. 10.

(b) show that the goods are or are likely to become the subject-matter of subsequent proceedings; or

(c) indicate as to which goods any question may arise in such proceedings;

(d) give substantial and clear evidence that, unless the order made, the defendant is likely to dispose or otherwise deal with the goods so as to deprive the plaintiff of the benefit of any judgment obtained;

(e) indicate that the plaintiff's case cannot be properly conducted unless the order, as sought, is granted.

Power of the court

Refusal of order If the plaintiff is unable to identify with certainty what he wants delivered up and is unable to give adequate reasons, this uncertainty may well cause the court to refuse an order. The court will be slow to order interim delivery up of the defendant's property unless there is clear evidence or inference that the property has been acquired by the defendant as a result of his alleged wrongdoings. The application is made by summons or notice under Order 25, rule 7, unless an emergency application is applied for *ex parte*. The court may order delivery up of goods following an application by any party to a cause or matter made under section 4, if the goods are to be the subject-matter of a cause of action or matter as to which any question may arise.[28]

Orders which may be made by the court Following application under section 33(1), SCA 1981 or section 4 of the Torts (Interference with Goods) Act 1977, the court, if satisfied that the orders, as sought, should be made, may grant an order directed against any person who has the possession of relevant property and may do so on such terms as it thinks right to meet the circumstances of the case including requiring a party to:

(a) give security for costs.[29] This is in respect of a section 33(1) order but within the inherent power of the court it would seem that it can extend to a section 4 order;

(b) give such undertaking as the court thinks fit to meet the circumstances of the case, such as an undertaking to indemnify a person if it transpires that the order should never have been granted;

(c) where the right of any party to a specific fund is in dispute, order the fund to be paid into court or otherwise secured;[30]

(d) pay all or any part of the costs of the proceedings.

Time Application should be made as soon as is reasonably possible, whether under the SCA 1981 or the Torts (Interference with Goods) Act 1977. Delay may prevent the grant of an interlocutory order.

Delay

[28] O. 29, rr. 2 and 2A.
[29] O. 29, r. 7A.
[30] O. 29, rr. 2 and 3.

The county court

The county court has similar powers to the High Court.
County Courts Act 1984, section 38 provides:

Power similar to that of High Court

"(1) Every county court, as regards any cause of action for the time being within its jurisdiction,—
  (a) shall grant such relief, redress or remedy or combination of remedies, either absolute or conditional; and
  (b) shall give such and the like effect to every ground of defence or counterclaim equitable or legal, as ought to be granted or given in the like case by the High Court and in as full and ample a manner.
(2) For the purpose of this section it shall be assumed (notwithstanding any enactment to the contrary) that any proceedings which can be commenced in a county court could be commenced in the High Court."

The general effect of this provision is to confer on the county court in respect of any cause of action within its jurisdiction, the power to grant remedies as could be given in a similar case in the High Court. The jurisdiction of the county court in respect of matters of contract and tort is limited by the amount of damages sought.

Jurisdiction

The general jurisdiction of the county court is exercised over:

  (a) matters where the claim does not exceed £5,000 which would, if in the High Court, be held in the Queen's Bench Division;
  (b) land on which the value does not exceed certain prescribed amounts according to the class of action;
  (c) matters where the subject-matter shall not exceed £30,000 and which would, in the High Court, be the subject of an action in the Chancery Division.

This work is concerned with the procedures, and the equitable and common law remedies, which are generally, unless excluded by statute, available in the county court.
The County Courts Act 1984, section 52(1) provides:

Powers before commencement of action

"(1) on the application of any person in accordance with county court rules, a county court shall, in such circumstances as may be prescribed, have power to make an order providing for any one or more of the following matters, that is to say—
  (a) the inspection, photographing, preservation, custody and detention of property which appears to the court to be property which may become the subject-matter of subsequent proceedings in the court, or as to which any question may arise in any such proceedings; and
  (b) the taking of samples of any such property as is mentioned in paragraph (a), and the carrying out of any experiment on or with any such property."

The provision is the same as SCA 1981, section 33(1)[31] save for

[31] For comment on the section, see p. 6.

wording which is different on account of the section dealing with the county court as opposed to the High Court. The procedure is governed by the County Court Rules.

Order 13, rr. 6 & 7

Application for an order Applications for orders under the County Courts Act 1984 are made under Order 13, rules 6 and 7 of the County Court Rules 1981, the relevant provisions of which provide:

Application for injunction

"6—(1) An application for the grant of an injunction may be made by any party to an action or matter before or after the trial or hearing, whether or not a claim for the injunction was included in that party's particulars of claim, originating application, petition, counterclaim or third party notice, as the case may be.

(2) Rule 1(6) shall not apply and, unless the registrar has power under any other provision of these rules to grant the injunction, the application shall be made to the judge.

(3) Where the applicant is the plaintiff and the case is one of urgency, the application may be made *ex parte* on affidavit but, except as aforesaid, the application must be made on notice, and in any case the affidavit or notice must state the terms of the injunction applied for.

(4) The plaintiff may not make an application before the issue of the summons, originating application or petition by which the action or matter is to be commenced except where the case is one of urgency and in that case—

   (a) the affidavit on which the application is made shall show that the action or matter is one which the court to which the application is made has jurisdiction to hear and determine; and

   (b) the injunction applied for shall, if granted, be on terms providing for the issue of the summons, originating application or petition in the court granting the application and on such other terms, if any, as the court thinks fit.

(5) Unless otherwise directed, every application not made *ex parte* shall be heard in open court.

(6) Except where the case is one of urgency, a draft of the injunction shall be prepared beforehand by the party making an application to the judge under paragraph (1) and, if the application is granted, the draft shall be submitted to the judge by whom the application was heard and shall be settled by him.

(7) The injunction, when settled, shall be forwarded to the proper office for filing."

Application for an injunction may be made before or after the trial. Thus it would appear to be concerned only with interlocutory matters.[32] Paragraph (2) excludes the general provisions in the County Court Rules which enable interlocutory application to be decided by the registrar, and hence application must be made direct to a judge (unless the registrar has power under another rule to grant the injunction). Unless an *ex parte*

Application direct to judge

---

[32] O. 6, r. 1.

Open court   injunction is applied for, the application is heard in open court[33] on notice and must state the terms of the injunction applied for.

***Ex parte* application**   Generally an application shall not be made except on notice but in cases of urgency, application may be **Affidavit in** made *ex parte*. In such a case, an affidavit in support must be filed **support** which should be similar in content to an affidavit in the High Court.[34] The affidavit must also state the terms of the injunction for which application is made. The injunction, if granted, shall be on terms as the court thinks fit and the court follows, generally, the High Court procedures.[35] A draft of the proposed order shall be supplied to the court.

Application of the Rules of the Supreme Court   Order 13, rule 7 provides:

Order 13, r. 7   "(1) Subject to the following paragraphs of this rule, the provisions of the RSC with regard to—
  (a) the payment into court of money in respect of which the defendant claims a lien on or other right to retain specific property (other than land) which the plaintiff seeks to recover;
  (b) the detention, custody, preservation or inspection of any relevant property;
  (c) the payment into court or securing of a specific fund which is in dispute in an action or matter;
  (d) the delivery up of any relevant goods under section 4 of the Torts (Interference with Goods) Act 1977;
  (e) the taking of any sample of or the making of any observation or experiment on any relevant property;
  (f) the sale of any relevant property (other than land) which is of a perishable nature or likely to deteriorate if kept or which for any other good reason it is desirable to sell forthwith;
  (g) the exercise of the powers conferred by sections 33 to 35 of the Supreme Court Act 1981;
  (h) the taking or making of any necessary accounts or enquiries,
shall apply in relation to proceedings or, as the case may be, subsequent proceedings in a county court as they apply in relation to proceedings or subsequent proceedings in the High Court."

In this paragraph "relevant property" and "relevant goods" **Meaning of** mean property (or, as the case may be, goods) which is or are the **"property" and** subject-matter of an action or matter, or as to which any question **"goods"** may arise therein.
The elements of Order 13, rule 7 generally provide that orders may be obtained in respect of detention, custody, preservation and inspection of any relevant property,[36] the

---

[33] O. 13, r. 6(6).
[34] See p. 11.
[35] See p. 16.
[36] O. 13, r. 7(1)(*b*).

payment into court or securing of a specific fund,[37] the delivery up of goods under section 4 of the Torts (Interference with Goods) Act 1977,[38] the taking of samples of or the making of any observation or experiment in connection with property,[39] or the exercise of powers conferred by sections 33 to 35 of the SCA 198 in relation to county court proceedings or subsequent proceedings under similar principles and circumstances as they would in an action in the High Court.[40] Application shall be made either by notice or *ex parte* in accordance with the County Court Rules, but the underlying principle of applying for an order with affidavit in support are the same as for the High Court.[41]

---

[37] O. 13, r. 7(1)(*c*).
[38] O. 13, r. 7(1)(*d*).
[39] O. 13, r. 7(1)(*e*).
[40] See pp. 6 *et seq.*
[41] See pp. 8 *et seq.*

3 ORDERS PRECEDING ACTIONS RELATING TO DEATH OR PERSONAL INJURIES

Supreme Court Act 1981, s.33(2)

Applies to death or injuries Derived from section 31 of the Administration of Justice Act 1970 and section 21(1) of the Administration of Justice Act 1969, section 33(2) only applies to actions and claims in respect of personal injury or death. It enables a person who wishes to bring a claim, to obtain, before commencing proceedings, disclosure of relevant documents from the potential defendant to the action. A potential plaintiff can accordingly assess the strength of his claim by obtaining early discovery.

Section 33(2) of the Supreme Court Act 1981 (SCA 1981) provides:

Power of High Court "(2) On the application, in accordance with rules of court, of a person who appears to the High Court to be likely to be a party to subsequent proceedings in that court in which a claim in respect of personal injuries to a person, or in respect of a person's death, is likely to be made, the High Court shall, in such circumstances as may be specified in the rules, have power to order a person who appears to the court to be likely to be a party to the proceedings and to be likely to have or to have had in his possession, custody or power any documents which are relevant to an issue arising or likely to arise out of that claim—

    (a) to disclose whether those documents are in his possession, custody or power; and

    (b) to produce such of those documents as are in his possession, custody of power to the applicant or, on such conditions as may be specified in the order—

        (i) to the applicant's legal advisers; or

        (ii) to the applicant's legal advisers and any medical or other professional adviser of the applicant; or

        (iii) if the applicant has no legal adviser, to any medical or other professional adviser of the applicant.

Reasonable basis for claim **"Person likely to be a party"** The phrase should be construed liberally and has been held to mean "a reasonable prospect of becoming a party." The claim should have a reasonable basis and not be irresponsible or speculative.[1] The Court of Appeal has

---

[1] *Dunning* v. *Board of Governors of the United Liverpool Hospitals* [1973] 1 W.L.R. 586.

granted discovery when the likelihood of proceedings being taken has depended on the information which would be revealed by the documents whose disclosure was sought. While this authority has been overruled on another point, the principle enunciated concerning this phrase is still sound law.[2] The person can be plaintiff, defendant or a third party, but is usually the plaintiff.

"Subsequent proceedings"   Under this section, the proceedings in respect of a death or injury claim will not have commenced.

"In respect of personal injuries"   The term "personal injuries" includes any disease and any impairment of a person's physical or mental condition.[3] It is sufficient that the nature and extent of the personal injuries are a necessary element in the plaintiff's claim, **Subsidiary claim**   even if the cause of action is not directly for damages for such injuries but is, for example, an action in negligence against a solicitor who conducted an action in respect of those injuries;[4] however, an action against an insurance broker for failure to effect a personal injury insurance policy was not regarded as a claim in respect of personal injuries.[5]

"Likely to be made"   The words "likely to be made" are to be construed as meaning "may" or "may well be made" if the documents in question indicate that the applicant has a good cause of action. It is immaterial that the likelihood of a claim being made is dependent on the outcome of the discovery. The **Claim dependent**   court may make an order if the only basis for submitting that a **on documents**   claim is not likely to succeed is the absence of the document or documents for which discovery is sought.[6]

"As may be specified in the rules"   Express provision is made in Order 24, rule 7A.

"Possession, custody or power"   The effect of the words **Any documents**   "possession" and "custody" is that any relevant document held by a person will fall within the definition. This includes documents that are or have been in a party's possession as opposed to control, though the documents can be both in the possession and custody of the same person, or in his custody which includes holding documents as a bailee or as an employee of a corporation which owns the documents. "Power" relates to documents which may not be in a party's possession or custody, but which the party has the right to obtain from another who possesses or is custodian of them. The above circumstances include possession by an agent of the defendant such as his solicitor.[7]

    The underlying purpose of the subsection is the production of documents, so that if a party does not have possession of

---

[2] *McIvor* v. *Southern Health and Social Services Board, Northern Ireland* [1978] 1 W.L.R. 757.
[3] SCA 1981, s.35(5).
[4] *Paterson* v. *Chadwick* [1974] 1 W.L.R. 890.
[5] *Ackbar* v. *Green(C.F.) & Co.* [1975] Q.B. 582.
[6] See above, n. 1.
[7] *Murray* v. *Walter* (1839) Cr. & Ph. 114.

documents, he may be ordered to produce them because he has the power to do this. A person being a defendant cannot be ordered to produce documents over which he has possession,
Defendant holding custody or power if he holds them in another capacity, *i.e.* not as
in another capacity defendant. Such is the case if he holds the documents as director or officer of a company which is not the subject of litigation.[8] It is a question of fact as to whether the documents of a subsidiary may or may not be under the control of the parent company.[9] Similarly it is a question of fact as to whether the documents are in the power of a controlling shareholder.[10]

"Documents"   The meaning of documents extends to anything upon which evidence or information is recorded in a manner in which it can be read or be capable of being read through the use
Recorded of equipment; thus it includes tape recordings, computer
information records, and the output of an electronic-encephalographic machine.[11]

The relationship between section 33(1) and section 33(2)

Whilst both subsections give power to the High Court prior to the commencement of proceedings in relation to discovery matters, section 33(1) relates to all classes of action whereas section 33(2) is limited to death or injury cases. The powers of the High Court appear to be different in that section 33(2) is limited to discovery of documents, while section 33(1) relates to any property. In the application of section 33 to the Crown, this is limited to property involving an action for personal injuries or death.[12]

Non-parties

It is often the case that there are documents in the possession of a person who is not a party to the proceedings. Save for the case of action for discovery (see Chapter 4) which is limited in its
Subpoena duces application, non-parties are summoned to trial with an order to
tecum produce documents under *subpoena duces tecum*. This can be most inconvenient for all parties to the litigation, as until the documents are produced in court, the parties do not know what they contain.
To avoid this inconvenience, once an action has commenced
SCA 1981, s.34(2) in respect of death or injury, any party to the proceedings may apply under section 34(2) for a similar order for disclosure against a non-party. The procedure is substantially the same as under section 33(1) which gives the High Court the same powers, the only difference between the two subsections being the underlying circumstances giving rise to their operation.
If all the information is available to the injured person's

---

[8] *B* v. *B* [1978] Fam. 181.
[9] *Lonhro* v. *Shell Petroleum Co.* [1980] Q.B. 358.
[10] *Tecnion Investments, Re.* [1985] B.C.L.R. 434, C.A.
[11] *Grant* v. *Southwestern and County Properties* [1975] Ch. 185.
[12] SCA 1981, s.35(4).

Assess strength of claim

advisers or his personal representatives at an early stage, they can then come to an opinion as to whether or not any claim is likely to be successful and, if so, against whom. It often happens in such cases where it is clear that a claim would not succeed, that an early decision will prevent waste of time, anxiety and expense. However, a view may be taken that a claim is likely to be successful and thus litigation may be commenced. If litigation ensues, this can often be conducted with a view to possible settlement.

Clarifies issues

If a settlement cannot be reached, preparation for the conduct of the trial will be with the benefit of the facts disclosed in relevant documents at an early stage, so that often the only issue will be whether the plaintiff contributed to his injuries, and if so, to what extent; this also aids assessment of the amount of damages. There is the added advantage that the trial can take place somewhat sooner than would be the case if discovery took place under the ordinary course of events.

Effect

The effect of the SCA 1981 (and rules), whether under section 33(2) or section 34(2), is to establish that in personal injury or death actions the court has power to order disclosure of documents by a likely party before action commences, and also immediately after action commences by a non-party. These powers do not, in general, apply to other classes of action, although there are exceptions.[13] The general rule is to obtain documents, either between parties after close of pleadings, or from non-parties through the *subpoena duces tecum* procedure at trial. Sections 33(2) and 34(2) of the SCA 1981 afford exceptions to the general rule.

Medical records

In many death or injury cases, evidence indicating whether personal representatives of the deceased or the injured party can successfully claim for damages will often be in documentary form, such as medical records. These records will show the extent of the injuries, possibly the cause, the likely prognosis for injury cases, as well as the degree of pain and suffering. It is therefore of importance to the advisers of a potential plaintiff or his personal representatives to be able to examine such records, with a view to being able to assess the position both as to liability and to *quantum* of damages.

Examples of applications

SCA 1981, section 33(2) applies to obtaining documents from parties likely to be a party to subsequent proceedings, whether as plaintiff, defendant or a third party. Examples which follow are given for injury cases when the plaintiff is normally the injured party, but the same examples could be used for cases of death or when the injured person is under a legal disability (*e.g.* a minor).

Records held by defendant employer

Example 1   In an industrial injury case when the plaintiff wishes to have access to the medical records kept by the factory doctor and his staff, the likely defendant being the employer.

---

[13] See Chap. 4.

Records held by a party associated with defendant

Example 2   An action against a surgeon for negligence. In such a case, the medical records may be held by the hospital where the operation took place. If, as is often the case, the hospital is likely to be joined as a co-defendant with the surgeon, then application can be made to view the documents in the hospital's possession.

Records held by a non-party

Example 3   The plaintiff has sustained injuries in a motor accident and commences action against the driver of one of the vehicles. As a result of his injuries, the plaintiff has undergone hospital treatment. The hospital, which will not be a party to the action, refuses to disclose the plaintiff's medical records concerning treatment for the injuries. In such an event, the action must be commenced first against the other driver, and then the plaintiff or the defendant may make an application, not under section 33(2) SCA 1981 but under section 34(2) SCA 1981, for the hospital to make the disclosure.[14]

Disclosure to legal, medical or professional advisers

Applicant precluded from viewing records

The court has power, under either section 33(2) or section 34(2) in relation to disclosure of documents, to make it a condition of any order that the documents are only to be disclosed to the applicant's medical and/or legal advisers. The effect of such an order is to preclude the applicant himself from seeing the medical records.[15]

Application for an order

Originating summons

Application under section 33(2)   The application is made by originating summons to which an acknowledgment of service must be returned. The person against whom the order is sought becomes the defendant and is served in the usual way. The summons should state that the application is made pursuant to Order 24, rule 7A(1) and it should specify the document or documents in respect of which the order is sought.[16]

Summons in the action

Application under section 34(2)   An application under section 34(2) is by summons in the action, directed to the person against whom the order is sought. It must be served on the defendant as if under an originating process. The summons should state that the application is made under section 34(2) SCA 1981 and should specify the document or documents in respect of which the order is sought. A copy of the summons and supporting affidavit must be served on every other party to the action.

Order 24, rule 7A provides:

Order 24, r.7A

"(1) An application for an order under section 33(2) of the Act for the disclosure of documents before the commencement of proceedings shall be made by originating

---

[14] *Walker* v. *Eli Lilly & Co.* [1986] E.C.C. 550.

[15] The subsections restore the legal position as found by the court in *Dunning* v. *United Liverpool Hospital's Board of Governors* [1973] 1 W.L.R. 586, which was later overruled.

[16] *Campbell* v. *Tameside Metropolitan Borough Council* [1982] Q.B. 1065.

summons and the person against whom the order sought shall be made defendant to the summons.

(2) An application after the commencement of proceedings for an order under section 34(2) of the said Act for the disclosure of documents by a person who is not a party to the proceedings shall be made by summons, which must be served on that person personally and on every party to the proceedings other than the applicant.

(3) A summons under paragraph (1) or (2) shall be supported by an affidavit which must—

  (a) in the case of a summons under paragraph (1) state the grounds on which it is alleged that the applicant and the person against whom the order is sought are likely to be parties to subsequent proceedings in the High Court in which a claim for personal injuries is likely to be made;

  (b) in any case, specify or describe the documents in respect of which the order is sought and show, if practicable by reference to any pleading served or intended to be served in the proceedings, that the documents are relevant to an issue arising or likely to arise out of a claim for personal injuries made or likely to be made in the proceedings and that the person against whom the order sought is likely to have or have had them in his possession, custody or power.

(4) A copy of the supporting affidavit shall be served with the summons on every person on whom the summons is required to be served.

Conditional order

(5) An order under the said section 33(2) or 34(2) for the disclosure of documents may be made conditional on the applicant's giving security for the costs of the person against whom it is made or on such other terms, if any, as the court thinks just, and shall require the person against whom the order is made to make an affidavit stating whether any documents specified or described in the order, or at any time have been, in his possession, custody or power and, if not then in his possession, custody or power, when he parted with them and what has become of them.

(6) No person shall be compelled by virtue of such an order to produce any documents which he could not be compelled to produce—

  (a) in the case of a summons under paragraph (1) if the subsequent proceedings had already been begun, or

  (b) in the case of a summons under paragraph (2) if he had been served with a writ of *subpoena duces tecum* to produce the documents at the trial.

(7) In this rule "a claim for personal injuries" means a claim in respect of personal injuries to a person or in respect of a person's death.

(8) For the purposes of rules 10 and 11 an application for an order under the said section 33(2) or 34(2) shall be treated as a cause or matter between the applicant and the person against whom the order is sought.''

It should be noted that an order for disclosure of documents is for discovery of particular documents, not general discovery.

Prerequisites of application

An application for an order under section 33(2) or section 34(2) SCA 1981 for the disclosure of documents must be:

(a) preceding the commencement of proceedings in the case of section 33(2);

(b) applied for by the person who appears to be likely to be party to subsequent proceedings in the case of an application under section 33(2). The person making the application in respect of an application under section 34(2) will be a party to proceedings already commenced and will be seeking an order against a non-party;

(c) in respect of personal injuries or a person's death;

(d) if applied for under section 33(2), against a person who appears to be likely to be a party to such proceedings, and shall be made defendant to the summons; and

(e) against a person who appears to be likely to have, or have had in his possession, custody or power over any relevant documents. For the purpose of the summons (a section 33(2) application) the party against whom the order is sought shall be the defendant. Thus, if a potential defendant is the applicant *qua* the summons, the plaintiff or a third party is the defendant.

Affidavit

The originating summons and the summons in the action must be supported by affidavit,[17] which should contain the following particulars:

(a) the name of the person against whom the order is sought;

(b) in the case of an application under section 33(2) SCA 1981, the grounds on which it is alleged the applicant and defendant are likely to be parties to subsequent proceedings in which a claim for personal injuries or death is likely to be made;

Contents of affidavit

(c) particulars of the accident or event giving rise to the claim, and if it has been made known that a claim is likely to be made, the letter or letters before action and the responses should be attached as exhibits;

(d) descriptions or specifications of the documents in respect of which an order is sought;

(e) evidence that the person against whom the order is sought is likely to have, or has had such documents, as described or specified in point 4 above in his possession, custody or power;

(f) evidence that such documents as described or specified in point 4 above are germane to an issue arising out of a claim for personal injury (or death) which is likely to be the subject of a subsequent action (section 33(2)) or an existing action (section 34(2)). If there is a Statement of Claim in existence or a draft statement[18] which is intended to be served, the facts set out in such statements should be adopted for the affidavit.

If the court makes an order under section 33(2), the

---

[17] O. 24, r. 7A(3).
[18] The rule states "if practicable:" r. 7A(3).

Affidavit of the defendant

defendant is required to make an affidavit stating whether any documents specified or described in the order are, or at any time have been in his possession, custody or power, and if not, when he parted with them and what has become of them.[19]

For the purpose of rules 10 (service of originating process) and 11 (service of process outside the jurisdiction) an application under section 33(2) or section 34(2) is treated as if an action between the applicant and the person against whom the order is sought had commenced.[20] Thus any document disclosed in the

Inspection by applicant

affidavit made in compliance with Order 24, rule 7A may be inspected by the applicant under rule 10 (or the court may order production under rule 11) and copies may be taken subject to privilege or the possessor showing good cause why the documents should not be disclosed.[21]

Non-compellable documents

The court cannot order a person to produce documents which he could not be compelled to produce if the subsequent proceedings had already begun.[22] Thus if the documents are not compellable after action has commenced, an applicant cannot get around this difficulty by applying under section 33(2) SCA 1981

Privilege

before the action has started. A claim for privilege from production of the documents can be made in the same way and to the same extent in relation to discovery of documents before action as after action has begun.

Powers of the court under section 33(2)

Order refused

On the hearing of the application, the court, if satisfied that discovery is not necessary, or not necessary at that stage, may dismiss or adjourn the application. In any case, the court may refuse to make an order if and so far as it is of the opinion that discovery or inspection is not necessary either for disposing fairly of the cause or matter or for saving costs.[23]

Legal aid

Where the applicant is legally aided, the court should bear in mind that it is in the public interest that there should be early disclosure of documents which might affect the bringing of legally aided proceedings, since it is undesirable that proceedings should be brought with legal aid if it was reasonably clear that the plaintiff had no substantial prospect of success.[24]

Court's discretion

In any application under section 33 or section 34, the court has the discretion to decline to make an order which, if complied with, would be injurious to the public interest, or would in any event be oppressive or not in the interests of justice. Guidelines for the court in this respect were laid down by the Court of Appeal in *Campbell* v. *Tameside Metropolitan Borough Council*.[25]

Campbell v. Tameside M.B.C.

It was held that the proper approach of the court was to weigh in the balance the public interest of the nation or the public service in non-disclosure against the public injustice in the production of the documents. In weighing the balance, the court should consider the significance of the documents in relation to their

---

[19] O. 24, r. 7A(5).
[20] O. 24, r. 7A(8).
[21] *Ibid.*
[22] O. 24, r. 7A(6).
[23] O. 24, r. 8.
[24] *Shaw* v. *Vauxhall Motors* [1974] 1 W.L.R. 1035.
[25] [1982] Q.B. 1065.

likely effect on the outcome of the case, and whether their absence would result in a complete or partial denial of justice to one or other of the parties or to both, and the importance of the particular litigation to the parties and the public. In making such an assessment, it is open to the court to inspect the documents concerned in private.

In *Barrett* v. *Ministry of Defence*,[26] Popplewell J. said that Order 24, rule 7 should be approached in a liberal and not a restrictive way. In this case a widow sought disclosure (under section 33(2)) of a full report of the Ministry of Defence into the death of her husband. The Ministry resisted the application. The Ministry conceded that the circumstances leading to the death of the husband—overdose of alcohol—were such that the Commanding Officer of the dead man had pleaded guilty at a Court Martial to negligent performance of his duty to discourage drunkenness. On the facts of the case as admitted, the court held that discovery, as sought, at this stage was wholly unnecessary either to enable the widow properly to plead her case or to decide whether she could properly pursue her claim, as there was ample evidence to enable her to do both.

The court will, if satisfied with the justice of an application, make the order as requested usually under the supervision of the applicant's solicitor, as he is an officer of, and therefore responsible to, the court.

In a case where it is probable that a defence under the Limitation Act 1980, section 11 will succeed and that an application by the prospective plaintiff to disapply the limitation period will not succeed, the court may exercise discretion to order discovery before action, where it cannot be said that the prospective plaintiff's claim is bound to fail, and where facts may emerge from the pre-action disclosure that are relevant to the limitation issues.[27]

Costs The person against whom the order is sought is entitled to his costs of and incidental to the application, and of complying **Delay** with an order. If, however, such a person does not reply or delays replying to a proper request to disclose documents, he may not be awarded his costs.

Security for costs In an order for discovery under section 33(2) or section 34(2), the applicant may be required to give security for the costs of the person against whom it is made or on such other terms as the court thinks just.[28]

County court The county court has similar powers to the High Court, and the provisions of the County Courts Act 1984 and County Court Rules[29] allow one to apply for an order under section 33(2) and section 34(2) SCA 1981.[30]

---

[26] *Daily Telegraph*, February 6, 1990.
[27] *Harris* v. *Newcastle-upon-Tyne Health Authority* [1989] 1 W.L.R. 96.
[28] O. 24, r. 7A(5).
[29] Rules set out on pp. 18 *et seq.*
[30] C.C.R., O. 13, r. 7(1).

4 ORDERS IN RELATION TO INFORMATION HELD BY OTHERS

In many cases, persons not parties to an action or contemplated action may have, or are believed to have, in their possession documents which, if in the possession of litigants, would be discoverable.

Anyone may be in such a position; examples are police reports of incidents or Customs holding import/export files. For evidence at trial, it is sufficient to serve such persons with a *subpoena duces tecum* for production of the relevant documents.

Documents needed to determine cause of action

This is of no assistance to a potential plaintiff who has reason to believe that another has in his possession documents which, if available to him, would enable such a plaintiff to determine whether he has a cause of action, and the identity of the person or persons against whom he should proceed. Without the documents, the action would be greatly impeded, if not frustrated.

The substantive action[1] may or may not be against the possessors of the information; the prospective plaintiff will not know this, and often the possessors of the information (*e.g.* a bank) will be innocent of any wrongdoing. The holder of the information may believe he owes a duty, in law or ethics, not to disclose the information. The innocent holder of information has not, as such, committed any tort, and is not in breach of contract *vis-à-vis* the potential plaintiff.

Duty to assist litigation

While the courts have developed the principle that all persons have a duty to assist parties in litigation by providing such relevant information as they may possess on request by *subpoena*, this is for trial of the substantive action. The action for discovery is another example of that principle and aids parties to litigation by giving them access to necessary information at a pre-action stage.

"Fishing expedition"

It is sometimes argued that a potential plaintiff should not be permitted to go on a "fishing expedition" to ascertain whether he has a cause of action against a person.[2] It also offends legal principles that the innocent possessor of information should be compelled to become the defendant in an action for discovery when he has committed no wrong, but may do so if he were to disclose the information which he possesses.

There is thus a conflict between the interests of the potential plaintiff, who needs to be helped in order to abate the wrong he believes he has suffered or is suffering, and on the other hand, the right of an innocent person to be protected from harassment

---

[1] *i.e.* between the injured party and the wrongdoer.
[2] *Loose* v. *Williamson* [1978] 1 W.L.R. 639.

in court. The courts and Parliament by legislation[3] have attempted to resolve this conflict with a system of checks and balances which ensure that both the potential plaintiff and the innocent party suffer as little inconvenience as is reasonable, but that the rightful interests of both, and indeed of potential defendants, may be preserved.

Discovery against non-parties

History The Judicature Act 1873 and successor statutes dealt with situations when discovery could be ordered *inter partes*. The Act did not affect pre-action discovery sought by a party against a person innocent of any wrongdoing and who was not contemplated as a party to a substantive action. The non-party would normally be innocent, for otherwise he could be sued and discovery flow in the normal way. There are two authorities leading to the present state of the law: *Upmann* v. *Elkan*[4] which was decided prior to the Judicature Act 1873, and *Orr* v. *Diaper*,[5] just after it. In *Upmann* v. *Elkan* it was held that Elkan (forwarding agents) must inform Upmann of the identity of the consignor of goods infringing Upmann's trademark. *Orr* v. *Diaper* followed this judgment.

Awareness creating duty These authorities decided that once a person is made aware of the likelihood of a wrongdoing in which he has become involved, albeit innocently, he is under a duty, if requested, to inform the wronged party of the identity of the wrongdoers,[6] and that a person may be made a defendant in an action for discovery even though he is neither a party nor an intended party to **Prevention of deadlock** another action, if to do so will enable the plaintiff after discovery has been made to continue with proceedings which, but for the discovery, would become deadlocked.[7]

Norwich Pharmacal v. Customs and Excise Commissioners

The general rule Until *Norwich Pharmacal Co.* v. *Customs and Excise Commissioners*[8] the only reported cases after *Orr* v. *Diaper*[9] were not solely concerned with the action for discovery. Today, this old form of action has become very significant, as a result of the increase in counterfeiting of products and the infringement of industrial and intellectual property rights. The House of Lords judgment in *Norwich Pharmacal*[10] provides that generally no independent action for discovery lies against a person against **Exceptions** whom no cause of action could be alleged. There are exceptions, and the circumstances in *Norwich Pharmacal*[11] offer an example

---

[3] *e.g.* the Supreme Court Act 1981 and see Chaps. 2 and 3.
[4] [1871] 7 Ch.App. 130.
[5] [1876] 4 Ch.D. 92.
[6] *Upmann* v. *Elkan*, see n. 4.
[7] *Orr* v. *Diaper*, see n. 5.
[8] [1974] A.C. 133.
[9] See above, n. 5.
[10] See above, n. 8.
[11] *Ibid.*

of such an exception. The judgment sets out the law in relation to the action for discovery as it is at present. The earlier authorities were considered and *Norwich Pharmacal*[12] is, in effect, a consolidation of those authorities which the House of Lords has approved.

Facts of *Norwich Pharmacal*

In this case, the Commissioners for Customs and Excise published information that a named compound "furazolidone" had been imported into the United Kingdom. Norwich Pharmacal owned a patent protecting the said compound. No licences had been granted for its importation. The Customs refused to disclose the importer's name to Norwich Pharmacal, hence an order for discovery of names and addresses was sought. The House of Lords allowed the order.

Elements of judgments

The five judges were unanimous in holding that the action for discovery existed in certain defined circumstances. Lord Reid[13] confirmed the general rule that discovery to find the identity of a wrongdoer is available against anyone with whom the plaintiff has a cause of action in relation to the same wrong. The action is not available against a person who has no connection with the wrong other than that he was a spectator or has some document in his possession relating to it.

The general rule admits of an exception and in the *Norwich Pharmacal* case, the respondent Customs and Excise came within that exception, namely that if, through no fault of his own, a person gets mixed up in the tortious acts of others so as to

Facilitating wrongdoing

facilitate their wrongdoing, whilst he may incur no personal liability, he comes under a duty to assist the person who has been wronged by giving him full information and in disclosing the

Cooperation in righting wrong

identity of the wrongdoers. Lord Reid said:[14]

> "I do not think that it matters whether he became so mixed up by voluntary action on his part or because it was his duty to do what he did . . . justice requires that he should cooperate in righting the wrong if he unwittingly facilitated its perpetration."

Actual involvement

Lord Morris of Borth-y-Gest further defined the circumstances which would result in a possessor of information falling within the exception to the general rule:[15]

> "At the very least the person possessing the information would have to have become actually involved (or actively concerned) in some transactions or arrangements as a result of which he has acquired the information."

Mere witness rule

Their Lordships also considered the respondent's argument that the case fell within the "mere witness" rule and therefore discovery could not be ordered against them. The "mere witness" rule provides that information cannot be obtained by discovery from a person who will in due course be compellable to give that information, either by oral testimony as a witness, or by *subpoena duces tecum*.

In relation to the particular information required by the plaintiff, the House found that the "mere witness" rule did not

---

[12] [1974] A.C. 133.
[13] *Ibid.* at p. 175.
[14] *Ibid.*
[15] *Ibid.* at p. 178.

apply in *Norwich Pharmacal*. Lord Reid,[16] Lord Cross of
Chelsea, Lord Morris of Borth-y-Gest and Lord Kilbrandon
decided that a witness was one who may be able to give testimony
in either pending or anticipated proceedings. In this case, there
were no pending proceedings and there would not be any
anticipated proceedings unless the appellants received the help of
Irrelevant that the courts. Viscount Dilhorne[17] was of the opinion that someone
involvement was who could be sued or is involved in the transaction is not a "mere
innocent witness," and the respondents in the case were involved and it
was irrelevant for the purposes of the "mere witness" rule that
the involvement was innocent and in ignorance of the
wrongdoing.

Developments following *Norwich Pharmacal*

In accordance with the rules in *Norwich Pharmacal*, an action for
General rule discovery will be maintained and discovery granted against
non-parties to the substantive action where the person against
whom discovery of information is sought had himself, albeit
innocently, been involved in the wrongful acts of another so as to
facilitate the wrongdoing.

"The person against whom"   "Person" refers to an individual:
Orr v. *Diaper*,[18] a partnership: *Upmann* v. *Elkan*,[19] an authority:
Norwich Pharmacal,[20] and a corporate body: *R.C.A. Corporation*
v. *Reddingtons Rare Records*.[21]

"Discovery of information"   It seems that any information
which would be discoverable as between litigants, can be the
basis for an action for discovery against a possessor of
information, subject to the defence of privilege and providing
that the circumstances are such that the case comes within the
exception to the general rule that discovery is not available where
Discoverable no cause of action is alleged. In actions for discovery, discovery
information has been ordered for names and addresses: *Upmann* v. *Elkan*;[22]
the registration number of a fishing vessel: *Loose* v. *Williamson*;[23]
and information concerning bank accounts, correspondence and
banking documents: *Bankers Trust Co.* v. *Shapira*.[24]
Orders refused   Orders in some circumstances have been refused: an order in
England for the recovery of land situated outside the jurisdiction
was not granted since the proper course was to sue in the foreign
court where the land was situated.[25] The order sought was in aid
of proceedings in an inferior or foreign court;[26] the order sought
was one which a foreign court has the power to compel discovery
itself.[27] An order in respect of information was not granted

[16] [1974] A.C. 133 at p. 174.
[17] *Ibid.* at p. 199.
[18] [1876] 4 Ch.D. 92.
[19] [1871] 7 Ch.App. 130.
[20] [1974] A.C. 133.
[21] *R.C.A. Corporation* v. *Reddingtons Rare Records* [1974] 1 W.L.R. 1445.
[22] See above, n. 19.
[23] [1978] 1 W.L.R. 639.
[24] [1980] 1 W.L.R. 1274.
[25] *Reiner* v. *Salisbury* [1876] 2 Ch.D. 378.
[26] *Derby* v. *Athol* (1749) 1 Ves. Sen. 202; *Bent* v. *Young*, (1838) 9 Sim 180.
[27] *Dreyfus* v. *Peruvian Guano Co.*, [1889] 41 Ch.D. 151.

in a copyright infringement case when the names and addresses of customers were sought since until such persons have notice of the claim, they are not wrongdoers.[28]

"Had himself, albeit innocently"   "Innocently" means involvement without knowledge of the wrongdoing being committed.

Active involvement   **"Been involved"**   "Involved" means becoming actually involved or actively concerned in some transaction or arrangement as a result of which the person concerned has acquired the information.[29]

Without lawful authority   **"In the wrongful acts of another"**   "Wrongful acts" refers to any acts which are contrary to the law and/or without lawful authority. It is not restricted solely to acts which are tortious.[30] In practice, most wrongful acts are likely to be unlawful acts for which there are civil remedies, since a plaintiff will tend only to seek an order for discovery so that he may commence civil proceedings. At the trial of an action for discovery, discovery will be granted if the plaintiff shows that there is prima facie evidence that the wrongful acts have been committed.[31]

Involvement crucial   **"So as to facilitate the wrongdoing"**   The possessor of information must have become involved in the wrongdoing to the extent that he facilitated its perpetration. The involvement of the possessor of information is crucial to the wrongdoing, it not being possible without such involvement. Anything less than this leads to the logical conclusion that the possessor of information need not contribute to the commission of the wrongdoing at all, which would appear to be contrary to the intention of the House of Lords in the *Norwich Pharmacal* judgment. As yet, there has not been a case before the courts to question the point where a possessor of information has become involved in the wrongful acts of another without in some way facilitating the wrongdoing. A person who is not a wrongdoer and has no connection with the wrongdoing cannot be made a co-defendant to a substantive action in order that discovery can be ordered against such person.[32]

Breach of foreign law   Discovery may be ordered of the name of a foreigner who is responsible for a breach of the law other than that of the United Kingdom; but orders should not be made at the interlocutory stage[33] unless the court is satisfied that the plaintiff would probably suffer irreparable damage if there was delay in ordering discovery.[34]

---

[28] *Roberts* v. *Jump Knitwear Ltd.* [1981] F.S.R. and Copyright Act 1956, s.5(3).
[29] *Norwich Pharmacal* [1973] 3 W.L.R. 178.
[30] *British Steel Corporation* v. *Granada Television* [1982] A.C. 1096; *Bankers Trust Co.* v. *Shapira* [1980] 1 W.L.R. 1274.
[31] *R.C.A. Corporation* v. *Reddingtons Rare Records* [1974] 1 W.L.R. 1445.
[32] *Wilson* v. *Church* [1878] 9 Ch.D. 552.
[33] *i.e.* when an interlocutory injunction is sought.
[34] *SKF Laboratories* v. *Global Pharmaceutical* [1986] R.P.C. 394.

Procedure prior to commencement of the action for discovery

Initial approach to holder of information

Parties considering embarking on an action for discovery should, having assembled the facts on which they rely, approach the party who has the information, and seek to obtain it before proceedings. Departments of State are not usually willing to disclose any such information but, if the matter is explained to the Department, it will often cooperate so that the information will be made available if the court is likely to make such an order.

In the *Norwich Pharmacal* case,[35] the defendants, the Commissioners for Customs and Excise, were alleged to be infringing, or contributory infringers of, the plaintiff's patents, thus giving the right for the plaintiffs to seek discovery. The allegation of infringement by the defendants was pleaded up to the House of Lords but in argument it was abandoned and the case proceeded as an action for discovery. The case initially proceeded after service of a writ, but in the ordinary course of action for discovery, this would be inappropriate.

Application by originating summons

Action for discovery against persons in the position of being holders of information who have been involved innocently in the tortious acts of others should be commenced by originating summons with the innocent party named as defendant, which is by making an application to the High Court[36] with affidavit in support. As a result of the nature of the action for discovery, there will not be any dispute as to fact.[37]

Originating summons

An originating summons may be issued out of the central office of a district registry in respect of proceedings intended to be in the Queen's Bench Division, or out of chancery chambers or one of the chancery district registries in respect of proceedings intended to be in the Chancery Division.

Statement of relief claimed

An originating summons must contain a concise statement of the relief or remedy claimed in the proceedings with sufficient particularity to identify the action for discovery in respect of which the plaintiff claims that relief or remedy.[38] The essence of the originating summons procedure is that there shall not be any dispute of fact to be tried by the court (if this is the case, one should proceed by writ).

No dispute of fact

An action for discovery is essentially one to ascertain facts. Though an originating summons is not a pleading,[39] the summons should set out the facts on which the plaintiff relies, but not the evidence by which they are to be proved. Points of law may be raised in the summons. In an action for discovery, the originating summons should contain the following:

Points of law

Contents of originating summons

(a) the plaintiff believes he has a cause of action, the nature of which should be specified, against, for example, an unknown person;

---

[35] See n. 29.
[36] O. 5, r. 3.
[37] O. 5, r. 4.
[38] O. 7, r. 3.
[39] *Lewis v. Packer* [1960] 1 W.L.R. 452.

(b) the defendant (to the action for discovery) has, in the course of his legitimate business dealings, acquired information which would identify the unknown person, and information about his wrongdoing, though unaware of the acts giving rise to the cause of action;

(c) the plaintiff is unable to conduct his action unless the unknown person is identified together with details of the wrongful acts.

Relief claimed

The above are the facts upon which the plaintiff relies. The relief claimed would be that the defendant (to the discovery action) should make available to the plaintiff such information as is necessary to establish the identity of the wrongdoer, together with the details of the wrongdoing, such as documents showing that goods have been imported to this country in infringement of the plaintiff's patent rights.

Affidavit in support

An originating summons must be supported by an affidavit,[40] which must contain statements of evidence to prove the facts on which the plaintiff relies as set out in the originating summons. If the deponent is not aware of a fact from his direct experience but relies on information given to him by another, the source of the information should be given.

Affidavit of company

If a company is seeking information in an action for discovery, it may well be necessary for several departments within the company to provide facts for the action. The affidavit in support of the originating summons may be sworn by the company secretary or a senior officer, who would swear to the effect that the information is within his own knowledge, or has been made available to him from within the company and from the company's records. The wording is as follows:

> "I am duly authorised by the plaintiff,   Ltd. to make this affidavit on their behalf. Save where indicated otherwise I make this affidavit from facts within my own knowledge, all of which are true to the best of my knowledge, information and belief."

If any information is from another department the wording should be: "I am informed from within the company that . . . "

Defendant challenging facts

If the defendant wishes to challenge any of the facts in the affidavit, then the actual sources within the company would make affidavits. It is rare for this to happen for if the defendant does not agree with facts, he will in his own affidavit state what he believes them to be.[41]

Hearsay evidence

An affidavit should not contain hearsay evidence, *i.e.* "I have been informed by A who was told by B." The contents of the affidavit should be such that they will, if accepted by the court, prove the facts set out in the originating summons. They should be fully detailed so as to show precisely, with conciseness, the details of the difficulty in which the plaintiff finds himself being unable to wage his action without the information sought.

Belief of wrongdoing

It will, therefore, be incumbent on the plaintiff to set out the wrong he is believed to be suffering, and the reason why he believes this to be so and why it is necessary that the defendant be ordered to give discovery. For example, that it is only by

---

[40] O. 28, r. 1A.
[41] *Re J. L. Young Manufacturing Co. Ltd.* [1900] 2 Ch. 753.

Burden on plaintiff obtaining discovery from the defendant that the plaintiff can obtain the information so as to wage his action. The action for discovery is treated as an exceptional measure by the court, and it is therefore for the plaintiff to establish why such an exceptional remedy is appropriate.

Costs of the action In the action for discovery the plaintiff seeking the name of the wrongdoer will have to pay the innocent defendant's costs of obtaining the information. If a defendant is reasonably doubtful as to whether he should give the information without a court order, he may require the plaintiff to apply to the **Defendant's costs** court for an order before he does so, and the plaintiff will have to pay his costs.[42] If however, the case is one where it is manifest that a court will make an order, the innocent defendant to the action may not be awarded costs.

Discovery costs A plaintiff, having obtained the name of a wrongdoer in an action for discovery in which he has to pay the costs, may recover **recoverable from** the costs of the action for discovery as part of his damages if he is **wrongdoer** successful against the wrongdoer, provided that the wrongdoer knows, or ought to know, that steps by way of investigation or discovery were likely to be made as a result of his wrongdoing.[43]

Service The originating summons is served using the same procedure for service of a writ,[44] that is service can be personal or **Body corporate** by post.[45] If the defendant to the action for discovery is a body corporate other than a limited company, one serves on a specified officer of the corporation or by delivery, as for personal service to an individual, or if a body corporate, one serves to its registered office or principal office of the body.[46]

In most cases, the action for discovery will be commenced *inter partes*, and will only arise because the defendant to the discovery action has refused to make the discovery. In such cases, **Service on** it is usual for a solicitor to be appointed to accept service of the **solicitor** originating summons on the defendant's behalf.

Ex parte application

An application can be made *ex parte*, but it would seem the only **Risk of destruction** reason for doing this would be if there was a substantial risk of **of evidence** evidence being destroyed. In most cases this would be unlikely, for if a defendant to a discovery action is innocent of any wrongdoing, there is no reason why he should not be willing to co-operate with the plaintiff, at least to the extent of holding the evidence until the plaintiff has obtained his order for discovery. There may well be cases, however, where certain individuals, whether for themselves or in the conduct of the business of a limited company, may be likely to destroy evidence. In such a case, an *ex parte* application may be sought, but there will be a very heavy onus on the plaintiff to prove the necessity for such proceedings.

In the event of *ex parte* proceedings being successful, the

---

[42] *Harrington* v. *North London Polytechnic* [1984] 1 W.L.R. 1293.
[43] *Morton-Norwich Products Inc.* v. *Intercen (No. 2)*, D.C. [1981] F.S.R. 337.
[44] O. 10.
[45] *i.e.* in the course of mail or by posting in the defendant's letter box.
[46] O. 65, r. 3.

Application to set aside

defendant would be faced with an order requiring discovery unless he showed good cause why this should not be done. In such circumstances, the defendant, if he had good reason, would apply to have the order set aside, and would then be in the position of any other defendant to a discovery action.

Affidavit in support

Filing of affidavit

Following service of the summons, it is acknowledged by the defendant as if it were a writ.[47] Within 14 days after acknowledgement of service, the plaintiff should file the affidavit in support in the court and serve it on the defendant.[48] If the defendant wishes to produce affidavit evidence, he must do so within 28 days of receiving the plaintiff's affidavit.[49] The plaintiff may, within 14 days of receipt of the defendant's affidavit, file an affidavit in reply, with a copy served on the defendant[50] and no further affidavit evidence shall be received without leave of the court.[51] An appointment for hearing the summons is obtained within one month from the expiry of the term within which copies of the affidavit must be served under Order 28, rule 1A.[52]

Discretion of the court

Powers of the court　　Following the hearing, the court will, as a matter of law and judicial discretion, make such order as it thinks appropriate, including ordering discovery as requested either in whole or in part, or may decline to make an order.

Documents outside jurisdiction

　　The court will not, save in exceptional circumstances, order a foreigner, in particular a foreign bank, who is not a party to the principal proceedings, to produce documents which are outside the jurisdiction and which concern business transactions outside the jurisdiction.[53]

Originating application

The county court　　The county court has similar powers to the High Court.[54] Application would be by originating application under C.C.R. Order 3, rule 4 accompanied by an affidavit in support, and the procedure is similar to that for the High Court. There would appear to be no reason why orders for discovery obtained in the county court should not be used, if the information obtained warrants it, for an action in the High Court.

---

[47] O. 12, r. 9.
[48] O. 28, r. 1A(4).
[49] O. 28, r. 1A(4).
[50] O. 28, r. 1A(5).
[51] O. 28, r. 1A(6).
[52] O. 28, r. 2.
[53] *McKinnon* v. *Donaldson, Lufkin and Jenrette Securities Corporation* [1986] Ch. 482.
[54] See pp. 21 *et seq.*

5 ORDERS TO PREVENT DESTRUCTION OR CONCEALMENT OF EVIDENCE

With the great increase in fraudulent trade, such as sale of counterfeit products, counterfeiters, knowing their trade is unlawful, take steps to destroy evidence which might incriminate them if they become aware that an injured party is likely to bring proceedings against them. In such cases, an order for discovery after commencement of an action is a sham, for by the time it is made, the unscrupulous defendant will have destroyed or hidden his documents, removed or destroyed infringing materials and have no evidence of value to be discovered.

Anton Piller order
To deal with this situation, there has been created the *ex parte* search and seize remedy for discovery, known as the Anton Piller order.[1] The making of such an order in an appropriate case is not a breach of Article 8 of the European Convention on Human Rights.[2] This remedy, as well as granting various injunctions, orders the defendant to permit the plaintiff entry on to the defendant's premises so that the plaintiff may inspect, photograph and, if necessary, take away documents and other things such as products which infringe the plaintiff's rights, all of which are relevant to his cause of action against the defendant. Since the order is *ex parte*, the defendant is not aware of its existence until the plaintiff and his solicitor arrive on the defendant's doorstep. The remedy may also be granted so as to compel inspection of premises to gain information as to goods or equipment which may be at the premises, but only if this evidence is vital to the applicant's case.[3]

The Anton Piller order is an extremely powerful measure available to the court, which is required to be satisfied on the affidavit evidence before it as to whether an application for an order shall be granted. The court weighs up the effect of the order on the defendants as against the potential damage a plaintiff will suffer if the unscrupulous defendant precludes the plaintiff from obtaining the evidence to prove his case. The courts are always anxious to emphasise that the Anton Piller order is not a search warrant but merely an order to the defendant to invite the plaintiff into his premises to carry out the search and seizure operation. However, in practical terms and in most cases, the Anton Piller order operates as a search warrant with the concomitant right to seize goods.

Not a search warrant

Having established the Anton Piller order as part of the legal

---

[1] *Anton Piller KG* v. *Manufacturing Processes* [1976] Ch. 55.
[2] *Chappell* v. *United Kingdom, The Times*, April 6, 1989, E.C.H.R.
[3] *Ex p. Matshini* [1986] F.S.R. 454.

Compliance with strict rules

its premature discharge to the advantage of the defendant. The reason for these rules is to protect the interests of a defendant who cannot be at the court when the order is granted and thus only the plaintiff's side of the case is heard. Further, there are strict rules as to what can be seized under the order and the manner of dealing with material thereafter. A failure to carry out these rules may result not only in the order being discharged but also in the solicitor responsible being held in contempt of court and fined (possibly imprisoned if the breach is very grave—though this has not yet been reported as happening). The responsibility for carrying out the order is that of the plaintiff's solicitor and he is answerable to the court as an officer of the court.

Background to the Anton Piller order

Though Anton Piller orders are a fairly recent phenomenon, they are founded on precedent as opposed to statute.

Kynaston v. East India Company

In *Kynaston* v. *The East India Company*[4] Eldon L.C. held that if the court could not attain justice without inspection of premises, then the court had authority to order inspection, taking care to impose as little inconvenience as possible on those in relation to whom the order was made. This case established that where a plaintiff would otherwise be denied a remedy, the court will grant an order that the defendant permits the plaintiff entry on to his premises. It will be noted that the order is for the defendant to invite the plaintiff to inspect—there is no right to inspect without the defendant's consent.

Early *ex parte* orders

The first *ex parte* order was made in *Hennessey* v. *Bohmann, Osborne & Co.*,[5] where the plaintiffs feared that if the defendants had notice of the action they would remove incriminating evidence, this being bottles and cases. Apart from an Irish decision,[6] there appear to be no further reported cases in which an *ex parte* order for inspection and discovery has been granted until 1974 and the case of *EMI* v. *Khazan*.[7] The earliest case to be reported is *EMI* v. *Pandit*.[8]

EMI v. Pandit

In *Pandit*, the plaintiffs EMI, who owned the copyright in certain sound music recordings, initially sued the defendants *inter partes* and were granted interlocutory injunctions and orders requiring discovery. The plaintiffs later applied to the court *ex parte*, submitting evidence tending to show that the defendant's affidavit in the interlocutory proceedings was false, that he had forged a document and that a probability existed that infringing material and relevant evidence vital to the plaintiff's case was at the defendant's address. The plaintiffs applied for an order under Order 29, rules 2(1) and (2), that persons authorised by the plaintiffs be at liberty to enter the defendant's premises and inspect and seize relevant photographs and other material. The

Fear of destruction of evidence

---

[4] (1819) Ch. 3 Swanston 248–256.
[5] (1877) 36 L.T. 51.
[6] *Morris* v. *Howell* [1888] 22 L.R.Ir. 77.
[7] [1976] R.P.C. 326; *A. & M. Records Inc.* v. *Darakdjian* [1975] 1 W.L.R. 1610; *Pall Europe* v. *Microfiltrex* [1974] which are also in respect of orders granted prior to *E.M.I.* v. *Pandit* but were only reported [1976] R.P.C. 326.
[8] [1975] 1 W.L.R. 302.

Prevent further relief plaintiffs feared that if they served notice on the defendant as required by Order 29, rule 2(5), he would destroy or remove all relevant documents and articles and that the plaintiffs would therefore be effectively debarred from obtaining further relief in the action. Templeman J. held that the court had jurisdiction to make an order.

Anton Piller v. Manufacturing Processes

In 1975 came the judgment in *Anton Piller KG* v. *Manufacturing Processes*.[9] This was the first case since 1888 before the Court of Appeal ordering the defendant to permit entry, search and seizure following an *ex parte* application. The plaintiffs, Anton **Facts of** Piller KG, were German manufacturers, who had appointed the **Anton Piller** defendants as the United Kingdom distributors of their products. In the course of the dealings between the parties, confidential information passed to the defendants, concerning the plaintiffs' new electric frequency converters for computers which the plaintiffs claimed was then being passed on to their competitors, thus potentially being very damaging to the plaintiffs.

Interim injunction The plaintiffs applied *ex parte* for an interim injunction to restrain the defendants from infringing their copyrights, from disclosing confidential information, and for an order for permission to enter the defendant's premises to inspect all such documents and to remove them into the plaintiffs' solicitors' custody. They submitted that such an order was necessary to prevent the defendants destroying any relevant documents which would tend to prove the plaintiffs' case. On the plaintiffs' undertaking to issue a writ forthwith, Brightman J. granted the interim injunction but refused to order inspection or removal of documents on the ground that:

> " . . . it seems to me that an order on the lines sought might become an instrument of oppression particularly in a case where a plaintiff of big standing and deep pocket is ranged against a small man who is alleged, on the evidence of one side only, to have infringed the plaintiff's rights."[10]

Ormrod Guidelines The plaintiffs appealed *ex parte* to the Court of Appeal. The appeal was allowed and in so doing the court through the judgment of Ormrod L.J. provided guidance for the future known as the "Ormrod Guidelines." These lay down the most exceptional circumstances which must exist before an order will be made, namely, where there is clear evidence shown by the plaintiff's affidavit, that:

Clear evidence may destroy documents (a) the defendants have in their possession incriminating documents or other material and that there is a real possibility that they may be destroyed before any application *inter partes* can be made; and

Strong prima facie case (b) the plaintiffs have a very strong prima facie case that the defendants are liable to the plaintiffs for some wrongdoing; and

Serious damage (c) the actual or potential damage to the plaintiff is very serious.

---

[9] [1976] Ch. 55.
[10] *Ibid.* at p. 60.

Enter premises, remove relevant materials

In such circumstances, the court has inherent jurisdiction to order defendants to "permit" the plaintiff's representatives to enter the defendant's premises to inspect and remove such material. Further, in such very exceptional circumstances, the court was justified in making the order sought on the plaintiff's *ex parte* application.

Lord Denning M.R., in his judgment, reiterated[11] the principles established in *Entick* v. *Carrington*[12] that:

> " . . . no court has in this land, any power to issue a search warrant to enter a man's house so as to see if there are paper or documents there which are of an incriminating nature, whether libels or infringements of copyright or anything else of that kind, no constable or bailiff can knock at the door and demand entry so as to inspect papers or documents. The householder can shut the door in his face and say 'Get out.' "[13]

Permission of defendant for inspection

He added that the order sought in the case preserved the *Entick* v. *Carrington* principle and that it only authorises entry and inspection by permission of the defendants, although it does bring pressure on the defendants since it orders them to give permission when failure to do so is a contempt of court. Lord Denning found that the court had jurisdiction to make such an order following the *East India Company*[14] decision.

Lord Denning also considered whether such an order could be made *ex parte* and he decided[15] that:

Circumstances in which *ex parte* order made

> " . . . such an order can be made by a judge *ex parte*, but it should only be made where it is essential that the plaintiff should have inspection so that justice can be done between the parties: and when, if the defendants were forewarned, there is a grave danger that vital evidence will be destroyed . . . so that the ends of justice be defeated: and when the inspection would do no real harm to the defendant or his case."

Enforcement of order

Finally he stressed that the plaintiffs must act in the enforcement of the order with due circumspection. On the service of the order:

(a) the plaintiffs should be attended by their solicitor who is an officer of the court;

(b) the plaintiffs should give the defendants an opportunity to consider the order and consult their own solicitor;

(c) if the defendants wish to apply to discharge the order as having been improperly obtained, they must be allowed to do so;

(d) if the defendants refuse permission to enter or inspect, the plaintiffs must not force their way in, they must accept the refusal and bring it to the notice of the court afterwards, if need be on an application to commit for contempt.[16]

---

[11] [1976] Ch. 55.
[12] [1765] 2 Wils. K.B. 275.
[13] See n. 11.
[14] 1821 3 Bli. (o.s.) 153.
[15] [1976] Ch. 55 at p. 61.
[16] *Ibid. per* Lord Denning M.R.

Only effective measure available

Shaw L.J., concurring with Lord Denning and Ormrod L.J., stated[17] that the overriding consideration is that such an order should only be resorted to when the normal process of law would be rendered nugatory if some immediate and effective measure was not available. The order made, therefore, was that the defendants should permit one or two of the plaintiffs and one or two of their solicitors to enter the defendants' premises for the purpose of inspecting documents, files or other material and removing those which belonged to the plaintiffs, or related to the plaintiffs' equipment as well as original documents associated therewith which had been supplied by the plaintiffs to the defendants. The plaintiffs were further required to give an

Indemnity

undertaking to indemnify the defendants in the event of their suffering damage if the order was wrongly served.

Development of the order

Exceptional remedy

Difficulty satisfying Guidelines

The Anton Piller order was regarded as a most exceptional remedy but since its inception it has become commonly used. The three prerequisites of the Ormrod Guidelines[18] are stringent and the courts have taken into account that it is often very difficult, if not impossible, for an applicant to meet them. Often the evidence that the applicant needs to satisfy the first and third Guidelines is to be found in the documents that are in the defendants' possession, and it is for these that the applicant seeks the order to pre-empt the defendant from destroying them. There has thus been some alleviation of the exacting requirements originally stipulated in the Ormrod Guidelines.

First Guideline alleviated

Establishing the first of the Ormrod Guidelines, *i.e.* that the defendants have, in their possession, documents and other material relevant to the action, and there is a real possibility that they may be destroyed by them, has been made considerably less stringent by subsequent authorities. Thus the possibility in the light of surrounding circumstances of destruction or removal of evidence was considered sufficient in *Universal City Studios Inc. v. Mukhtar & Sons*.[19]

The Court of Appeal held that while in the original *Anton Piller* case there was clear evidence of the possibility that the evidence might be destroyed or disappear, it is seldom that one can get actual evidence of a threat to destroy material or documents, so it is necessary for it to be inferred from the evidence which is before the court. If it is clearly established on the evidence before the court that the defendant is engaged in a nefarious activity which renders it likely that he is an untrustworthy person, this will satisfy the first Guideline. If the plaintiff's affidavit evidence is such that it shows that the defendant is trading in a manner in which no respectable businessman would engage, this is sufficient for establishing the first Guideline.[20] The making of an Anton Piller order is only justified when there is a paramount need to prevent a denial of

---

[17] [1976] Ch. 55 at p. 62.
[18] *Ibid.*
[19] [1976] 1 W.L.R. 1540.
[20] *Dunlop Holdings and Dunlop* v. *Staravia* [1982] Com. L.R. 3, C.A.

justice to the plaintiff, which cannot be met by order for delivery up or preservation of documents. Even where the plaintiff has strong evidence that an employee has taken specific confidential information, the court must employ a graduated response. There must be proportionality between the perceived threat to the plaintiff's rights and the remedy granted. The fact that a plaintiff has behaved wrongfully in his commercial relationship does not necessarily justify an Anton Piller order. In many cases it will be sufficient to order delivery up of the plaintiff's documents pending further order, or to allow the plaintiff's solicitor to make copies.[21]

Yousif v. Salama

    The Court of Appeal decided in *Yousif* v. *Salama*[22] that the conditions for the issue of an Anton Piller order were:

(a) a prima facie case must be established following the first Ormrod Guideline;

(b) the evidence sought to be preserved must be essential to the plaintiff's case; and

(c) there must be prima facie evidence that the documents or articles sought are at risk of destruction or concealment.

Present-day guidelines

Subsequently the guidelines now for the granting of an Anton Piller order are that the plaintiff must establish:

(a) that he has evidence to indicate an extremely strong prima facie case of infringement of his rights;[23]

(b) that the damage to him, potential or actual, is very serious;[24]

(c) that he has clear evidence that the defendants have, or are likely to have, in their possession incriminating documents or materials which are essential to the plaintiff's case;[25]

(d) there is prima facie evidence that the documents or things are at risk of being destroyed or concealed[26] or that the defendant is engaged in the sort of activity which by its nature reflects on the untrustworthiness of the defendant and thus he could not be trusted to preserve evidence which would be utilised against him in the action;[27] and

(e) there must be a paramount need to prevent a denial of justice to the plaintiff which can only be met by ordering search and seize, delivery up or preservation of documents. The fact that a plaintiff has behaved wrongfully in his commerical relationship does not necessarily merit an Anton Piller order. [28]

Emergency remedy

    Interlocutory injunctions are emergency remedies. The plaintiff is asking the court to interrupt its routine proceedings and allow the plaintiff's application to be heard with priority because of the damage that will be suffered it it were not. If the court is asked for an immediate remedy because of the

---

[21] *Lock International* v. *Beswick* [1989] 1 W.L.R. 1268.
[22] [1980] 1 W.L.R. 1540.
[23] *Anton Piller KG* v. *Manufacturing Processes* [1976] Ch. 55.
[24] *Ibid.*
[25] *Ibid.*
[26] *Yousif* v. *Salama* [1980] 1 W.L.R. 1540.
[27] See above, n. 20.
[28] See above, n. 21.

importance and urgency of the matter to the plaintiff, then it is incumbent on the plaintiff to show that he has treated the matter with immediacy. In the case of an Anton Piller order, one is also seeking a remedy whereby one inspects the premises of another and takes items therefrom, without the defendant's case being heard. It is therefore incumbent on all applicants for these orders to give the fullest information.

Extension of the order

Use in any civil action

In the example given the plaintiff has suffered from his goods being counterfeited by the defendant and is applying for an Anton Piller order to claim an injunction to restrain the defendant from infringing his trademark rights and also passing off, as well as the other elements required in such an order. The Anton Piller process may, however, be used in any form of civil action where the facts justify it. Examples are listed below.

Intellectual property Anton Piller orders have been granted in cases concerning other forms of intellectual property such as patent, design and copyrights.

Confidential information Anton Piller orders[29] have been granted to prevent misuse of confidential information[30] and also wrongly on transpiring the information was not confidential. What is or is not confidential information arises normally through contract between the parties. With regard to employees there is generally a stricter duty of confidentiality during employment than if it had ceased. Once it has ceased it is necessary to have regard to the circumstances of each case to determine whether a matter is confidential or not, the circumstances being:

(a) the nature of the employment. If employed in a capacity where confidential material is habitually handled this may impose a high obligation of confidentiality;

(b) the nature of the information. It will only be protected if it can be properly classed as a trade secret or which requires protection as such;

(c) whether the employer impressed on the employee the confidentiality of the information;

(d) whether the relevant information can easily be isolated from other information which the employee is free to use or disclose.[31]

Criminal acts When a crime has been committed but not a civil wrong, *e.g. ex parte Island Records*[32] where the crime was under a statute (Copyright Act 1956) passed for the benefit of the class of individual who was wronged.[33] The law concerning criminal acts

[29] *Anton Piller KG* v. *Manufacturing Processes* [1976] Ch. 55.
[30] See *Manor Electronics* v. *Dickson, The Times,* February 8, 1990; *Lock International* v. *Beswick*, above, n. 21.
[31] *Faccenda Chicken* v. *Fowler* [1986] 3 W.L.R. 288.
[32] [1978] Ch. 122.
[33] But see the House of Lords judgment in *Lonhro* v. *Shell Petroleum Co.* (1981) 3 W.L.R. 33 which has cast some doubt on *Island Records* [1978] Ch. 122 and *RCA Corp.* v. *Pollard* [1983] Ch. 135.

and civil wrongs is in an unsettled state and it appears that an Anton Piller order will be granted when the defendant has committed a criminal act, provided that the plaintiff can establish that he has a right of action against the defendant within the civil courts jurisdiction.

Family law   The Family Division of the High Court also has jurisdiction to grant an Anton Piller order if there is a serious risk of relevant documents being destroyed by one of the parties in an action. In many matrimonial disputes the bitterness between the parties is such that they will disobey a court order, rather than disclose, for example, details of their financial position, hence the Anton Piller order is of great assistance in such cases. *Emanuel* v. *Emanuel*[34] and *K.* v. *K.*[35] were matrimonial cases in which the court held that the Anton Piller order is appropriate if the prima facie evidence is strong.[36]

Enforcement of a judgment   An Anton Piller order may be used for the purpose of obtaining documents which are essential to the execution of a court judgment and which otherwise would be unjustly denied to the judgment creditors.[37]

Refusal to grant Anton Piller orders

Technical reasons

The court has discretion in every application for an Anton Piller order to grant or refuse it or to grant it on such terms as the court thinks fit. The court's discretion must be exercised with regard to natural justice. Thus, if the facts of a particular application justify the grant of an order, it must be granted. In each case, however, the judge may require that certain elements of the order, as proposed to him, be varied, *e.g.* the number who shall attend the search and seizure operation may not be as many as the plaintiffs would wish.

Discretion of judge

Judicial discretion bears heavily on an application in considering whether, in fact, the evidence adduced comes within the guidelines; or whether there has been full material disclosure.[38] If a judge is not satisfied with any of these matters he may refuse an order. It is, therefore, useful to their case for the plaintiffs to view their position as if they were appearing before a very strict judge, and then only if they are satisfied that they have the evidence both to justify a claim for the order and for disclosure of material should the application be made.

Reasons for failure to file affidavits

There are exceptional cases where the plaintiff has not been able to assemble all the facts or make affidavits; in such circumstances there should be full disclosure of these matters by counsel to the court. Also counsel should give the reasons why it is appropriate to apply before his "tackle" is in order, and what action is being taken to remedy the matter. In these exceptional

---

[34] [1982] 1 W.L.R. 669.
[35] (1983) 13 Fam. Law 46.
[36] See also *Kepa* v. *Kepa* [1983] F.L.R. 515.
[37] *Distributori Automatici Italia S.p.A.* v. *Holford General Trading Co.* [1985] 1 W.L.R. 1066.
[38] See p. 63.

cases the court is accepting an undertaking by counsel on behalf of the plaintiff and his instructing solicitor that the necessary affidavits and other documents will be made and filed and will be in accord with what counsel has told the court.[39]

Adjournment

If a plaintiff is refused an order by the judge because a vital element is missing, counsel can ask for an adjournment to remedy the matter, with leave to reapply to the same judge as soon as this has been done.

Different jurisdictions

The English court refused to grant an Anton Piller order for the inspection of premises in Scotland, on the basis that the plaintiff should apply to the courts of that country.[40] However, the court granted an order in respect of a foreign defendant to permit inspection of a flat in the defendant's name, in Paris by a French advocate (also a member of the English Bar).[41] The circumstances of these cases are unusual. An Anton Piller order being *in personam* it should not normally be the subject of an application against a party over whom the court has no jurisdiction. Jurisdiction over a foreign party not resident in the jurisdiction should not be assumed. The court will not grant an order against an English defendant who is said to control the foreign party.[42]

"Fishing expedition"

An Anton Piller order will be refused if it appears that the object of the application is to find out what claims may be made against a defendant.[43] Accordingly writs should be drafted in such manner that it is clear what the action is against the defendant.

Privilege against self-incrimination

In *Rank Film Distributors* v. *Video Information Centre*,[44] the House of Lords held that an Anton Piller order should not be executed if the defendant was able to show that if he complied with the order he might incriminate himself and thus become liable to prosecution. A few months after the decision, section 72 of the Supreme Court Act 1981 was enacted which provides that the right of such a defendant to refuse to comply with an order is not permissible in intellectual property cases in civil proceedings in the High Court. In all other types of case, such as matrimonial dispute[45] and enforcement proceedings,[46] the decision in *Rank Film Distributors* v. *Video Information Centre*[47] continues to apply.

Representative actions

In counterfeiting cases it is common to find a chain of traders who have handled the same bogus goods. An Anton Piller order is not usually a suitable vehicle for a representative action because some of the traders may have handled the goods not realising that they were counterfeit and as such it is difficult to assert that they would destroy or remove the evidence.[48] In *EMI Records* v.

---

[39] *W.E.A. Records* v. *Vision Channel 4* [1983] 1 W.L.R. 721.
[40] *Protector Alarms* v. *Maxim Alarms* [1978] F.S.R. 442.
[41] *Cook Industries Inc.* v. *Galliher* (1979) Ch. 439.
[42] *Altertext* v. *Advanced Data Communications* [1985] 1 W.L.R. 457.
[43] *Hytrac Conveyors* v. *Conveyors International* [1983] 1 W.L.R. 44.
[44] [1982] A.C. 380.
[45] *Emanuel* v. *Emanuel* [1982] 1 W.L.R. 669.
[46] See above, n. 37.
[47] See above, n. 44.
[48] *Rogers (Jeffrey) Knitwear Productions* v. *Vinola (Knitwear) Manufacturing* [1985] J.P.L. 184.

Kudhail[49] an order was granted against dealers in cassette recordings under their own brand name, but which recordings infringed the plaintiff's copyright.

Anton Piller orders in jurisdictions outside England, Wales and Northern Ireland

Common law actions

In many countries, especially those deriving their legal system from that of England, the courts have followed the principles enunciated by the English courts, and Anton Piller orders have been granted in:

Australia: *EMI (Australia)* v. *Bay Imports Pty.*[50]

Canada: Certain provincial courts have adopted the Anton Piller procedure where their legal system derives from the law of England.

Hong Kong: The first Anton Piller order was granted in Hong Kong in 1978 and has been commonplace since then. The courts have tended to follow United Kingdom judicial authority, and following the passing of the Supreme Court Act 1981, section 72 of which alleviated the position created by the decision in *Rank Film Distributors* v. *Video Information Exchange*[51] the Hong Kong Supreme Court (Amendment) (No. 3) Ordinance 1982 was passed incorporating the same provision.

Malaysia: *Television Broadcasts* v. *Mandarin Holdings Sdn. Bhd.*[52] The first reported case was *Lian Keow Sdn. Bhd.* v. *Paramfoths.*[53]

New Zealand: *Thorn EMI Video Programmes* v. *Kitching & Busby.*[54]

Nigeria: *Ferodo* v. *Unibros Stores.*[55]

Scotland: *British Phonographic Industry* v. *Cohen.*[56]

Singapore: *Art Trend* v. *Blue Dolphin (Pte.).*[57]

South Africa: *House of Jewels & Gems* v. *Gilbert, ex parte Matshini* [1986] F.S.R. 454.[58]

Unless bound by statute there appears to be no reason why any country deriving its law from that of England should not grant Anton Piller orders.

---

[49] [1983] Com. L.R. 280.
[50] [1980] F.S.R. 328.
[51] [1982] A.C. 380.
[52] [1984] F.S.R. 111.
[53] [1982] 1 M.L.J. 217.
[54] [1984] F.S.R. 342.
[55] [1980] F.S.R. 489.
[56] [1984] F.S.R. 159.
[57] (1983) 2 M.L.J. 93.
[58] (1983) 4 S.A.L.R. 824.

Europe: There are many countries in Western Europe which have "search and seizure" systems similar to an Anton Piller order, but conducted by the public authorities. For example, one commences a trademark action in France, by means of the *saisie contrefaçon*. This is a process where the plaintiff requests the public authorities to seize products and papers from the premises of the defendants. This is done and the items seized are examined by a court-appointed expert who reports to the court as to whether or not the goods in the example infringe the plaintiff's trademark. The court is not bound to follow the report but usually does. It is necessary to inquire in each country whether this system exists: thus it exists in certain cantons of Switzerland but not all.

County court: The county court also has jurisdiction to grant such orders,[59] but this is not often exercised owing to the limitations of jurisdiction within the county court.

---

[59] s.38 of the County Courts Act 1984, App. E and County Court Rules, App. B.

6 APPLICATION FOR AN ANTON PILLER ORDER

Procedure governed by Order 29

An Anton Piller application is normally made in the High Court, the procedure being governed by Order 29 of the Rules of the Supreme Court. The application is often made in the Chancery Division, but any division of the High Court has jurisdiction, although the procedure varies according to the division in which the application is made.

In *Refson & Co.* v. *Saggers*[1] Nourse J. said

"In the generality of cases the court has no jurisdiction to grant an injunction or any other form of relief before the issue of an originating process. . . . If the court agrees to make an exception under Order 29, rule 1(3) in return for an undertaking forthwith to cure what would otherwise be a defect in its jurisdiction, it is manifestly a serious matter if it is let down by a default on the undertaking."

Ex parte applications of the nature of Anton Piller and Mareva orders should always be made with these words in mind. It is desirable that the solicitor and counsel acting for the plaintiff in such an application should only have a professional as opposed to a personal connection with the parties.[2]

Ex parte procedure

The Anton Piller order is always sought by *ex parte* application (indeed it would have little value if it were not) and usually before an action has commenced, but there can be occasions when an Anton Piller order is sought after an action has been commenced.[3] In cases of extreme urgency, counsel can appear before the court with a draft writ, no affidavit, not even an unsworn draft, and only instructions as to the nature of the case. The court has granted an Anton Piller order on this basis.[4] The Court of Appeal confirmed that in the circumstances of that case an order should be granted, but such circumstances must be very rare and every effort should be made to have a complete case to present.

Extreme urgency

Anton Piller orders are exceptional remedies and a plaintiff should do all he can to have his counsel fully armed with the appropriate documents. The order is discretionary and any failure to have all relevant material in order can create extra difficulties, with the possibility of the order not being granted.

Plaintiff's case fully prepared

[1] [1984] 1 W.L.R. 1025 at p. 1029 and at p. 156, below.
[2] *Manor Electronics* v. *Dickson* [1988] R.P.C. 618.
[3] *Emanuel* v. *Emanuel* [1982] 1 W.L.R. 669; *EMI* v. *Pandit* [1975] 1 W.L.R. 302.
[4] *W.E.A. Records* v. *Visions Channel 4* [1983] 1 W.L.R. 721.

Exceptional remedies are only granted in exceptional cases and it is incumbent to do all that is reasonable to have one's "tackle" in order, if necessary delaying the application for a day or so, but obviously not in the case where it is feared the defendant will be bent on destroying evidence. This is unusual, as in most cases the defendant is caught by surprise.

Application to judge at home

If the court is not sitting, the application for an *ex parte* injunction may be made to a judge at his home. In such a case the solicitor should telephone the Royal Courts of Justice or district registry who will give them the telephone number of the appropriate judge. The material parts of the draft order will be read to the judge, who may require the solicitor, with counsel, to attend at his home. Only in cases of very exceptional urgency should the court be asked to act without a sight of the material parts.[5]

In such cases where it is not possible for documents to be issued owing to the court offices being closed, the draft writs and affidavits should be retained by the judge and sent by him to the central office at the earliest opportunity with instructions to treat them as issued and filed at the time when they passed into the judge's possession.[6] If draft writs and affidavits only are available, or affidavits are not even in draft, there must be an undertaking to issue the writ and sworn affidavits "forthwith" or

Expedition

"as soon as possible". This is an undertaking to expedite the matter and if the plaintiff's solicitor fails to do so he is prima facie in breach of his duty to the court.[7]

Appeal

If the order is refused at first instance, the Court of Appeal has jurisdiction to hear an appeal. Application for appeal should be made to the Court of Appeal within seven days of the date of refusal.[8] It is usual for the appeal court to hear matters in open

Hearing *in camera*

court. If it is desired that the appeal shall be heard *in camera*, counsel must inform the Registrar of Civil Appeals to that effect, and give his written reasons stating why he personally considers that this is necessary.[9] The court may agree with counsel and the matter shall so proceed, or the court can make the application to be heard *in camera* a preliminary point. It may well be that, if the decision is to hear the matter in open court, the plaintiff will abandon the appeal rather than risk the facts of the matter being made public.

Review by judge of first instance

If a defendant who is the recipient of an Anton Piller order wishes to appeal against its grant, such appeal in the first instance must be to the judge who granted the order *ex parte* or, if he is not available, to another judge. If the judge hearing the appeal refuses to discharge the order, then the defendant can appeal to the Court of Appeal. The judge, at first instance, should always hear the defendant who wishes the order to be discharged. An *ex parte* order is essentially of a provisional nature made by the judge

[5] *Refson and Co.* v. *Saggers*, see above, n. 1.
[6] *Channock* v. *Hertz* [1988] 4 T.L.R. 331 and *In re N (an infant)* [1967] Ch. 512.
[7] *Refson and Co.* v. *Saggers*, see above, n. 1.
[8] O. 59, r. 14.
[9] *Practice Note; (Court of Appeal Anton Piller Orders)* [1982] 1 W.L.R. 1420.

on the plaintiff's evidence which is before him. When the judge reviews this provisional order following submission by the defendant, he has only then heard both sides. Thus his review of the matter cannot be considered as appeal from the *ex parte* order but rather a completion of the application for the order.[10]

Costs of attendance   A party seeking relief in respect of allegations that an Anton Piller order was improperly obtained or a party served as a matter of comity against whom no relief is sought, will not be awarded costs of attendance; but a person not a party to the action against whom no relief is sought or obtained will be awarded costs immediately, and, in an appropriate case, costs will be paid on an indemnity basis.[11]

Urgency   An Anton Piller order should only be applied for in cases of urgency and is sought because there is fear of evidence being destroyed, but the usual order comprises several elements including interlocutory injunctions and orders to the defendant. Further, the plaintiff is always required to give undertakings in case it is later found that the order should not have been granted Order 29, rule 1(3) provides "the injunction applied for may be granted on terms providing for the issue of the writ or summons and such other terms, if any, as the court think fit."

Applications in the Chancery Division

Form of application   The application is made usually by motion, with affidavits in support, accompanied by a draft order which it is hoped the court will grant, and also a draft writ for the substantive action which the plaintiff proposes to serve. If the case has already been commenced, the application should be *ex parte* but by summons.[12] As an example take the case where a company is suspected of making and dealing in counterfeit engineering parts under the plaintiff's trademark "Notreve" and also using the plaintiff's identification letters and numbers. The documents with the motion should contain a draft order which the plaintiff hopes the court will grant. Such draft order of the court may contain the following:

Example

Contents of draft orders

    (a) a note referring to the court reading the draft writ and affidavit evidence with exhibits;
    (b) undertakings by the plaintiff and undertakings by the plaintiff's solicitor;
    (c) injunction against the defendant:
       (i) order to the defendant concerning disclosure and preservation of documents and materials,
      (ii) order to the defendant to permit the plaintiff and his solicitor inspection of the defendant's premises and to search for documents and materials and to remove them, and
     (iii) order to the defendant to make an affidavit concerning names, addresses, etc., of those receiving or passing to the defendant counterfeit parts and confirming they do not have any documents or

---

[10] *W.E.A. Records* v. *Visions Channel 4 Ltd.* See above, n. 4.
[11] *Piver (L.T.) Sàrl* v. *S. & J. Perfume Co.* [1987] F.S.R. 159.
[12] *EMI* v. *Pandit* [1975] 1 W.L.R. 302.

infringing parts in their possession (this last will arise as by then the search and seizure operation will have taken place).

Such an order could thus be set out:

IN THE HIGH COURT OF JUSTICE

CHANCERY DIVISION

MR. JUSTICE NICKLEBY (sitting *in camera*)
20th day of SEPTEMBER 1990

IN THE MATTER OF AN INTENDED ACTION
B E T W E E N   CONWAY LIMITED (Intended plaintiff)
and
JUPITOR LIMITED (Intended defendant)

UPON MOTION made by Counsel for the intended plaintiff(s) (hereinafter called the plaintiff)

Court reading the papers AND UPON READING [Draft Writ of Summons and the Affidavits]
AND the plaintiff by [his her its their] Counsel undertaking

Writ
(1) forthwith on or before September 27, 1990 to issue a Writ of Summons claiming relief similar to or connected with that hereafter granted
(2) to make and file an Affidavit [verifying what was alleged by Counsel] [in the terms of the draft Affidavit of
]

Service of notice of motion by the solicitor
(3) to serve upon the Intended Defendant(s) (hereinafter called the defendant(s)) by a Solicitor of the Supreme Court of Judicature being a member or employee of the firm of Messrs. Jarndyce & Co. the plaintiff's solicitors a copy of the said Affidavit and the copiable Exhibits thereto and Notice of Motion for October 2, 1990

Future order as to damages
(4) to obey any Order this Court may make as to damages if it shall consider that the defendant(s) shall have sustained any damages by reason of this Order which the plaintiff(s) ought to pay

Undertakings in respect of innocent third parties
[(5) to obey any order this Court may make to damages if it shall consider that any innocent parties other than the defendant(s) shall have sustained any damages by reason of this Order which the plaintiff(s) ought to pay]

AND the Solicitors for the plaintiff(s) by Counsel for the plaintiff(s) being their Counsel for this purpose undertaking

Explain order in everyday language
(1) to offer to explain to the person or persons served with this Order its meaning and effect fairly in everyday language and to advise the person on whom the same is

Advice to defendant served of his right to obtain legal advice before complying with this Order provided that such advice is obtained forthwith

Safe custody
(2) to retain in their safe custody until further order all

articles and documents taken or delivered to them pursuant to this Order

Answer defendant's queries   (3) to answer forthwith any query made by the defendant(s) as to whether any particular [document/article] is within the scope of this Order

List things prior to removal **Defendant's copy**   (4) to make a list of all articles and documents obtained as a result of this Order prior to removal of any such articles or documents into their safe custody and provide to the defendant or the person served with this Order a copy thereof prior to such removal

Return originals to defendant   (5) to return the originals of all documents obtained as a result of this Order within 2 working days of removal of the same

Ownership in dispute   (6) where ownership of any article obtained as a result of this Order is disputed to deliver up an such article to the custody of solicitors acting on behalf of the defendant within 2 working days of receipt of any undertaking in writing from the defendant's solicitors to retain the same in safe custody and production in required to the Court

IT IS ORDERED

Injunction   (1) that the defendant(s) [and each of them] be restrained until after October 2, 1990 or until further Order in the meantime from doing (as regards the defendant(s) whether by   directors or servants or agents or any of them or otherwise howsoever) the following acts or any of them that is to say

     (i) using the plaintiffs' trade marks and part numbers and letters details being set out in the draft writ to describe parts not of the plaintiffs' manufacture or otherwise representing that parts not of the plaintiffs' manufacture or merchandise are the plaintiffs' goods

     (ii) destroying defacing or parting with the possession custody or control of any infringing parts or any documents relating to the manufacture purchase sale or supply thereof

     (iii) directly or indirectly informing or notifying any person company or firm of the existence of these proceedings or of the provisions of this Order of the plaintiffs' interest in these proceedings or otherwise warning any person company or firm that proceedings may be brought against [him her it them] by the plaintiff(s) otherwise than for the purpose of seeking legal advice from [it his her their] lawyers

Further orders   (2) that the defendant(s) do disclose forthwith to the person serving this Order upon [him her its them]

Orders to disclose   (a) all infringing parts in their possession custody power or control,

     (b) all invoices books of sale order books and other documents in their possession custody power or control relating to the manufacture purchase sale or supply by them of infringing parts,

     (c) to the best of the defendants' knowledge and belief

     (A) the names and addresses together with telephone, telex and fax numbers of all persons who have

supplied or offered to supply [him her its them] with
infringing parts

(B) the names nad addresses together with telephone,
telex and fax numbers of all person to whom [he she
it them] has/have supplied or offered to supply any
infringing parts

(C) full details of the dates and quantities of each offer to
supply and supply referred to in (A) and (B) hereof

Delivery up to plaintiff's solicitor

(3) that the defendant(s) do deliver forthwith to the plaintiffs'
solicitors all infringing parts and all documents relating to
the manufacture purchase sale or supply thereof which are
in [his her its their] possession custody or power and if any
such item exists in computer readable form only the
defendant(s) shall cause it forthwith to be printed out and
deliver the print out to the plaintiffs' solicitors (or failing a
printer) to be displayed in a readable form

(4) that the defendant(s) and each of them whether by
[himself herself itself themselves] or by any person
appearing to be in control of the premises hereafter

Invitation to plaintiffs

mentioned do permit the persons serving this Order upon
them and such other persons duly authorised by the
plaintiffs (such persons not to exceed [four] in number
altogether) to enter forthwith at any time between 9
o'clock in the morning and 6 o'clock in the evening the
premises known as Priory House, Stirling Road,
Strathmore [and any other premises or vehicles to the
extent that any of the said vehicles or premises are in the
power possession occupation or control of the
defendant(s)] for the purpose of looking for inspecting
photographing and taking into the custody of the
plaintiffs' solicitors all items and materials referred to in
paragraph 3 above or which appear to the plaintiffs'
solicitors to be such items or materials

(5) that within 7 days after service of this Order the
defendant(s) do make and serve on the plaintiffs' solicitors

Defendant's affidavit

an affidavit or affidavits setting out all of the information
to be disclosed pursuant to this Order and exhibiting
thereto all relevant documents AND the defendant(s) is
are to be at liberty to move to vary to discharge this Order
upon giving to the solicitors for the plaintiffs 24 hours
notice of intention so to do

Elements of the order

Reading of draft Writ of Summons and the affidavits   The
order sets out that the court has read the draft writ and the
affidavits attached to the order. The purpose is to confirm that
the court is fully aware of the plaintiff's case, as set out in the
writ, and the affidavit evidence is such, or should be such, that it
is plain why an Anton Piller order should be granted. It is on the

Importance of affidavit evidence

evidence as set out in the affidavits and only that, on which the
court will judge the matter. The affidavits may be in draft form
or just facts submitted by counsel, which will be required to be
confirmed by sworn affidavits. On any review of the matter, the
court may be asked by the defendant to consider evidence that
the plaintiff failed, in the defendant's opinion, to disclose in his

affidavits. If the court considers that the evidence should have been included, the order may be discharged.[13]

Draft Writ of Summons   The writ is in the form of that which will be served on the defendant to commence the substantive action. The writ[14] sets out briefly the plaintiff's claim.

Amendment

The writ   If the plaintiffs consider, after the order has been granted, that the writ could properly include other matters they must issue a new writ or go back to the court for amendment. If one serves the writ with the order but in a form not approved by the court, the order is likely to be discharged.

Affidavits   These must be sworn by persons who have knowledge of the matter or have access to such knowledge and are in a responsible position such as one of the plaintiff's solicitors, or an in-house legal adviser or a senior executive. In any case, the person must have gained the knowledge personally by perusal of documents or by talking to persons who are aware of the facts. As has been noted, the court may accept draft affidavits if there has been no time to get them sworn. In *W.E.A. Records* v. *Visions Channel 4*[15] a draft writ alone was submitted to the court and counsel had to inform the court of the nature of the case. The Court of Appeal allowed the order to be issued.[16]

Persons in responsible position

Draft affidavits

Undertakings by the plaintiffs and their solicitors   An Anton Piller order, if wrongly granted or improperly carried out, may cause the defendant serious damage. Accordingly, undertakings are required which are given by counsel in open court on behalf of the plaintiff and his solicitor. It is for the plaintiffs' solicitors to ensure the undertakings are carried out. These undertakings become part of the order. The usual undertakings are as follows:

Usual undertakings

(a) to issue the writ in terms of the draft writ forthwith;[17]
(b) to serve upon the defendant notice of motion for a given date—usually seven days from the date of the order, but it can be shorter or longer. The plaintiff is then required to return to the court *inter partes* in order to obtain continuing interlocutory relief, by which date the Anton Piller order will have been executed;
(c) the order, with the affidavit, must be served by a solicitor who is a member or employee of the practice, (which must be named) which represents the plaintiff. It should not be served by anyone else.[18] It is also desirable that any expert accompanying the solicitor be named together with the total number of the party accompanying the solicitor.[19] The order should be addressed to the defendant, its

---

[13] See p. 62 under Affidavits.
[14] For an example of a writ and consideration of elements, see p. 60.
[15] See above, n. 4.
[16] For further consideration of what affidavits should disclose see p. 63.
[17] See pp. 65 and 152 for the meaning of "forthwith".
[18] *International Electronics* v. *Weigh Data* [1980] F.S.R. 423.
[19] *Vapormatic Co.* v. *Sparex* [1976] 1 W.L.R. 939.

servants or agents and it may provide that it may be served on the person appearing to be in charge of the premises;[20]

Undertakings as to damages

Undertakings by solicitors

(d) if, following application by the defendant, the court is of the opinion that the order was wrongly granted, then the plaintiff must undertake to pay any damages the court may order. The plaintiff's solicitors are also required to give undertakings, which they do through the plaintiff's counsel, at the time of the hearing. The court must be satisfied that the plaintiff is good for sums which may be due upon this undertaking as to damages. It is customary to file a copy of the plaintiff's most recent annual accounts. This will be by way of exhibit to the affidavit in support. However, in *Salford Plastics* v. *Greene*[21] although the plaintiff defaulted in respect of his undertaking to produce his accounts, the order was not discharged. Failure to produce accounts can be very serious both for the plaintiff and also his legal adviser;[22] and

Safe custody

(e) the plaintiff's solicitor must make a list of all things obtained prior to removal to give a copy to the defendant and to undertake to keep in safe custody anything obtained as a result of the order (following the "search and seizure" operation). The undertaking with regard to safe custody and non-disclosure of the defendant's documents is permanent unless discharged by order of the court. The originals of the documents must be returned within two working days.

Undertakings personal to the solicitor

The last undertaking is personal to the solicitor and as far as safe custody is concerned, while he may permit his client, the plaintiff, to have copies of documents seized for the purpose of the case, it is the solicitor's responsbility to see that these documents are not improperly used. The solicitor is responsible personally to the court if there is failure to comply with the undertaking by the client, even though the client would also be liable.

Advice to the defendant

(f) In addition, the solicitor must undertake at the time of serving the order to advise the defendants as to the meaning and effect of the Order in *every day language* that they may seek legal advice before complying with the terms of the order. Failure to do so or do so properly is a contempt of court[22a] as is failure to answer any queries of the defendant as to whether any item is within the scope of the Order;

(g) if ownership of any article is disputed it must be delivered to solicitors for the defendants within 2 working days of such solicitors agreeing to retain them in safe custody and to produce to the Court if required. If solicitors are not appointed by the defendant, the plaintiffs' solicitor should apply to the court for instruction.

---

[20] *Gates* v. *Swift* [1981] F.S.R. 57. This case sets out the order which should be considered only in the light of the form on p. 53 which is issued by the Drafts Department of the Chancery Division of the Royal Courts of Justice.

[21] *Salford Plastics* v. *Greene* (1986) 11 E.I.P.R. D. 197.

[22] *Manor Electronics* v. *Dickson*, *The Times*, February 8, 1990; [1988] R.P.C. 618

[22a] *VDU Installations* v. *Integrated Computer Systems & Cybernetics*, *The Times*, August 13, 1988.

Contempt of court

Failure on the part of either the plaintiff or his solicitor to comply strictly with these undertakings is contempt of court, and apart from any penalty for contempt the Anton Piller order will, in most instances, be discharged, with the possible consequence of having to pay damages to the defendant as well as costs.

See *Manor Electronics* v. *Dickson*[23] in which Scott J. said:

> "It is important and has to be understood by all practising solicitors and barristers to be important that procedural undertakings included in ex parte orders should be scrupulously honoured: ignorance and convenience are no excuse."

Injunction against the defendant

The injunctions in the order are for a short period of time,[24] but in most cases once the matter becomes *inter partes*, the parties agree that the interlocutory injunctions will subsist until after

Discharge or variation

trial. The injunctions may be discharged or varied on application by the defendants and may be the subject of appeal in the usual way. It would be unusual for an injunction to be discharged on the grounds that damages are an adequate remedy if the allegation is that the defendant is making and selling or selling counterfeits of the plaintiff's product.

Restraint of infringement

Form of the injunction   The first injunction is in common form restraining the defendant from infringing the trade mark "Notreve" (a registered trade mark) or passing off in respect of the plaintiff's part numbers and letters or trade marks not registered.

Restraint of destruction

The second injunction operates so as to keep in being parts which infringe the plaintiff's rights and any related documents, in the sense that none may be destroyed, defaced or disposed of. This has the effect that any such things should be available for the search and seizure operation.

Restraint of communication

The third injunction forbids the defendant from informing anyone whether directly or indirectly of the existence of the order or the proceedings. An exception is made in that the defendant is able to consult his legal adviser. The purpose behind this injunction is to stop the defendant from getting in touch with those who may supply him or to whom he may supply infringing parts. The importance of this injunction is not so much that the defendant will naturally obey it (some will, but in counterfeit cases may not), but that he should be warned when the Anton Piller order is served that if, for example, he telephones anyone to

Warning to defendant

warn them of what has happened, the recipient of the message may not be relied upon to refrain from informing the plaintiff's solicitor if later he is approached for evidence; in consequence, the defendant could find himself facing contempt proceedings.

Continuance of injunctions

Following the return date, the parties may agree to continue certain of the injunctions. It should not be necessary to continue all the injunctions and orders, for the defendant should have complied with some and those will no longer be required. If it

---

[23] See n. 22 and p. 151.
[24] *i.e.* until the return date.

later transpires that the defendant had failed to comply, he will be liable to face contempt proceedings.

In addition to the injunction there are certain orders with which the defendant must obey.

Order to produce relevant documents and materials   When the solicitor serves the order he should draw the attention of the defendant, *inter alia*, to that part of the order which directs the defendant to produce all infringing parts in the possession, custody, power or control of the defendant. In addition he must produce all invoices, books of account and other documents relating to the manufacture, purchase, sale or supply by the defendant of infringing parts. It is the duty of the defendant to help the plaintiff in his task even though it reveals information damaging to the defendant.

Duty to help plaintiff

Names and addresses   The defendant is required to give full details of the persons to whom he has supplied, or from whom he has obtained, infringing parts together with their names and addresses, telephone, facsimile and telex numbers.[25] There is authority to the effect that such an order should not be made on an *ex parte* application,[26] but it does not appear to have been followed.

Full details necessary

Order permitting entry, search and seizure   The order does not give the plaintiff the right, as with a search warrant, to enter forcibly but it is an order of the court instructing the defendant to allow the plaintiff to carry out "search and seizure" of relevant documents and other things such as infringing parts. An order should not contain a provision to the effect that the plaintiffs' representatives have a right to be admitted to premises, *i.e.* not invited.[27]

No right to use force

Search and seizure   The order is that the defendant permits the solicitor serving the order and others named or enumerated in the order (including representatives of the plaintiff):

(a) to enter named premises of the defendant between 9.00am and 6.00pm. The order should have been so drafted that search may be made at any office or part of the defendant's premises where there is good reason for considering that relevant material lies. It may also be appropriate to include in the order a person's home, but the evidence to justify this must be very compelling for a court to grant it;

All relevant premises covered

(b) to search for relevant documents and infringing parts; and
(c) to remove those found to the plaintiff's solicitor's custody.

Prior to the "search and seizure" operation taking place, the plaintiffs and their solicitor should plan the operation very carefully if they are to achieve the greatest benefit from it.[28] In the course of the search and seizure operation, the plaintiff's

---

[25] *EMI Records Ltd* v. *Spillane* [1986] 1 W.L.R. 967.
[26] *Wilmot Breedon* v. *Woodcock* [1981] F.S.R. 15.
[27] See above, n. 22.
[28] See p. 67.

Custody of relevant documents solicitor will be likely to take into custody infringing parts and documents relevant to the case. It may be a difficult question to decide what may be taken and the manner of dealing with it, but what are known as the Scott Guidelines[29] should be followed.

If the defendant does not permit the search and seizure operation, he is in contempt of court, and while some defendants refuse immediate compliance and make an urgent application to have the order set aside, until the order is set aside the defendant is liable to be punished for contempt of court.

Non-compliance is contempt

Defendants are at liberty to move to vary or discharge of order The order ends with the declaration that the defendant may apply for discharge of the order upon giving the plaintiff 24 hours' notice of his intention to do so. If the defendant intends to seek discharge of the order following service he must do so forthwith, for until it is discharged the defendant is in contempt of court. It is also important that if for any reason there is delay occasioned by the defendant in allowing the order to be carried out, he should not regard it as an opportunity to make away with relevant material, for if he does so the penalty upon him will be severe.[30]

Application must be without delay

The terms of the writ

The writ in the hypothetical case discussed above could be as follows:

IN THE HIGH COURT OF JUSTICE   1989 D No.1234

CHANCERY DIVISION

BETWEEN   CONWAY LIMITED Plaintiffs
                                                  and
                                          JUPITOR LIMITED Defendants

To the defendants Jupitor Limited

[Then the usual wording for a writ followed by:]

The plaintiff's claim is for

Injunction

1. An injunction to restrain the defendants whether acting by their directors, servants or agents or otherwise howsoever, from doing any one or more of the following acts, that is to say:
   (i) offering for sale or selling engineering parts which are not the parts of the plaintiffs under or by reference to the plaintiffs' registered trademark "Notreve" or a mark confusedly similar thereto of by reference to part numbers which commence with the letter groups CON, CO, CONW and/or CANW;
   (ii) offering for sale or selling any engineering parts which are not the parts of the plaintiffs' under or by reference to the corresponding part number of the plaintiffs;

[29] See p. 75.
[30] See above, n. 4.

(iii) selling or supplying a response to an order for an engineering part placed by reference to the said trademark or a mark confusingly similar thereto or to a part number of the plaintiffs any part which is not the part of the plaintiffs;

(iv) infringing the plaintiffs' registered trademark "Notreve" and passing off or attempting to pass off or causing, enabling or assisting others to pass off parts bearing the plaintiffs' part numbers and letters not of the plaintiffs' manufacture or merchandise as for the plaintiffs' goods.

Delivery up

2. Delivery up or destruction upon oath of all infringing copies of any one or more of the aforesaid parts used or intended to be used to infringe the plaintiffs' right as set out aforesaid.

Damages

3. An enquiry as to damages including additional damages to be awarded to the plaintiffs by reason of the defendants' acts of infringement conversion and passing off or, alternatively, at the plaintiffs' option an account of profits and payment of all sums due upon such enquiry or account together with interest pursuant to section 35(A) of the Supreme Court Act 1981.

Disclosure of information

4. An order that the defendants do disclose to the plaintiffs upon oath all information known to them and all documents in their possession, custody, powers control relating to:

(i) the sale or supply by the defendants of engineering parts not of the plaintiffs' manufacture or merchandise as and for the plaintiffs' goods, and

(ii) further or other relief,

(iii) costs.

Elements of the writ

Paragraph 1 This is a claim for an order to restrain the defendant from offering or dealing generally in the course of trade, with parts which are in infringement of the plaintiff's registered, common law or unregistered marks. The unregistered **Unregistered marks** are those letter symbols accompanied by numbers which **marks** the plaintiff will use in identifying the various parts he manufactures. He may use them on his drawings, parts manuals, invoices to customers and the like. In the case given by way of example, it will be the plaintiff's contention that in his particular trade, his part numbers and letter codes are used only by him for parts for the type of machinery in which he deals, and that this is well known to the trade; the consequences being that if anyone in that trade, experienced in dealing with parts, saw an order for "CON 1234 bush", he would assume that to be one of Conway Ltd.'s parts.

In many cases such examples of common law marks will not occur, but the practitioner should ask his client about this as very often the client will not realise the significance of his position.

Paragraph 2—"Delivery up or destruction" This claim is in common form but the Anton Piller order will require such delivery up to the plaintiff, so that the evidence is not destroyed.

Paragraph 3—"Enquiry as to damages"   This is in common form.

Paragraph 4—"An order that the defendants disclose"   This is ancillary to the Anton Piller order and by the time of the return date following the order, this disclosure should have been made.

Continuance of order to disclose   The writ, however, is of a continuing nature, *i.e.* to the end of the action, and the defendant is required to make disclosure to the plaintiff of information available, or which should be available to him at the time of the action. Thus if the defendant has traded in parts covered by the terms of the writ which he has forgotten about, and some of these, after the date of the Anton Piller order and writ, are returned to the defendant by a dissatisfied customer then the defendant should disclose this further information which comes into his possession to the plaintiff, as well as tendering them for removal and inspection.

Particulars of allegations   The writ is in wide terms and one has to look to the affidavits attached to the order,[31] for particulars as to what the plaintiff is alleging, though it is clear that there is an allegation of the infringement of the trademark "Notreve". The statement of claim will later be served and that will contain particulars, but prior to the action the particulars are set out in the affidavits in support of the order.

Further consideration of affidavits in support

The matter of who should swear the affidavits in support of an Anton Piller order has already been discussed[32] together with the use of draft affidavits. It is appropriate to consider what these affidavits should contain in some detail.

The underlying principle is that the affidavits should include such material as is necessary to comply with the guidelines for granting an Anton Piller order.[33] These should show that, if the facts set out and the opinions given in the affidavit are right or sound, then:

Contents of affidavit in support

(a) the case is one of urgency and importance and the acts complained of may have serious consequences to the plaintiff;

(b) the intended defendant is likely to destroy or in other ways render unavailable pertinent evidence. As it is unusual to have direct evidence to prove this likelihood, it is sufficient to show that the defendant has been shown to be untrustworthy in other or even related matters.[34] This can be adduced if the facts alleged against the defendant show that he is engaging in dishonest or a nefarious activity and is therefore the sort of person who might well destroy evidence;[35]

(c) the plaintiff's case is such that the evidence shows that there is an extremely strong prima facie case of

---

[31] See below.
[32] See p. 56.
[33] See p. 44.
[34] See above, n. 12.
[35] *Dunlop Holdings and Dunlop* v. *Staravia* [1982] Com.L.R. 3.

infringement of the plaintiff's rights. It cannot go further
than that as the defendant may be able to show that he was
not the party to be sued or he was licensed to do that
which took place or he may raise some other defence;

(d) injunctive relief is necessary because, in the circumstances
of the case, damages would not be an adequate remedy.
The damage is very serious to the plaintiff if the activity is
not abated;

(e) the defendant is liable to the plaintiff in the terms of the
draft writ; and

(f) there is full disclosure of material facts so that the Anton
Piller order will be not only granted, but also not
susceptible to discharge on the application of the
defendant, without even any enquiry as to the merits of
the original order. The disclosure goes beyond what is
required to prove the case.

**Just and
convenient**
The ultimate test for the exercise of the court's discretion is
whether, in all the circumstances, the case is one in which it
appears to the court "to be just and convenient" to grant the
injunction.[36] "Thus the conduct of the plaintiffs may be
material" *per* Kerr L.J.[37] This case was concerned with a Mareva
injunction but the same principle applies to an Anton Piller
application.

Material disclosure

**Disclosure of all
relevant facts**
It should be in the forefront of an applicant's mind that the court
must be fully informed of all facts that are relevant to enable the
court to come to a decision as to whether or not to grant the
order.[38] There are facts, which are additional to those required to
prove the plaintiff's case, which need to be disclosed. There is
some judicial variance as to what is material disclosure and how
far it can affect the court's discretion; in these circumstances it is
better to submit as much evidence as possible. The plaintiff
should, so far as it is reasonably possible, put forward all facts so
as to minimise the grounds for having the order discharged. In
making the plea before the court, it is important that all matters
are put to the judge by counsel even though he is disinclined to
hear them.

Any dispute as to whether a plaintiff has made full and frank
disclosure in obtaining an Anton Piller order should not, save for
an application to discharge the order, be investigated at the *inter
partes* interlocutory hearing, as its purpose is to regulate what is
to happen in the future not the past.[39] It is no answer to say that
the order has been justified by the results of its execution.[40]

The following are some of the matters to which the plaintiff
must address himself:

---

[36] SCA 1981, s.37.
[37] *Ninemia Maritime Corporation* v. *Trave Schiffahrtsgellschaft* [1983] 1 W.L.R.
1412 at 1426.
[38] Browne-Wilkinson J. in *Thermax* v. *Schott Industrial Glass* [1981] F.S.R. 289.
[39] *Dormeuil Frères* v. *Nicolian International (Textiles)* [1988] 1 W.L.R. 1362; but
contrast with *Manor Electronics* v. *Dickson*, n. 22 and *Lock* v. *Beswick* where it
was clearly shown that the material non-disclosure has attended the obtaining
of *ex parte* relief.
[40] See n. 22.

<table>
<tr>
<td>

Plaintiff to investigate the case

Particulars about the defendant

Plaintiff's reputation

Misleading terms

No evidence of likelihood that materials would be destroyed

No disclosure of previous dispute

</td>
<td>

(a) The plaintiff has a responsibility to investigate the case as fully as possible before applying for the order; the results of the investigation should be reflected in the affidavits.[41]

(b) There should be included in the affidavits facts about the defendants, the nature of their trade, how long they have been in business, and the facts and reasoning that leads one to conclude that they may be infringing the plaintiff's right, together with copies of their recent accounts if available. Also included should be facts or opinions which lead to the conclusion that they are likely to destroy or make away with relevant evidence. The application will not fail if some of these facts are not available but the affidavit should acknowledge that a search has been made.

(c) Evidence of the plaintiff company's reputation and the way in which its parts (using the example of counterfeit parts as referred to in the draft writ[42]) are designed and sold, as well as evidence of its financial position. The most recent accounts should be sufficient to show the plaintiff is good for any award against it, if called upon to honour its indemnity which it undertakes as one of the conditions for the granting of the order. Failure to disclose the financial position of the plaintiff could be a reason for refusing to grant an order.

(d) In *Thermax* v. *Schott Industrial Glass*[43] an Anton Piller order was set aside because there was a failure to disclose that the intended defendant was part of the Karl Zeiss Group, nor was it disclosed that before the *ex parte* proceedings had commenced the plaintiff had been refused permission to enter the defendant's premises because of the confidential information there. Although it was truthful, the affidavit filed had been couched in such terms that the court could be misled. The order was set aside but if there had been full disclosure it is doubtful if the order would have been made.

(e) In *Jeffrey Rogers Knitwear Productions* v. *Vinola (Knitwear) Manufacturing Co.*,[44] the order was discharged because, *inter alia*, there was nothing to support the claim that the defendants might destroy evidence.[45]

(f) There was no disclosure in *Wardle Fabrics* v. *Myristis*[46] of the fact that in a previous dispute between the parties, the defendant had honoured the plaintiff's rights. As a result, the order was discharged but Goulding J. stated that if he had known of that fact he would have still granted the order. In later proceedings, citing the defendant for contempt of court for failing to obey the order before

</td>
</tr>
</table>

---

[41] *Rogers (Jeffrey) Knitwear Productions* v. *Vinola (Knitwear) Manufacturing Co.* [1985] J.P.L. 184 and *Practice Note* (1983) 1 All E.R. 1119, which though issued by the Queen's Bench Division by para. B(3) may also apply in the Chancery or any other division.

[42] See p. 60.

[43] See above, n. 38.

[44] See above, n. 41.

[45] But note that it does not appear from the judgment that *Dunlop Holdings and Dunlop* v. *Staravia* [1982] Com.L.R. 3 was cited to the court.

[46] *Wardle Fabrics* v. *Myristis* [1984] F.S.R. 263.

discharge, the defendant was required to pay the plaintiff's costs of the application.

Not material disclosure

(g) The court has held[47] that the following facts (either individually or collectively) are not to be categorised as "material disclosures" for the purpose of refusing to discharge an order:

  (i) the parties had traded together;
  (ii) the quantifiable damage to the plaintiff/defendant (costs were only £6–7000);
  (iii) the nett value of the plaintiff's premises were incorrectly stated. This is relevant when considering the plaintiff's worth and therefore being able to satisfy any undertaking given in the order as to damages/costs to the defendant; and
  (iv) there had been a dispute regarding a poaching of a member of staff from the plaintiff by the defendant.

In the same case, the affidavit dated May 18, stated that the plaintiff had learned of the defendant's tortious activity in the "past few days" when they had known of it since the beginning of May. This was held to be a material non-disclosure but did not apparently affect the grant of the order. This authority is difficult

Booker McConnell v. Plascow

to distinguish from the Court of Appeal decision in *Booker McConnell* v. *Plascow*[48] which held that, in the event of material non-disclosure, the Anton Piller order should be discharged without investigation of its merits, if for that reason it should not have been made.[49] *Booker McConnell* is worthy of study: it is a case in which the proceedings were described by the Court of Appeal as "far from satisfactory," though some of the leading advocates and solicitors in Anton Piller matters were engaged in the court of first instance and in executing the order. *Columbia Picture Industries* v. *Robinson*[50] offers an example of an Anton Piller order where there was not proper disclosure.[51]

The matters referred to above, should, if they exist, be included in the affidavits as should also any matters, which, however fanciful, might be considered material. The more recent authority *Manor Electronics* v. *Dickson*[52] indicates that the court is tending to take a very severe view of any apparent laxity by solicitors and counsel. In this case the Anton Piller and writ were issued but not executed or served for five days. This was not "forthwith" and the plaintiff's solicitors were held to be in breach of their undertaking.

Accordingly one should so prepare one's case that the order be executed and writ and other papers served within two days of the order being made.

Exhibits

Exhibits attached to the affidavit form part of the affidavit and should be filed in the court. The affidavits and the exhibits form the evidence which the defendant must receive.

It may be necessary to disclose to the court highly

---

[47] *Galley Cosmetics* v. *Number 1* [1981] F.S.R. 556.
[48] [1985] R.P.C. 425.
[49] *Gom Automation* v. *Giles* [1985] 8 E.I.P.R. D. 139.
[50] [1987] Ch. 38.
[51] See Scott Guidelines, p. 75.
[52] See n. 22.

Confidential information

confidential technical information to prove that the defendant's copies of the plaintiff's products are not made in accordance with the plaintiff's specification. It could be damaging if the defendant becomes aware of the plaintiff's information, as this could enable him to use it improperly. In an appropriate case, application should be made to the court that the information be disclosed only to the defendant's counsel or solicitors with an order that the defendant shall not be permitted to receive that information. The court will not wish to agree to such order but may do so if the grounds are sufficiently strong and that the defendant will not be disadvantaged by only his legal advisers being made aware of the specified technical information.[53]

No information must be given to the court *ex parte* which the plaintiff is not prepared to disclose to the defendant's legal adviser.[54] A defendant, on receipt of an Anton Piller order must, in complying with its terms, deliver up any material required and also make an affidavit. This matter is considered in Chapter 7.

Change of circumstances or matter relating to plaintiff's affidavit

In respect of Anton Piller orders a plaintiff has a duty to inform the court as soon as he becomes aware that the court has been misled or not fully informed of any material facts at the *ex parte* application—as also any charge in material circumstances.[55]

---

[53] *Amber Size Co.* v. *Menzel* [1913] 2 Ch. 239.
[54] See above, n. 4.
[55] *Commercial Bank of the Near East* v. *A* (1989) 139 New L. J. 645.

7 SERVICE AND EXECUTION OF THE ANTON PILLER ORDER

Preparatory work required

An Anton Piller order should be served as soon as possible after it is granted, preferably within 2 days.[1] In order that the search and seizure operation is executed efficiently and in compliance with the law, much preparatory work should be done before the application for the order is made, based on the assumption it will be granted. Detailed information such as the names and addresses of relevant people who are to be served with the order should be acquired, and a full list of what to look for and request should be made. A list of questions should be prepared to put to the defendant and his employees. When the order has been accepted by the defendant and the plaintiff's party admitted to the building, each member of the party should have been allotted a list of his duties beforehand and be ready to carry out its requirements.[2]

Attendance at the search and seizure operation

Naming of parties in attendance

The solicitor who is to serve the order may be named, but the firm of which he is a member *must* be named in the order. If an expert is necessary, he should also be named, as well as any special authority he may be given (such as to operate a particular computer system). It is also usual to ask for the assistance of some of the plaintiff's employees to assist with identification of documentation and material. There should be at least one person to take notes of all that is said and what takes place. It is useful to have a pocket recorder, as well as a camera.

Police presence

The number of those to attend at the execution of the order is specified in the order. It is common to inform the local police that an Anton Piller order will take place; they may decide to send an officer to prevent a breach of the peace. Also the local police may be able to advise whether there is likely to be trouble. It is important, however, that the execution of the order does not appear to be part of a police activity, otherwise the order may be discharged.[3] Many Anton Piller orders are served without the police being informed; it is a matter for the plaintiff's solicitor's judgment as to whether or not there may be trouble, and he should inform himself of any facts which could help him come to an opinion on these matters before the order is obtained.

[1] See *Manor Electronics* v. *Dickson* [1988] R.P.C. 618.
[2] See also conduct of the search operation, p. 74.
[3] *I.T.C. Film Distributors* v. *Video Exchange, The Times*, June 17, 1982.

Service

Proper procedure to be followed

The Anton Piller order is addressed to the defendant, his servants or agents, and the manner and circumstances in which an order is served are of very great importance, for if there is failure to do this properly, the order is likely to be discharged, whatever the merits of the case.

Though there is no rule of law to the effect, a solicitor should never attempt to execute an Anton Piller order alone. It should be borne in mind that those receiving Anton Piller orders

Responsibilities of serving solicitor

may react violently to the order, and further, if there is a dispute later as to what took place, the solicitor, if alone, is at a disadvantage when giving evidence. The solicitor serving the order is in charge of the operation. He is, as such, responsible to the court for the execution of the order, and if anything wrongful occurs, either by him or a member of his party, he will be personally liable to the court.

In *A.B.* v. *C.D.E.*[4] an Anton Piller order was obtained against an ex-employee of the plaintiff with his new employer being joined as third party. The solicitor responsible for conducting the "search and seizure" operation visited the third party with a policeman who confirmed that the solicitor had a

A.B. v. C.D.E.

right of search. The solicitor did not take copies of the affidavit evidence given in support of the application for the Anton Piller order, as required by the order, nor did he inform the third party of the right to consult a solicitor. These failures were heavily criticised. The order was discharged on the grounds that there was no power to grant interlocutory relief against a party against whom there was no cause of action, *i.e.* the third party employer, as the affidavit evidence disclosed. In any event, the order in the case would have been discharged because of failure to serve it properly.[5]

Attendance must be made during normal business hours. On reaching the defendant's premises the solicitor in charge should

On whom to serve the notice

ask to see the most senior person present (*e.g.* the managing director). If proper inquiries have been made earlier, the name of the managing director and most senior people in the company will be known and should be asked for by name. Often it will be difficult to gain audience with the managing director or other higher official of the company. Once it is stated or a message passed that there is an order of the court to be served, with the possibility of penalties if it is not, then the person required to be seen will, if he is at the premises, usually make himself available. In certain cases, and prior investigation will reveal whether this i necessary, it may be advisable to have a member of the party at the rear of the premises to prevent persons responsible from avoiding service.

In *EMI Records* v. *Kudhail*[6] an Anton Piller order was granted against certain named defendants and those selling

EMI Records v. Kudhail

cassettes under the "Oak Record" label since anyone selling under that label was selling products in breach of the plaintiffs'

---

[4] *Sub nom.* [1982] R.P.C. 509.
[5] See also *Booker McConnell* v. *Plascow* [1985] R.P.C. 425 where similar facts arose.
[6] [1983] Com.L.R. 280.

copyright. Photocopies of the order were made and a letter attached giving a full explanation of the legal position. The solicitors for the plaintiffs gave the named defendants and each trader selling the "Oak Record" cassettes a photocopy of the order and letter. The legal position was explained verbally and all the cassettes bearing the "Oak Record" label were seized under section 18 of the Copyright Act 1956 (which provides that the ownership of goods which infringe a copyright belong to the copyright owner).

Ex parte Seatrade

In *Ex parte Seatrade*[7] a secretary to the senior director was served with the order as she was the only person in the office at the time the plaintiff's solicitor arrived to serve the order. If

Procedure following service

whoever receives the solicitor appears to be in charge, even if only temporarily, owing to more senior people being too busy or absent, he or she must be given a copy of the order and the

Explanation of order

affidavits with exhibits (if any). The solicitor must next explain very clearly the nature of the order. He should advise that a failure to comply with the order could lead to contempt of court proceedings. He should go through each feature of the order and explain its meaning in "easy to understand English." If the person in charge claims not to understand English, then the well-prepared solicitor will have been aware of this possibility and have an interpreter with him. If, however, the solicitor is caught

Interpreter

by surprise then he should stay on the premises and summon an interpreter. In such cases, the element of surprise is likely to be lost and the person denying knowledge of English will probably understand sufficient to appreciate what is happening and inform others in his own language. The consequences of being in contempt of court should also be explained. Finally the solicitor

Legal advice

must explain very carefully that the defendant has the right to seek legal advice, but if he wishes to avail himself of the opportunity he must do so forthwith, *i.e.* by telephone.

Defendants can be reminded that though the respondents to Anton Piller orders may go to the court which granted the order

Risk of contempt

to have it discharged, until the order is lifted, refusal to obey puts them in danger, not only of contempt proceedings, but also of adverse inferences being drawn against them.[8] If such respondents are allowed to delay matters, the purpose of the order and procedure would be largely lost.[9] The solicitor should advise the particular individual to whom he is speaking that if he causes the company to refuse to obey the order, *i.e.* by refusing entry, he may also be in contempt and is personally answerable to the court for such contempt. If the situation is that he has standing instructions to admit no one without permission from his superior, it could be wrong to threaten the person with contempt of court proceedings.

No authority to admit

If the solicitor is speaking to a person who feels that he or she does not have the authority to allow execution of the order, then that person should be advised to get in touch with someone who has such authority or, failing that, contact the company's solicitors to seek immediate advice. A well-prepared Anton Piller party will have attempted to find out the name of the defendant's

---

[7] (1986) (unrep.).
[8] *Anton Piller KG* v. *Manufacturing Processes* [1976] Ch. 55 at p. 61.
[9] *Columbia Picture Industries* v. *Robinson* [1986] 3 All E.R. 338.

solicitors beforehand, and should, if possible, be armed with their address and telephone number. In *Ex parte Seatrade*[10] the director's secretary, as no one else was in the office, took this action, and the company's solicitor advised her to let the order be carried out, which she then permitted. She let the party use the firm's photocopier, for which a charge could have been levied.

In those cases where a defendant's solicitor is contacted by a member of the defendant's staff with an inquiry as to what to do, it may be useful if the plaintiff's solicitor explains the position to the defendant's solicitor direct. Following that conversation, the **Advice from** plaintiff's solicitor should withdraw from the room to allow the **defendant's** defendant's solicitor to advise his client privately. If the **solicitor** defendant's solicitor cannot be contacted immediately, four hours should be allowed for advice to be sought.

Refusal to admit If in the result the defendant declines to obey the order, the **Anton Piller party** plaintiff's solicitor and his party must retire. The remedy is to bring the defendant before the court for contempt, which should be done immediately with a warning to the defendant that these steps are being taken. In *Wardle Fabrics* v. *Myristis*[11] the defendant's managing director refused to allow the plaintiff's solicitor and representatives to search the premises. On being summoned for contempt, the defendant was required to pay the costs of the contempt application on a full indemnity basis. In this case, the order was discharged as there had not been full disclosure by the plaintiff, but Goulding J. held that as long as the order stood, failure to obey was a contempt. The fact of discharge was, however, of value in considering the level of penalty.

The fact that a plaintiff cannot insist on "search and seizure" appears to be a weakness in the system, but in practice it is rare for the defendant to destroy evidence in the intervening period. As a practical matter, it is difficult to destroy the evidence without this being apparent to an examiner of records.

Position of the defendant

If a solicitor is contacted by a client, being a defendant to an Anton Piller order, prior to the "search and seizure" operation commencing, he should make himself available, if required, to attend on his client, or otherwise try to advise him by telephone. **Attendance of** On the assumption that he will attend on his client, he should ask **defendant's** to speak to the plaintiff's solicitor with the order, explain that he **solicitor** will be attending and to defer the operation until his arrival. He should also advise his client to take no action and to inform no one of what has occurred.

On arrival at the defendant's premises, the solicitor should ask the plaintiff's solicitor to explain everything which must be done under the order, even if the explanation is repeated for the second time. The defendant's solicitor should check in detail what is being told to him, as this may give grounds for discharge of the order. Having received the information, the defendant and his solicitor should consider the order very carefully not only to

[10] See above, n. 7.
[11] [1984] F.S.R. 263.

Defects in order

establish what must be done, but to ascertain if there are any defects, especially with regard to material disclosure. There may also be a good reason for the order being discharged[12] because the defendant is not liable to the plaintiff. Before advising a defendant to refuse to comply with an Anton Piller order, his solicitor should bear in mind the words of Lord Denning in the *Anton Piller* case:[13]

Risk on refusal

"The order serves to tell the defendants that, on the evidence put before it, the court is of the opinion that they ought to permit inspection—nay it orders them to permit— and that they refuse at their peril. It puts them in peril not only of proceedings for contempt but also of adverse inferences being drawn against them, so much so that their own solicitor may often advise them to comply."

Further comments in *Columbia Picture Industries* v. *Robinson*[14] were made by Scott J. who said:[15]

"If the respondents to an Anton Piller order were to be allowed to delay their execution while application to apply to discharge was being made, the purpose of Anton Piller orders and procedure would be largely lost."

Privilege against self-incrimination

Plaintiff's solicitor informed of application for discharge

In certain circumstances, the defendant need not comply with elements of the order if to do so would tend to incriminate him.[16] If the defendant's solicitor is of the view that the order should be discharged and application made to that effect, and the client agrees, his solicitor should inform the plaintiff's solicitor as follows:

(a) the defendant will seek to have the order discharged immediately as there are strong grounds—of which the plaintiff's solicitors should be informed—for contending that it would never have been granted if all information had been before the court;

(b) in these circumstances it is inappropriate to carry out the Anton Piller order now;

(c) his client has no wish to be in contempt of court and his client is prepared to enter into an undertaking not to do anything that will affect the position by disposing of evidence or informing anyone of the Anton Piller order.

If an Anton Piller order is granted wrongly because the court was not informed of all the facts and the plaintiff's solicitor is made aware of this, he may well agree to abstain from insisting on execution of the order for to do so could place his client at risk of paying full costs to the defendant.[17]

Expeditious application

It is incumbent on the defendant to bring the matter before the court with all speed, *i.e.* in a day or two, at most, and any failure to do so will be regarded adversely by the court, for the defendant is in contempt of court prior to any discharge.

Defendant's solicitor/counsel bear a very heavy

---

[12] See above, n. 4.
[13] See above, n. 8.
[14] See above, n. 9.
[15] *Ibid.* at p. 368.
[16] See p. 47.
[17] *WEA Records* v. *Vision Channel 4 Ltd.* [1983] 1 W.L.R. 721.

responsibility and they should advise their client that disobedience to an Anton Piller order, such as refusing to permit search and seize, places the client in contempt of court. However, if an application is made to discharge the order at once the courts have tended not to punish for contempt.

Variation or discharge While the defendant may apply for discharge immediately following receipt of the order, he also has the right at any time to apply for the order to be varied or discharged on giving 24 hours' notice to the plaintiff's solicitor.

Application for discharge

This will not be granted if the application is made a considerable time after the order was issued.[18] Any application for discharge will be made *inter partes*. The defendant may bring evidence in affidavit form to show why the order should not have been granted *ab initio*. The grounds for discharge may include those matters set out on pp. 64, 65 and see the Scott Guidelines.[19]

High Court judge

Application for discharge should be made to the judge who granted the order or if not available, another High Court judge. An appeal should not be made to the Court of Appeal until the case has been heard *inter partes* by the court of first instance. In a case when the order is not discharged, providing the defendant has acted with expedition, the court will not, except in exceptional circumstances, exact penalties for contempt, especially if the defendant has acted on the advice of his lawyers.

No penalties for contempt

Compliance with the order A defendant, in addition to admitting the plaintiff's solicitor and party to his premises, must also comply with the other elements of the Anton Piller order. It is not sufficient for him just to admit the party and leave them to get on with the work. The defendant should permit the plaintiff's solicitor to search the premises, and also take documents and other materials covered by the order; the defendant should also, voluntarily, deliver up such materials. It is for the defendant to decide (with the aid of his legal adviser if present) what is or is not an infringement, a relevant document or material required to be disclosed in his affidavit and what ought to be delivered to the plaintiff's solicitor.

Responsibilities of defendant

If the defendant takes a very narrow view of what is an infringement, for example not disclosing parts or papers marked "Motreve" or "Knotreve" as not being infringement of the plaintiff's mark "Notreve," then he may expect, if this failure is discovered, an application to be made to commit him for contempt. Quite clearly such marks are confusingly similar to the plaintiff's trademark "Notreve."

Narrow view of infringement

In respect of documents, the court by the Anton Piller order is seeking to ensure preservation of documents, not only of direct evidence, but even those which do not necessarily form the subject-matter of the action, *e.g.* a particular document which may be the best evidence from which inferences may be drawn. An Anton Piller order in respect of identified computer programs may include, as part of the order, that the defendant print out material in a computer-readable form. If the defendant's

Computer programs

---

[18] See above, n. 9 at p. 378.
[19] As set out in *Columbia Picture Industries* v. *Robinson*. See above, n. 9 and p. 75.

computer is to be used, the order should so specify. This part of
the order can also include computer-readable material in his
possession.[20] It may be appropriate for the plaintiff's computer
expert to be at the search and seizure operation and possibly to
operate the defendant's computers and software. If this is
required there must be a full explanation to the judge with the
expert named in the order. If the running of the computer costs
money, or the plaintiff wishes to make photocopies of documents
on the defendant's premises (unless the order so provides, which
is unusual, the defendant may refuse), but the defendant can
charge for all such use on a reasonable basis.

The defendant's affidavit   The defendant is required to swear
an affidavit in the terms of the order[21] as well as comply with its
other terms.

The final part of the Anton Piller order instructs the
defendant within seven days of the order to make and file an
affidavit. This is a very important part of the order. It requires

Full declaration   the defendant to make a full declaration within the terms of the
order and any default on his part is a contempt of court. In the
example given,[22] the defendant must reveal names and addresses
and other information of those whom he has supplied, or those
who have supplied the defendant, with infringing material, and
state that the defendant does not have any other relevant
documents or infringing parts or items which have not been
disclosed. If the defendant discloses that there are documents or
infringing parts in his possession then these should have been
delivered to the plaintiff's solicitor by then.

A summary of the course of events is as follows:

Summary
(a) The plaintiff's solicitor arrives and is admitted to the
office of desirably the most senior person at the
defendant's premises. Having explained the order to such
a person, and informed the defendant of his right to take
legal advice, the defendant should then ask the plaintiff's
solicitor to retire in order that he can consult his solicitor.
(b) At the time the defendant telephones his solicitor, which
should be immediately upon the plaintiff's solicitor
retiring, he should have with him the copy of the order,
the draft writ and affidavits, including any exhibits in
support.
(c) The defendant's solicitor, on having the paper read to
him, should offer to come round to his client's office, and
if this can be done in a reasonably short time then he will
do so.
(d) If the defendant's solicitor is unable to go to the premises
or to send anyone, he should advise the defendant to
admit the party, and while cooperating with them as
required by the order, take a full note of what transpires.
The solicitor should also advise his client of the
consequences of disobeying the order, but also of his right
to apply to the court to have it varied or discharged. It is

[20] *Gates* v. *Swift* [1981] F.S.R. 57.
[21] See p. 55.
[22] See p. 55.

desirable that both solicitors agree with each other as to what is going to happen.

Procedure following execution of the order   The *ex parte* order,[23] including the injunction, is granted for a short period and on the return date the defendant has an opportunity to seek to have the injunction lifted and the order discharged, but the search and seizure element of the order by this time may have been carried out, and application for discharge of that element should be made as soon as possible following service.[24] The injunction cannot be continued beyond the return date without further order being sought.[25] In most cases the parties agree as to the continuance of the injunction and the matter proceeds to trial (or settlement) in an orderly way, with the plaintiff having discovered the evidence and also the defendant having entered into an affidavit in compliance with the order.

Conduct of the search operation

The search by the plaintiff's solicitor and party may take place once a defendant consents to it. It is important that prior to the plaintiff's party visiting to serve the order, full preparation is made to conduct the search and seizure operation. A check-list should be made of the type of documents and other items that are required for the plaintiff's case and for which search should be made and delivery up given, with the visitors ready to examine all of these. A list of questions should be prepared, the answers to which will indicate what the defendant has in his possession. A list of places to search such as safe, filing cabinets and stores should also be made.

Check-list

An Anton Piller order is set out on p. 53 and a combined Anton Piller/Mareva Order at p. 121. The elements of the order must be read out to the defendant and he is asked to comply item by item, this involving the production of documents and other items in accordance with the order. In addition the searching party may search the premises. This should be done with a representative of the defendant. Anything may be searched if it likely to or may be used to obtain required material. The files and items should be examined very thoroughly and any documents or items likely to be of value to the plaintiff's case taken into custody. A note should be made of the files from which documents are drawn. The plaintiff's party should be careful to restore to the proper place anything not required. The premises should be left in a similar state as that in which they were found. This procedure may take several days. With counterfeit cases especially, one should search the places of manufacture and where parts are stored.

Search

Any documents or parts which come within the terms of the order may be seized. If there is a tool which can only be used for manufacturing counterfeit products and has no other purpose, this is of value as evidence and may be seized. Tools which can

Items to be seized

---

[23] See p. 53.
[24] If search and seizure has been refused, see above, p. 70.
[25] *Bolton* v. *London School Board* [1878] 7 Ch.D. 766.

used for conventional purposes as well as for making counterfeits should not be seized, though a photograph may be taken of such a tool and notes made of the detail and its location.

Examination of files

In particular when examining files, it is useful to see if papers have been deliberately removed as this can indicate that the defendant had been engaged in an activity which he would rather conceal. It is not wrong to remove papers before the order, but one finds that in company files it is difficult to remove all such incriminating papers. Thus, in one example, the defendant had caused all green copies of documents to be removed from his file and left only white. The green documents related to exports often of counterfeit products. This was clear as some torn-off corner pieces were left in the file. However, some of the "green copies" had been photocopied on white and filed with the word "green" written on them. These white "green" copies had not been removed and contained evidence of value to the plaintiff. These facts clearly indicated that the defendant had been engaged in a nefarious activity which he was trying to conceal, and inferences adverse to the defendant could be drawn by the court.

Monitoring

The carrying out of the search and seizure operation of an Anton Piller order should be monitored with great care, and questions have arisen as to what may lawfully be seized under an Anton Piller order and also how long such material can be retained. The leading authority on this matter is *Columbia Picture Industries* v. *Robinson*.[26] In this case in which both a Mareva injunction (see Chapter 8) and an Anton Piller order were served, the plaintiff's solicitor was found to be in breach of his

Columbia Picture Industries v. Robinson

undertaking under the order. The solicitor also failed to carry out the terms of the Mareva injunction, to the disadvantage of the defendant. Aggravated damages were ordered to be paid by the plaintiffs to the defendants. (The plaintiffs would presumably recover this sum together with any related expenses from their solicitor). The case was one in which material was seized and retained for an inordinate number of years and where some items had been lost. In addition it was suggested that some items seized were irrelevant to the issue between the parties. For details of this case, see p. 141.

Scott Guidelines as to seizures

The *Colombia Picture Industries* authority sets down[27] guidelines with regard to material which can be seized under an Anton Piller order. These are known as the Scott Guidelines.

The five criteria essential to the execution of an Anton Piller order are:

(a) the order must be drawn so as to extend no further than the minimum extent necessary to achieve its purpose, namely, the preservation of documents or articles which might otherwise be destroyed or concealed. Once the plaintiffs' solicitors have satisfied themselves what material exists and have had an opportunity to take copies thereof, the material ought to be returned to its owner;

[26] *Columbia Picture Industries* v. *Robinson* [1986] 3 All E.R. 338.
[27] *Ibid.* at p. 371.

(b) a detailed record of the material taken should always be made by the solicitors who execute the order before the material is removed from a defendant's premises;

(c) no material should be taken from a defendant's premises unless it is clearly covered by the terms of the order;

(d) seized material, the ownership of which is in dispute, should be handed over to the defendant's solicitors on their undertaking for its safe custody and production;

(e) the affidavits in support ought to err on the side of excessive disclosure. In the case of material falling into the grey area of possible relevance, the judge, not the plaintiffs' solicitors, should be the arbiter.

(a) **Relevant material**   The plaintiffs' solicitors should take what they consider to be relevant material. No material should be taken from the respondents' premises by the executing solicitor unless clearly covered by the terms of the order. The solicitor in charge of execution, having established what material exists, both by way of being delivered to him by the defendant, his employees and by operation of the search procedure, must then decide what is relevant. As it is also the duty of the solicitor to remain on the premises of the defendant for as short a time as possible, it is **Generous** permissible to have a fairly generous interpretation of what is **interpretation** relevant so as to include what might turn out to be irrelevant. It is most important that documents should only be taken if covered by the order and, in particular, it is quite wrong to take papers whose absence would embarrass the defendant in the conduct of his legitimate business, unless they include matters which are the subject of the order. It also follows that it is wrong to take **Personal papers** personal papers such as documents relating to the defendant's matrimonial problems. Anton Piller orders are to preserve evidence that might otherwise be destroyed—it is quite improper for them to be used as an instrument of coercion or to close down a business.

    If there is doubt as to whether material seized is relevant to the issues of the case, the judge should be asked to decide. In **Caution** effecting a search of the defendant's premises, the plaintiff's solicitor will try to err on the side of caution and take any material likely to be of probative value. Thus it is likely that much of the material will not ultimately be required.

(b) **Copies and retention**   Material taken should be copied and then the material ought to be returned to its owner. The material should be retained for only a relatively short period of time. By leave of the defendant, copies may be taken on his photocopying machine, for which a reasonable charge may be levied. Documents may, with the consent of the defendant, be copied on the premises of the defendant or otherwise the plaintiff may have them taken away and copied. In any event copies should be made and once made, the originals should be returned **Return of originals** to the defendant. An exception to this may arise in, for example, the case where ownership is in dispute, or in the case of material, the subject of copyright where it is not appropriate for the material to be returned.[28] Having taken copies of the documents

[28] See below, p. 77.

and returned the originals, the solicitor should then return all copies of documents which are not relevant to the proceedings.

(c) Record It is essential that a detailed record of the material taken should always be made by the solicitors who execute the order before the material is removed from the defendants' premises. So far as possible, disputes as to what material is taken, can be avoided by providing adequately detailed receipts recording what is taken.

A record of documents and material to be taken should be strictly compiled and in some detail. Thus simply the contents of File A would not be sufficient as this gives no indication of what is in the file, but the contents of a file relating to the export of identified material between given dates and to whom, and giving the number of documents would be because this lists each document. If possible, the list of documents and material should be agreed with the defendant. It is most important that disputes as to what is taken should not, so far as is possible, be dependent on the oral testimony of the plaintiff's solicitor and the defendant. A solicitor's sworn testimony as to what has been taken is more likely to be preferred to the evidence of a defendant which is not corroborated, and this is unfair to the defendant.

(d) Consent of defendant The respondent (defendant) to the order should not be required to give the solicitor performing the seizure operation a consent to material being removed unless the respondent's solicitor has been present to confirm and ensure that the consent was a free and informed one.

There have been occasions when a defendant has been "persuaded" to sign a document to the effect that he has consented to the plaintiff's solicitor taking away material even though outside the terms of an order. The intention underlying such consent may have been to cover any documents seized which were not included in the order.

The court will not be prepared to accept that a "consent" such as this had been freely and effectively given unless the defendant's solicitor had been present to confirm that the defendant has an opportunity of considering the position and that his consent was freely given.

(e) Ownership of seized material in dispute Seized material, the ownership of which is in dispute, should not be retained by the plaintiff's solicitor pending trial. If the proper administration of justice requires that material taken under an Anton Piller order should, pending trial, be kept from the defendant, then as soon as the solicitor for the defendant is on the record, the plaintiff's **Delivery to** solicitor should deliver the material to such solicitor on the **defendant's** undertaking for its safe custody and production, if required, in **solicitor** court.[29]

Use of information by the plaintiff

Information obtained under an Anton Piller order must always be used only for the purposes of the action which is the subject of

[29] See above, n. 26 at pp. 371 and 376.

the order. It is of great value not only for the trial but also when interviewing witnesses, who are often reminded of what they had forgotten, or say they had forgotten, when they are shown relevant documents.

    If the plaintiff, in obtaining the information under the order becomes aware of the possibility of criminal offences being **Possibility of** committed, the information obtained should not be used in **criminal** connection with any criminal proceedings without leave of the **proceedings** court. See *General Nutrition* v. *Pradnip Pattni*[30] in which the court refused leave to permit the plaintiff to pass to the police copies of documents found in an Anton Piller search which indicated that criminal acts may have taken place. This was followed by *EMI Records* v. *Spillane*[31] in which Sir Nicholas Browne-Wilkinson V.-C. said:[32]

> "So long as documents are held solely as the result of discovery, particularly discoveries under compulsion under an Anton Piller order, it would be quite wrong to authorise their use in criminal proceedings brought under fiscal laws, and having no connection with the original cause of action.'

    One of the implied undertakings that a solicitor gives when obtaining discovery in the ordinary course of any civil proceedings is not to use any of the material discovered for a purpose other than the proper conduct of the action for which **Undertaking as to** discovery is given. This undertaking must be strictly respected. **use of material** In circumstances where documents obtained under an Anton Piller order reveal a breach of an earlier order made in different proceedings but between the same parties concerning the same or similar subject-matter, the implied undertaking may be varied or discharged by the court.[33]

    The above authorities are to be distinguished when **Customs and** considering *Customs and Excise Commissioners* v. *A.E. Hamlin &* **Excise** *Co.*[34] in which, while affirming that the documents could only be **Commissioners** v. disclosed pursuant to an order of the court, the court gave **Hamlin** permission in the circumstances of this particular case for its evidence to be released to the prosecution authorities. In *Custom and Excise Commissioners* v. *Hamlin Slowe*[35] the V.C. decided that the earlier *Hamlin* case should not be followed but held that after the action giving rise to the Anton Piller order was settled, Hamlin's the solicitors for the plaintiffs held the seized documents to the order of the defendants and as they had not consented to the production of the papers to the Commission in the exceptional circumstances of the case, it was proper for the court to authorise disclosure of the documents. In *L. T. Piver* **L. T. Piver** v. *Sarl* v. *S. & J. Perfume Co.*[36] it was held that a person who, in **S. & J. Perfume** the execution of an Anton Piller order, sees an article proving infringement of the rights of someone other than the plaintiff, may properly report the matter to the person concerned, although he may not lawfully seize the article in question.

---

[30] [1984] F.S.R. 403.
[31] [1986] 1 W.L.R. 967.
[32] *Ibid.* at p. 977.
[33] *Crest Homes* v. *Marks* [1987] A.C. 829.
[34] [1984] 1 W.L.R. 509.
[35] 1986 F.S.R. 346.
[36] [1987] F.S.R. 159.

Use for further action

Leave of the court

It is said[37] that when information is obtained pursuant to an Anton Piller order there is no implied undertaking that the information will be used solely for the purpose of the existing proceedings, and unless an order specifically restricts use of information it may be used for further action without leave. A study of relevant judgments leads to the view that it is prudent always to ask the court for permission to disclose or use information obtained for further proceedings and consent will be given if there is a close connection with the original cause of action. Thus if, in the example given,[38] one finds evidence of counterfeit products being sold or being purchased by the defendant, one may use with leave documents which reveal the identity of the suppliers to the defendants or their customers in order to commence further proceedings against others. Whilst the statement in *The Supreme Court Practice 1990* may be correct in law, this will be of little value to a plaintiff if his order is discharged because a judge, in his discretion, takes a different view, since the consequences of having an order discharged can be calamitous.

Goods emanating from abroad

If, following an Anton Piller order in England, evidence found indicates the goods emanated from abroad, the court will normally give leave for the plaintiff to use the evidence for proceedings in the courts of other jurisdiction.[39] *Sony Corporation* v. *Anand* indicated that it is not necessary to seek the consent of the court in such circumstances. However, this case which gave leave for information collected under the order to be used not only for civil but criminal proceedings should be followed with care, and it is better to seek leave if one is taking action outside the jurisdiction, in this case in Hong Kong.

Action after the search and seizure operation

Continuing compliance

After the operation has finished, the activities of the defendant should be kept in mind to make certain that he is complying with the terms of the order. This is a continuing activity until trial. In this respect, his affidavit is a most important part of the process. In a big case with many documents it may take a very long time for the plaintiff to identify all that he needs for his case. As documents are studied, the plaintiff should bear in mind the defendant's affidavit to make certain he has complied with the order with regard to disclosure. Any failure should at once lead to request for an explanation, and if it is not given or is unsatisfactory, application should be made to the court with a view to ordering the defendant to do that which he has so far failed to do. In addition, the court may order cross examination of a defendant on any affidavits filed by him in purported compliance with a discovery order.

---

[37] *The Supreme Court Practice 1990*, p. 518.
[38] See p. 60.
[39] [1981] F.S.R. 398.

8 ORDERS BRINGING ABOUT PRESERVATION OF ASSETS: The Mareva Injunction or Order

Transfer of assets abroad

With the great increase in rapid communication between countries, monetary assets can be moved from one country to another within minutes. This has led to a practice whereby companies, knowing they are in debt in the United Kingdom, will transfer their assets, usually cash, out of their United Kingdom bank account direct to a place where it will be difficult if not impossible to trace. Action such as this can easily defeat the claims of any creditors in the country where the assets were situated. In such cases, a plaintiff having successfully obtained a judgment ordering the defendant to pay him, will find that the judgment may become worthless.

"Asset freezing" order

To deal with this situation there has been created the *ex parte* "asset freezing" order known as the Mareva injunction.[1] As the order comprises more than just an injunction it will be generally referred to in this work as a "Mareva order," though sometimes "Mareva injunction" will also be used. The injunction, as well as the various orders that go with it, instructs those who have assets of the defendant in their possession not to dispose of them, save under the circumstances set out in the order. Since the order is *ex parte*, the defendant is not aware in some cases of its existence until after the plaintiffs have enforced it, usually through the defendant's bank.

Extreme powers

The Mareva order and the Anton Piller order are said to be at the extremity of the powers of the court, and though ancillary to the substantive action which brings these operations into being, often decisive in their effect, as settlement quickly follows their execution. Donaldson L.J. has described them as the "law's two nuclear weapons."[2] The court has to be satisfied on the affidavit evidence before it as to whether an application for a Mareva order should be granted. The court weighs up the draconian effect of the injunction as against the very great damage a plaintiff will suffer if the unscrupulous defendant precludes the plaintiff from obtaining his award by removing assets from the jurisdiction of the court.

Strict rules

Having established the Mareva order as part of the legal system, the courts have evolved strict rules with which applicants must comply, if an injunction is to be granted, and must follow in the execution of the order. These not only protect the defendant

---

[1] *Mareva Compania Naviera S.A. of Panama* v. *International Bulk Carriers S.A.* (1975) 119 S.J. 660.
[2] *Bank Mellat* v. *Nikpour* [1985] F.S.R. 87 at p. 92.

in so far as he is not left penniless and unable to carry on his business, but also look to the interests of innocent third parties caught up in the order. Neither the defendant nor a third party (whether innocent or not) can be in court when the order is granted and thus only the plaintiff's side of the case is heard. Further, there are rules as to what can be the subject of a Mareva order and the manner of dealing with such assets. A failure to carry out these rules may not only result in the injunction being discharged but the plaintiff, or indeed the solicitor responsible, being held in contempt of court and fined. Damages may also be payable to the defendant[3] and innocent third parties will have to be indemnified in full.

History of the Mareva injunction

Though Mareva orders are a fairly recent phenomenon, they derive from the old laws. A form of securing assets to satisfy a debt was in existence under Roman law and in use during the Roman occupation when London became a centre of commerce. In Tudor times it was used in the City of London by a process **"Foreign** called "foreign attachment." It was originally used to compel a **attachment"** defendant to appear and bail was required in order to secure attendance. It was later extended to cases where the defendant was not to be found within the jurisdiction. In such cases, the plaintiff was allowed to attach instantly any money or goods of the defendants within the jurisdiction as soon as the plaint was issued. It is described in Bohun's *Privilegia Londini*[4] and updated in Pulling's *The Laws, Customs, Usages and Regulations of the City and Port of London.*[5] The system existed in many cities in England as well as in Scotland, Jersey and the maritime ports of Northern Europe. Settlers from England to the 13 colonies of America took British law with them and the process of attachment became part of the law of the United States of America.[6]

Though Mareva orders as such are relatively new, the need **Lister & Co. v.** for them at least since the Second World War was long required, **Stubbs** but it was thought they could not be granted owing to the ruling in *Lister & Co. v. Stubbs.*[7] Prior to this decision it seems that they were available, though they appear to have fallen into disuse. *Lister & Co. v. Stubbs,*[8] is a Court of Appeal judgment arising out of an action by the plaintiff suing the defendant for money; it was highly probable that the plaintiff would succeed in his action. The plaintiff applied for an order that the defendant give security to satisfy any eventual award, but the court would have none of it. It was stated by Cotton L.J.:[9]

Security for   "I know of no case where, because it was highly probable
eventual award   that if the action were brought to a hearing the plaintiff

---

[3] *Columbia Picture Industries* v. *Robinson* [1986] 3 All E.R. 338.
[4] (3rd ed., 1723), pp. 253 *et seq.*
[5] (2nd ed., 1842), pp. 187 *et seq.*
[6] *Ownbey* v. *Morgan* [1921] 256 U.S. 94. See also Lord Denning, *The Due Process of Law* (1980), pp. 137 *et seq.*
[7] *Lister & Co.* v. *Stubbs* [1890] 45 Ch.D. 1.
[8] *Ibid.*
[9] *Ibid.* at p. 13.

could establish that a debt was due to him from the defendant, the defendant has been ordered to give security until that has been established by the judgment or decree."

Lindley L.J.[10] went even further:

Refusal to stretch principle

"We should be doing what I conceive to be a very great mischief if we were to stretch a sound principle to the extent to which the Appellants (the plaintiffs in the court below) ask us to stretch it, tempting as it is to do so."

So the law stood both at common law and under the Judicature Acts in 1890.

There is, and has been for centuries, an exception to what the Court of Appeal found to be the law in *Lister & Co.* v.

Exceptions *Stubbs*.[11] It arises in Admiralty law[12] and more recently there has been an exception under the Matrimonial Causes Act 1973.[13] *Nippon Yusen Kaisha (N.Y.K.)* v. *Karageorgis*[14] is the first reported case this century, with what is now known as a Mareva injunction being sought and indeed granted.

Nippon Yusen Kaisha v. Karageorgis

In this case, a Japanese company entered into a charterparty with the defendants who defaulted on payment of the hire. The defendants ceased business but it was known that they had funds in a London bank. N.Y.K., the plaintiffs, issued a writ in London claiming damages for breach of contract, and sought for leave to effect service out of the jurisdiction. The plaintiffs applied *ex parte* and before service of the writ for an order "freezing" the funds in the defendants' London bank to prevent the defendants removing them from the jurisdiction. Donaldson J. refused to grant the injunction at first instance, but the Court of Appeal granted it. Lord Denning M.R. in his judgment said:[1]

Review of practice

"We are told that an injunction of this kind has never been granted before. It has never been the practice of our English court to seize assets of a defendant in advance of judgment or to restrain the disposal of them. . . . We know, of course, that the practice on the continent of Europe is different. . . It seems to me that the time has come when we should revise our practice. There is no reason why the High Court or this court should not make an order such as is asked for here; it is warranted by section 45 of the Supreme Court of Judicature (Consolidation) Act 1925 which says that the High Court may grant a mandamus injunction or appoint a receiver by an interlocutory order in all cases in which it appears to the court to be just or convenient to do so. It

Power to grant injunction

seems to me that this is just such a case. There is a strong prima facie case that the hire is owing and unpaid. If an injunction is not granted, these monies may be removed out of the jurisdiction and the ship-owner will have the greatest difficulty in recovering anything. Two days ago we granted an injunction *ex parte* and we should continue it."

[10] *Lister & Co..* v. *Stubbs* [1890] 45 Ch. D. 1. at p. 15.
[11] *Ibid.*
[12] See p. 84.
[13] See p. 85.
[14] [1975] 1 W.L.R. 1093.
[15] *Ibid.* at p. 1094.

A month later came the case which gives the name to the Mareva injunction or Mareva order.

The *Mareva* case[16]

Facts

The *Mareva* was a cargo ship and her owners had let the vessel to the defendants, International Bulk Carriers S.A., on time-charter for a voyage to the Far East. She was let on daily rates payable at half-monthly intervals in advance. The date of first payment was the date of delivery of the vessel to the defendants which took place in Rotterdam. Bulk Carriers sub-chartered the *Mareva* to the Government of India who paid 90 per cent. of the freight U.S.$174,000 to a bank in London to the credit of Bulk Carriers. The ship loaded fertiliser in Bordeaux and then sailed to India. Bulk Carriers paid the first two instalments (amounting to U.S.$107,800) of the hire fees to the plaintiffs, but then defaulted and told the owners that they were unable to pay more. They also said that they had been unable to obtain financial support and that the vessel should complete its voyage to India.

Ex parte application to restrain disposal of money

The owners treated this action of Bulk Carriers as a repudiation of the charter. They commenced action by writ and applied for leave to serve outside the jurisdiction and, at the same time, moved for an injunction *ex parte* to restrain the disposal of any money which was in the defendants' United Kingdom bank account on the grounds that there was grave danger of it being dissipated. The money in the United Kingdom bank was largely the hire fees paid by the Indian Government. At first instance, Donaldson J. felt that he did not have power to grant the injunction but, on account of a conflict, as he saw it, between the Court of Appeal judgment in *Lister & Co.* v. *Stubbs*[17] which held that a freezing injunction could not be granted, and *Nippon Yusen Kaisha (N.Y.K.)* v. *Karageorgis*[18] to the opposite effect, he granted an interlocutory injunction for a short period in order to allow the owners to appeal. Donaldson J. felt that the *N.Y.K.* decision could have been decided differently if the *Lister* case had been cited to the court.

Judicature Act 1925, s.45

The Court of Appeal, on hearing the appeal, considered whether or not there was power to grant the injunction. The court took account of the *Lister* case but also section 45 of the Judicature Act 1925 which repeats section 25(8) of the Judicature Act 1875. Section 45 provided, *inter alia*:

> "A mandamus or an injunction may be granted or a receiver appointed by an interlocutory order of the court in all cases in which it shall appear to the court to be just and convenient."

Beddow v. Beddow

Section 25(8) of the Judicature Act 1875 was considered by Sir George Jessel M.R. in *Beddow* v. *Beddow*.[19] In interpreting this section, Sir George Jessel said,[20] "I have unlimited power to grant an injunction in any case where it would be right or just to

---

[16] See above, n. 1.
[17] See above, n. 7.
[18] See above, n. 14.
[19] [1878] 9 Ch.D. 89.
[20] *Ibid.* at p. 93.

do so." Lord Denning in the *Mareva* case adopted these words and added:[21]

Legal or equitable right

"There is only one qualification to be made. The court will not grant an injunction to protect a person who has no legal or equitable right whatever . . . but, subject to that qualification, the statute gives wide general power to the court."

It is well summarised in *Halsbury's Laws of England*:[22]

Court's jurisdiction

"Now, therefore, whenever a right which can be asserted either at law or in equity does exist, then whatever the previous practice may have been the court is enabled by virtue of this provision in a proper case, to grant an injunction to protect that right. In my opinion that principle applies to a creditor who has a right to be paid the debt owing to him, even before he has established his right by getting judgment for it. If it appears that the debt is due and owing—and there is a danger that the debtor may dispose of his assets so as to defeat it before judgment—the court has jurisdiction in a proper case to grant an interlocutory judgment so as to prevent him disposing of those assets. It seems to me that this is a proper case for the exercise of this jurisdiction . . . I would, therefore, continue the injunction."

The other judges followed Lord Denning and the interlocutory injunction was continued.

Admiralty matters having the effect of a Mareva order

Arrest of ship

In Admiralty it has long been the position that if a ship was the subject of some claim, an injured party can obtain a writ whereby the ship, and, in an appropriate case, its cargo, are arrested by the Admiralty Marshal. Examples giving rise to this situation are when the ship has collided with another and may be liable for damage sustained, it is the subject of an action for salvage, or there is a potential liability arising out of any contract with which the ship is concerned, whether on a charterparty, or arising out of a bill of lading concerning loss of cargo, or for wages of the crew and other situations for the classification is not closed. Following arrest, the owners lodge security so that the ship may be released.

Steamship Mutual Underwriting v. Thakur Shipping

In *Steamship Mutual Underwriting Association (Bermuda)* v. *Thakur Shipping Co. (No. 1)*,[23] the applicants for the order were also applying to the court for a declaration which, if granted, could have had the effect of rendering the defendant liable to the plaintiffs in damages. The court refused to grant a Mareva injunction in respect of the defendant's assets, as the plaintiffs failed to show that at the time of making the Mareva application they had any claim for damages against the defendant.

---

[21] *Mareva Companies Naviera S.A. of Panama* v. *International Bulk Carriers S.A.* (1975) 119 S.J. 660, at p. 661.
[22] (3rd ed.) Vol. 21, p. 348.
[23] [1986] 2 Lloyd's Rep. 439, C.A.

Statutory provision having the effect of a Mareva order: Matrimonial Causes Act 1973, s.37

Another exception to the rule in *Lister & Co.* v. *Stubbs*[24] is afforded by statute, namely section 37(2)(a) of the Matrimonial Causes Act 1973 which provides:

Claim for financial relief

"(a) if it is satisfied that the other party to the proceedings is, with the intention of defeating the claim for financial relief, about to make any disposition or to transfer out of the jurisdiction or otherwise deal with any property, [the court may] make such order as it thinks fit for restraining the other party from so doing or otherwise for protecting the claim."

The court thus has jurisdiction under section 37(2) to make an order restraining a party to financial proceedings (in the case of a matrimonial dispute) from disposing of property situated outside England and Wales, whether real or personal.

Irrespective of the M.C.A. the court has jurisdiction in an appropriate case to grant both Anton Piller and Mareva orders in matrimonial disputes.[24a]

The elements of the section

Proceedings for financial relief   Financial relief means awards relating to alimony pending suit (divorce, nullity or judicial separation) or relief after such proceedings, adjustments for property in connection with such proceedings, or relief in respect of proceedings for failure to maintain wife or children and variation of any such awards.

Awards pending suit

By one party against another   Proceedings can be brought by the male as well as the female party to the proceedings.

Intention of defeating the claim   The court has held[25] that to give to the meaning of "intention" a requirement that there is an element of purpose or design, places too narrow a construction on it. It is not sufficient for the person against whom the order is sought to prove absence of direct purpose or malignant design. He/she (though there is no reported case where the wife has been the respondent) must prove that he did not know, or it was not reasonable to expect that the disposition would defeat the applicant's claim, or that there were other funds available, or that the applicant consented to the disposition.

Proof of intention

About to make any disposition or transfer   The Act not only gives the court jurisdiction to grant an order restraining a party from disposing of the property, but also to restrain it from so doing if it is thought that such a disposition is likely to take place. In *Smith* v. *Smith*[26] there was no evidence that the husband was about to deal with the house or with the capital sum in respect of the sale. The wife applied for an injunction restraining him. The

Restraint against future disposals

---

[24] See above, n. 7.
[24a] But see Chap. 5, p. 46, n. 36.
[25] *Jordan* v. *Jordan* (1965) 109 S.J. 353.
[26] *Smith* v. *Smith* (1973) 115 S.J. 525.

wife's case was that the husband was the kind of man who was likely to dispose of assets simply to defeat the wife's claim, and that he had shown no responsibility to provide for wife and children. The fact that he opposed the wife's application was sufficient grounds for granting the injunction sought. "Disposition" includes all dispositions other than testamentary disposition. Application for relief under the section can be made in respect of any disposition of property which took place less than three years before the date of the application.

Or otherwise deal with any property   In *Quartermain* v. *Quartermain*[27] the house had been charged to a bank to secure the husband's overdraft and the bank forced a sale thus realising their security. The proceeds, after the bank had taken what was due to them, were £10,000. There was no direct evidence that the husband was about to dispose of the money, but the wife feared he might do so. The court found that as the husband was a party to the transaction of charging the house to the bank, there was, in these circumstances, a transaction coming within the words "otherwise deal with any property" in section 37(2)(*a*) of the Matrimonial Causes Act 1973, and an interim injunction was made whereby £8,000 of the £10,000 could not be the subject of disposition.

Quartermain v. *Quartermain*

Such order as it thinks fit   Whilst the court has jurisdiction to make an order in respect of property situated outside England and Wales, it will not make an order which would be incapable of execution and thus ineffective.[28]

Ineffective order

     In certain circumstances the intention of defeating a claim for financial relief is presumed, and the court has power to set aside a transaction which has the effect of disposing of property, and also to make a preservation order in respect of that property.

Power to set aside transaction

County court
Whilst the county court has jurisdiction to issue Mareva orders it is inappropriate to use the procedure where relatively small sums are involved. Where the claim was for £2000, the court refused an order.[29]

Development of the Mareva order

Both the *N.Y.K.*[30] and *Mareva*[31] cases were decided *ex parte*. It is probable in both cases that the defendant submitted to judgment and the funds frozen would be used to pay the judgment debts and costs.

The Pertamina

     It was not until 1977 that the Court of Appeal heard a case when both sides were represented. This case was *Rasu Maritima S.A.* v. *Perusahaan Pertambangan Minyakdangasbumi Negara (Government of Republic of Indonesia Intervening)*.[32] Rasu, a

---

[27] (1974) 118 S.J. 597.
[28] *Hamlin* v. *Hamlin* [1986] Fam. 11.
[29] *Sions* v. *Price, The Independent*, December, 1988, C.A. See Lord Denning, *The Due Process of Law* (1980), p. 136.
[30] See above, n. 14.
[31] See above, n. 1.
[32] [1978] Q.B. 644; [1977] 3 W.L.R. 518.

Liberian company, claimed damages for nearly £2 million for breach of a charterparty in respect of the hire of the *Pertamina*. The defendants were an Indonesian state-owned company. The plaintiff had sought to attach assets of the defendant round the world, stating that the defendants were disposing of them or putting them out of reach of creditors. The plaintiff identified certain of the defendants' assets at Liverpool awaiting shipment.

Clear claim At first instance, the judge granted an interlocutory injunction. The defendants applied to have it discharged and this was granted with a stay to enable the plaintiffs to appeal, which they did. The court upheld the judge below, for, on the facts of the case, it was clear that the defendants had claims against the plaintiff.

Unfettered discretion
" . . . the situation is such that I do not think it would be proper in this case for equity to intervene to assist one side or the other. . . . I think the courts have a discretion, in advance of judgment to issue an injunction to restrain the removal of assets—whether the defendant is within the jurisdiction or outside it. This discretion should not be fettered by rigid rules. It should be exercised when it appears to the court to be just and convenient."[33]

(The judge at first instance held that to sustain a Mareva order, the plaintiff would have to show that money due could be demanded under the Order XIV procedures. The Court of Appeal considered this too).

The Siskina The House of Lords in *The Siskina*,[34] while allowing the appeal of the defendants, did not cast doubt on the validity of granting a Mareva injunction as is made clear by Lord Hailsham, L.C.[35] In 1979 came the next landmark in the development of the Mareva order in *Third Chandris Shipping Corp.* v. *Unimarine*

Third Chandris* v. *Unimarine *S.A.*[36] By this time:

"The use of the remedy [the Mareva injunction] greatly increased. Far from being exceptional, it has now become commonplace. At present, applications are being made at the rate of about 20 per month. Almost all are granted."[37]

Denning Guidelines On appeal, guidelines were laid down for the grant of a Mareva order. These, known as the "Denning Guidelines," are as follows:

Full and frank disclosure
(a) the plaintiff must make a full and frank disclosure of all relevant matters in his knowledge which are material for the judge to know;[38]
(b) what is material evidence is to be decided by the court, not the plaintiff and it is thus advisable to put in too much evidence rather than too little;
(c) the duty of disclosure applies not only to facts which the

---

[33] *Per* Lord Denning [1977] 3 W.L.R. 518 at pp. 529, 530.
[34] *Siskina (Owners of cargo lately laden on board)* v. *Distos Compania Naviera S.A.* [1979] A.C. 210.
[35] *Ibid.* at p. 261.
[36] [1979] 3 W.L.R. 122.
[37] *Ibid.* as *per* Mustill J. at p. 126.
[38] See above, n. 36, at p. 137. See *Negocios Del Mar S.A.* v. *Doric Shipping Corporation (The "Assios")* [1979] 1 Lloyd's Rep. 331.

plaintiff knows but also those which would come to his knowledge if proper enquiries were made;

(d) the extent of the enquiries depends on the circumstances of the case;

(e) the court will ensure that the party seeking the order is deprived of any advantage arising from a breach of the duty to disclose;

(f) the question whether a fact not disclosed is sufficiently material to justify immediate discharge of the order depends on the importance of that fact to the issues to be decided; and

(g) the court has a discretion to continue the injunction or grant a new one.[39]

If proceedings between the parties are taking place, or in contemplation, in another jurisdiction this is highly material when applying for a Mareva order, since the court will have to be satisfied that such an injunction will not be oppressive to the defendant. Failure to disclose such proceedings (as also proceedings within the jurisdiction) may result in discharge of the injunction or denial of a continuation thereof.[40]

Where there has been non-disclosure of material facts at the *ex parte* application, but full disclosure at the *inter partes* hearing, the court has a discretion whether or not to continue the Mareva injunction or discharge it, and re-grant the injunction on full disclosure being made as if it had been made at the *ex parte* application. This last discretion is to be exercised sparingly; generally it will not be right to require a defendant to wait until trial and then seek damages for non-disclosure. The parties may have to be restored to their position as existed prior to the *ex parte* application being made, and the plaintiff has himself to blame if the assets are disposed of. Further post-trial damage may not adequately compensate the defendant for his loss.[41]

In respect of both Anton Piller and Mareva orders a plaintiff has a duty to inform the court as soon as he becomes aware that the court has been misled or not fully informed of any material facts at the *ex parte* application—as also any change in material circumstances.[42]

Particulars of claims

(a) The plaintiff should give particulars of his claims against the defendant, stating the grounds of his claim and the amount thereof and fairly stating the points made against it by the defendant.

Proof of assets

(b) The plaintiff must give some grounds for believing the defendant has assets within the jurisdiction.[43] In most cases the plaintiff will not know the extent of the assets. He will only have indications of them. The existence of a bank account in England is enough even though in overdraft.

---

[39] *Brink's Mat* v. *Elcombe* [1988] 1 W.L.R. 1350.

[40] *Behbehani* v. *Salem* [1989] 1 W.L.R. 723.

[41] *Ali Fahd Shobokshi Group* v. *Moneim* [1989] 1 W.L.R. 710. See also the rules relating to disclosure in respect of disclosures for Anton Piller orders which often apply to Mareva orders.

[42] *Commercial Bank of the Near East* v. *A.* (1989) 139 New L.J. 645.

[43] Later developments have shown these may not be necessary: see p. 96, under "International aspects."

Risk of removal

(c) The plaintiff should give some grounds for believing that there is a risk of the assets being removed, before the judgment or award is satisfied so as to defeat the purpose of the award. The mere fact that a defendant is abroad is not by itself sufficient. But some foreign companies invite comment if they are registered in countries where the law is so loose that little or nothing is known about it.

Undertaking as to damage

(d) The plaintiff must give an undertaking as to damages in case he fails in his claim or the injunction turns out to be unjustified. In a suitable case, this should be supported by a bond or other security. In general, undertakings given by a plaintiff as a condition of the grant of a Mareva must be strictly carried out. The authorities, with reference to failure of a plaintiff or his adviser to carry out the undertakings in respect of Anton Piller orders, may be said to apply according to circumstances to Mareva orders.

No delay

(e) To be effective, the application and execution of a Mareva injunction must be swift and secret. If there is delay, or an advance warning given, the assets could be removed rendering the injunction ineffective.

Since the Denning Guidelines were formulated, further developments are:

Injunction after judgment

(a) A Mareva injunction may be granted after judgment if there are grounds for believing that the debtor intends to dispose of assets in order to avoid the judgment debt.[44]

No substitute for full trial

(b) A Mareva order is an adjunct to an action and not a substitute for relief to be obtained at trial. A plaintiff should press on with his case quickly. Where a plaintiff has still not set down his case for trial two-and-a-half years after the grant of the order, the court may discharge it.[45] In *Re D.P.R. Futures*,[46] a Mareva order was continued on a limited cross undertaking as to damages.

Ancillary right of action

Pre-existing cause of action

A Mareva order, like an Anton Piller order and as contrasted with an action for discovery, is not a right of action in itself but ancillary to a substantive action and thus the applicant for the order must have a pre-existing cause of action against a defendant.[47] However, the pre-existing cause of action can include a threatened invasion of the plaintiff's legal or equitable rights or interest.[48]

Lord Diplock in *The Siskina* said:[49]

---

[44] Added by *Orwell Steel (Erection and Fabrication)* v. *Asphalt and Tarmac (U.K.)* [1984] 1 W.L.R. 1097.

[45] Added by *Lloyd's Bowmaker* v. *Britannia Arrow Holdings, The Times*, March 19, 1987.

[46] [1989] 1 W.L.R. 778.

[47] But see *Chief Constable of Kent* v. *V.* [1983] Q.B. 34; [1982] 3 W.L.R. 462 and judgment of Lord Denning at p. 463; also *Bank of Queensland* v. *Grant* [1984] 54 A.L.R. 306.

[48] See above, n. 34.

[49] *Ibid.* at p. 256.

Enforcement of legal or equitable right

"A right to obtain an interlocutory injunction is not a cause of action. It cannot stand on its own. It is dependent on there being a pre-existing cause of action against the defendant arising out of an invasion, actual or threatened, by him of a legal or equitable right of the plaintiff for the enforcement of which the defendant is amenable to the jurisdiction of the court. The right to obtain an interlocutory injunction is merely an ancillary and incidental to the pre-existing cause of action."

In *Chief Constable of Kent* v. *V.*,[50] Lord Denning M.R. held that under section 37(1) of the Supreme Court Act 1981 it was no longer necessary that the injunction should be ancillary to an action claiming a legal or equitable right, but his was a dissenting voice. Nevertheless, one can envisage that circumstances may arise when the court will, if it is to do justice, need the wide interpretation claimed by Lord Denning, and it does not strain the language of section 37(1) to do so. In Donaldson L.J.'s judgment, dissenting from that of Lord Denning he said:[51]

Wider interpretation

"I am quite unable to see how it can appear to the court to be just and convenient to make such an order, save in the enforcement or protection of a legal or equitable right or interest. Were it otherwise, every judge would need to be issued with a portable palm tree."

This, however, is a fairly apt description of the judicial discretion which brought into being both Anton Piller and Mareva orders. In *Bank of Queensland* v. *Grant*[52] the court held that the plaintiff seeking a Mareva order must show a vested or accrued cause of action, though there might be circumstances when this is not necessary. A Mareva order was not available to restrain the defendant's wife from proceedings to register the matrimonial home in her name following a maintenance agreement which effectively deprived the defendant of assets.

No accrued cause of action

Supreme Court Act 1981, s.37

Following the *Third Chandris* case there was enacted the Supreme Court Act 1981, section 37 of which provides:

Statutory provision regarding injunctions and receivers

"(1) The High Court may by order (whether interlocutory or final) grant an injunction or appoint a receiver in all cases in which it appears to the court to be just and convenient to do so.

(2) Any such order may be made either unconditionally or on such terms and conditions as the court thinks just.

(3) The power of the High Court under subsection (1) to grant an interlocutory injunction restraining a party to any proceedings from removing from the jurisdiction of the High Court, or otherwise dealing with, assets located within that jurisdiction shall be exercisable in cases where that party is, as well as in cases where he is not, domiciled resident or present within that jurisdiction."

[50] See above, n. 47.
[51] *Ibid.* at p. 469.
[52] [1984] 54 A.L.R. 306.

Section 37 of the Supreme Court Act 1981, though in very
different language from section 45 of the Judicature Act 1925,
substantially replaces it. Section 45 replaced the equivalent
section 25(3) of the Judicature Act 1873. It is to be noted that the
statutory principle upon which the court acted in granting
injunctions was intended to do away with certain technical
difficulties concerning them prior to the Judicature Act 1873.[53]

It is not necessary now to attempt to distinguish between the
Lister case and the *Mareva* case, as section 37(3) of the Supreme
Court Act 1981 makes express provision for the Mareva order.

The elements of section 37

"The High Court may by order grant an injunction . . . in
any case where it appears to be just and convenient to do
so."

This indicates very wide powers and follows the judgment of Sir
George Jessel M.R. in *Beddow* v. *Beddow*.[54]

**No new
jurisdiction**

"Interlocutory or final"   These are thought to be descriptive
words which relate to the practice before the passing of the Act
and they do not create a new jurisdiction to grant injunctions.
The power to grant an injunction may be exercised, not only
before judgment, but after judgment to assist the process of
enforcement and the words interlocutory or final do not have the
effect of removing or diminishing this power.[55]

**Discretionary
powers**

"Just and convenient"   This is generally a reference to the
discretionary powers the court has when considering the grant of
an injunction. A comprehensive review of the law was set out in
American Cyanamid Co. v. *Ethicon*.[56]

Undertakings

**"Unconditionally or on such terms and conditions as the court
thinks just"**   In most, if not all, cases of an interlocutory
injunction, the court will only grant the injunction to the party
who seeks it subject to entering into suitable undertakings.
Normally the plaintiff will give undertakings for damages to the
defendant and banks or other innocent party.[57] Where a
defendant seeks damages arising out of an undertaking the onus
of proof in on him to show that the damage sustained would not
have occurred but for the order.[58]

**"Removing from the jurisdiction of the High Court . . . or
otherwise dealing with"**   With the first Mareva injunction, the
assets (the subject of the application) were likely to be removed
from the jurisdiction of the High Court, *i.e.* abroad. This is no
longer a necessary requirement. "Otherwise dealing with" is not

[53] *Fletcher* v. *Rodgers* [1878] 27 W.N. 97, C.A.
[54] [1878] 9 Ch.D. 89.
[55] *Stewart Chartering* v. *C. & O. Managements S.A.*; *Venus Destiny, The* [1980] 1
W.L.R. 460 and *Faith Panton Property Plan* v. *Hodgetts* [1981] 1 W.L.R. 927.
[56] *American Cyanamid Co.* v. *Ethicon* [1975] A.C. 396.
[57] *Z* v. *A–Z and AA–LL* [1982] Q.B. 558 held that a Mareva order could issue out
if there was a danger of the assets being dissipated within the jurisdiction as
well as being removed from it.
[58] *Financiera Avenida S.A.* v. *Shiblaq, The Times*, November 21, 1988.

No need for risk of disposal abroad

to be construed *eiusdem generis* with "removing from the jurisdiction of the High Court," so that the assets no longer have to be at risk from being sent abroad.[59]

"Jurisdiction" has now been held to include a court, being a member of the Brussels Convention which will enforce the English order.[60] "Dealing with" includes disposing, selling, charging "salting away" or placing out of reach of the plaintiff assets of the defendant.[61]

"Assets"   In addition to money held in bank accounts, the following have been assets "frozen" under a Mareva Order:

Examples of assets

motor vehicles, jewellery, *objets d'art*, choses in action,[62] real property, although the interest of the property arising out of the order is not registrable;[63] an aeroplane;[64] removable and disposable chattels which have been purchased out of the proceeds of an illicit enterprise may become the subject of an order. The plaintiff must produce evidence that the assets in

Evidence of ownership

question are in fact those of the defendant; it is not sufficient for the plaintiff to show that there is a serious issue to be tried as to ownership of the assets.[65]

Bill of exchange   Mareva orders will not generally be granted in respect of a bill of exchange, but the holder of a bill can be enjoined from disposing of moneys recovered in an action on the bill.

Irrevocable letters of credit and performance bonds, guarantees issued by banks   The nature of these instruments is such that when used in commerce they are treated by business people as bank guarantees that will be honoured. For a bank to fail to do so for whatever reason will reflect on its probity and reputation to a very serious degree. It will be most exceptional for a Mareva order to be granted in such circumstances that a bank is unable to honour these instruments. If the court is to be asked *ex*

Validity of instrument in issue

parte to issue an injunction restraining a bank from paying out on any such instrument as referred to above then the validity of the instrument must be in issue, otherwise the order will be refused. An injunction may, in a proper case, be placed on the freedom of the person who receives payment from the bank.

Fraud

The exceptional case will arise in the case of fraud. The evidence must be very clear as to both the fact of fraud and that the bank knows of it. Nothing else will suffice. The uncorroborated statement of a customer is not sufficient.[66]

Wide scope

Section 37(3) gives statutory authority to the power to grant Mareva injunctions or orders.

The courts have interpreted section 37 as applying to all types of injunction not just the Mareva, and have interpreted their powers to mean that if the order is to be granted, the

---

[59] See n. 57.
[60] See "International Aspects" below, pp. 96 *et seq.*.
[61] *C.B.S. United Kingdom* v. *Lambert* [1983] Ch. 37.
[62] *Ibid.*
[63] *Stockler* v. *Fourways Estates Ltd.* [1984] 1 W.L.R. 25.
[64] *Allen* v. *Jambo Holdings* [1980] 1 W.L.R. 1252.
[65] *Allied Arab Bank* v. *Hajjar* [1987] 3 All E.R. 739.
[66] *Practice Note to Bolivinter Oil S.A.* v. *Chase Manhattan Bank* [1984] 1 W.L.R. 392.

plaintiff must at the time of the application for an injunction have a cause of action in being.[67]

"Domiciled, resident or present within that jurisdiction"   The provision makes it clear that the defendant may be of any nationality and either resident here or abroad; likewise with

Foreign company   domicile. This is important in cases where a foreign company may have a branch office or representative in the jurisdiction. The court at one time refused to make orders in respect of assets outside the jurisdiction.[68] However in *Derby & Co.* v. *Weldon (No. 3)*[69] it was held at first instance that the court will in an appropriate case grant a Mareva order if the defendant has assets outside England and Wales, provided that the defendant is resident or domiciled in a Brussels Convention country. On appeal the court held that the assets should normally be within the jurisdiction but in an appropriate case, the court had power to make an order concerning any foreign assets in order to achieve the purpose of the injunction.[70]

Statutory provision enacts common law   The underlying purpose behind subsection (3) is to put into statutory effect the grant of Mareva orders which developed through judicial decisions. The provision substantially states the law as the courts developed it up to the date of the passing of the Act. There was doubt up to that time as to whether or not a court had the power to grant a Mareva order otherwise than in respect of assets being sent out of the jurisdiction; this doubt has now been resolved and the order is now commonly granted in respect of property within or outside of England and Wales.

Position of third parties

The object of a Mareva injunction is to prevent the disposal of the assets of the defendant. These assets will often consist of cash held in bank accounts and securities, all of which may be held by others for the defendant. These third parties are served with the order and are required, in so far as it affects them, to comply with

Communication with third party   its terms. Third parties will be informed by telephone, telex or other means, but any such form of communication must be followed by serving the full order. In addition, at the time of serving the order the plaintiff should explain to the recipient in everyday English the full meaning of the order and also advise him to take legal advice if he is in doubt as to his position. If the evidence indicates that a defendant will, if he disposes of money owed to him by a third party, be in breach of a Mareva order, the court may, with the approval of the third party, order that the

---

[67] *The Niedersachsen* [1983] 2 Lloyd's Rep. 600 at p. 614; *Siporex Trade S.A.* v. *Comdel Commodities* [1986] 2 Lloyd's Rep. 428; *C.D.N. Research and Development* v. *Bank of Nova Scotia* [1981] 122 D.L.R. (3d) 485; *Bank of Queensland* v. *Grant* [1984] 54 A.L.R. 306.
[68] *Intraco* v. *Notis Shipping Corp. of Liberia, Bhoja Trader, The* [1981] 2 Lloyd's Rep. 256.
[69] [1989] 2 W.L.R. 412.
[70] See "International aspects", p. 96.

money be paid into court or into a frozen bank account of the defendant at a bank which has notice of the order.[71]

Action required of the bank or other third party   As the bank is required to perform its obligations, it is entitled to recoup its expenditure of so doing and the plaintiff must undertake to indemnify it. The bank or the innocent third party must be told with as much certainty as possible and as soon as possible what

Advice as to procedure they should do. The plaintiff should, so far as it can, identify the bank account by branch/number and should give any other details within his knowledge, together with any other assets

Costs which should come within the order. The plaintiff must pay the costs of any search. The affidavit of the plaintiff in support of the

Details of assets application should set out with as much detail as possible details of the defendant's assets and where they are located.

The bank officials or others concerned (third parties) should be informed of the significance of the Mareva order in "easy to

Significance of order explained understand" English. In particular, they should be informed in both general and detailed terms how it affects the defendant: what they must do and what they cannot do. Third parties should be advised that the order applies to them as soon as they have notice of it and that they must not deal with the defendant's assets which include any bank accounts and cheques presented for payment against it. Thus cheques for payment are "stopped" and credits made to the account come into it and are then

Duty to preserve assets "frozen." If the defendant, on being made aware of the order, tries to divert credits elsewhere, the bank should not permit this. Any failure by a third party to do what he reasonably can to preserve the assets of the defendant will render him liable to be found in contempt of court.

In the draft order, the plaintiff should specify with as much

Details of third parties detail as he can the name and address of the bank where the defendant's account is believed to be held and other details such as the account number. Similarly with other third parties, details should be given of name and addresses of the same, and particulars of the assets which they are believed to hold so that such third parties are in no doubt as to what is required of them under the order.

Indemnity for expenses incurred The plaintiff will be required to undertake, as part of the order, to indemnify any third party affected by the order in respect of any expense reasonably incurred in complying with the order and all liabilities which arise in consequence. What is a "reasonable expense" varies from case to case; thus with a very

"Reasonable expense" small building society it could be reasonable for them to seek "outside" legal advice, but with a large clearing bank this is not necessarily the case. A branch manager of such a bank should have been instructed as to what to do if he receives a Mareva order and can always telephone "Head Office" legal department for assistance.

The order is in being from the moment it is pronounced. A third party on receipt may take advice as to his position and what he must do. If during that time any of the assets in his possession

Responsibilities of third party or control are allowed to be dissipated, the innocent third party will be liable not only for contempt of court, but also to the

[71] *Bank Mellat* v. *Kazmi* [1989] 2 W.L.R. 613.

plaintiff for any extra expense incurred as a result of the assets leaving the third party's control, together with the value of those assets if in consequence they are no longer available to satisfy the plaintiff's claim. The third party may always seek a variation or discharge of the order if he wishes but until such event occurs he is bound by its terms.

No general restraint

For shares and similar securities held by a bank, while there may be a general restraint on the defendant, the bank should generally only be restrained in respect of accounts held by the bank, other assets should only be restrained if specifically identified, and held by the bank, *e.g.* share certificates. With regard to accounts, the restraint on the defendant should be such that he is restrained from drawing on any "time notice or demand deposits" which may be held by the bank in his sole name up to the maximum sum stated in the order.

Currency

If the bank is served with an order expressed in one currency but holds accounts in another, the bank should convert to the currency specified in the order at the buying rate as at the date of service, to meet the sum stated in the order, and put a stop on the account to that extent.

Joint account

If the defendant is found to have moneys in a joint account or that of a third party these can be the subject of a Mareva order, but the order must provide that it is applicable to joint accounts.[72]

Transfer of assets without knowledge

A Mareva order prevents a bank, or others who hold assets to the order of a defendant, from assisting in or disposing of the assets. A person may still hand over assets to the defendant unless such person knows or ought to know that the handing over of the assets will facilitate their disposition.[73] One should be very wary before handing over such assets in the knowledge that a Mareva order exists in respect of them.

Terms of the order

Wide terms

A Mareva injunction can be couched in the widest terms, and it may restrain the defendant from dealing in any way with any of his assets and may require him to disclose where those assets are and who has control of them in any country. The court has a discretion as to how far the order will apply to all countries.[74]

In following the judgment of Denning, Kerr L.J. in *Z Ltd.* v. *A–Z*[75] [1982] 1 Q.B. 558 set out the guidelines to be followed concerning the logistics and machinery of the jurisdiction when dealing with a Mareva order, especially in so far as banks an innocent third parties are concerned.

Kerr Guidelines

The guidelines are are follows:

1.   The Mareva order shall not be issued in certain circumstances:
      (a) where there is no real risk of the assets of a defendant being dissipated and the plaintiff uses the procedure to exert pressure on the defendant;

---

[72] *Z.* v. *A–Z* and *AA–LL* [1982] Q.B. 558.
[73] *Law Society* v. *Shanks* [1987] 131 S.J. 1626.
[74] See "International aspects" below, and *PCW (Underwriting Agencies)* v. *Dixon (P.S.)* [1983] 2 All E.R. 697, C.A.
[75] [1982] Q.B. 558, at 585.

Trap for payee

(b) where a person makes a payment which he regards as unjustifiable having previously obtained an *ex parte* injunction, so that the plantiff obtains the benefit for which he has made the payment but the money is "frozen" as soon as it is received by the defendant.

The effect of such conduct is to use the order as a trap for the payee.

Sum certain

2. The Mareva order should be granted only when it appears likely that the plaintiff will recover judgment for a certain or approximate sum, and when there is reason to believe the defendant may take steps to ensure that assets within the jurisdiction[76] are no longer available or traceable.

Costs payable by plaintiff

3. The costs incurred by a bank or innocent third party are payable by the plantiff for searching through its records.

Duties of plaintiff and legal adviser

4. It is the duty of the plaintiff and his legal adviser to consider very carefully the following:

(a) if a Mareva order is justified in the sense of being reasonably necessary in a particular case to achieve the objects for which the procedure is designed;

(b) the extent of the injunction to safeguard the plaintiff against a real risk of the defendant deliberately taking steps to avoid judgment;

(c) taking account of the foregoing, what way and to what extent should the injunction apply to assets of the defendant within the jurisdiction;

Identification of assets

(d) the extent the assets are known or suspected to exist, they should be identified even if value unknown, and if they are known or suspected to be in the hands of third parties then location and identity should be defined if possible;

Service on defendant

(e) how soon and in what manner the defendant can be served expeditiously both within the writ (if not already served) and the injunction. Generally there should be an undertaking about service on the defendant as part of the order;

(f) the third parties it is appropriate to serve with a copy of the order;

Draft affidavit

(g) the facts that should be contained in a full or draft affidavit in support of the *ex parte* application; and

(h) the application which should contain the full draft of the order for consideration by the court.

International aspects

A plaintiff may, if the circumstances of the case are appropriate, seek a Mareva-type remedy in more than one jurisdiction and he is entitled to the relief in a jurisdiction in which he is not resident. Thus, if a plaintiff commences proceedings in Gibraltar

Relief in several jurisdictions

---

[76] In the light of the later authority *Derby* v. *Weldon*, (see above, n. 69), "jurisdiction" seems to be wider than just the courts in England and Wales.

to "freeze" the assets of a defendant which comprise a ship trading between Gibraltar and Liverpool, the plaintiff can be granted a Mareva application in England and Gibraltar in respect of the assets even though he is pursuing the action in but one of the jurisdictions.[77]

A Mareva order will be granted and continued in an appropriate case to prevent assets of an insolvent defendant from being removed from the jurisdiction, to the disadvantage of creditors within the jurisdiction, even though the United States Bankruptcy Court had ordered the removal to the Southern District Bankruptcy Court of New York.[78]

Derby v. *Weldon*

A worldwide Mareva order preventing the dissipation of assets can be granted against a foreign company with no assets in England, if that foreign company is resident in a Brussels Convention country.[79] In *Derby* v. *Weldon (No. 3 and 4)* at first instance,[80] a Mareva order was granted in respect of a Luxembourg company but not one of Panama. Following the grant of the order, a receiver was appointed by the English court in respect of the Luxembourg company on the basis that any of the courts in Luxembourg would recognise and enforce such an order. The court will be slow to grant a Mareva order which cannot be enforced, for making an unenforceable order brings the law into disrepute. The Court of Appeal has in two judgments permitted a Mareva Order to be granted in respect of assets world wide, both these authorities deriving from section 37(1) of the Supreme Court Act 1981.

In *Derby* v. *Weldon (No. 1)* [1989] 2 W.L.R. 276 the first two defendants, British citizens residing in England were the subject of a Mareva Order at first instance restraining them from removing assets out of the United Kingdom, France, West Germany, Luxembourg, Eire, Denmark and the Netherlands. At the *inter partes* stage this was varied to apply only to assets within England and Wales. The defendants appealed against the granting of the order and the plaintiffs cross appealed to enlarge the jurisdiction. The Court of Appeal decided that there could be an order having effect worldwide in an exceptional case.

In the present case the judge at first instance had found that the claim was a very large (about £34 million) insufficiency of English assets, and there was a real risk of dissipation of foreign assets before trial. In these circumstances the Court of Appeal

---

[77] *House of Spring Gardens Ltd.* v. *Waite* (1985) 129 S.J. 64.
[78] *Felixstowe Dock & Railway Co.* v. *United States Lines Inc.* [1989] 2 W.L.R. 109.
[79] The Brussels Convention is the Convention on Jurisdiction and the Enforcement of Judgments in Civil and Commercial Matters 1968, enacted by the Civil Jurisdiction and Judgments Act 1982. By Title III of the convention, *inter partes* judgments, both final and interlocutory, are recognised and enforceable in Member States of the EEC (known as Brussels Convention countries). Consequently, a Mareva order is subject to the jurisdiction of a Brussels Convention court, which may enforce the order of an English Court. The English Court takes the view that, by reason of the Brussels Convention concerning enforcement of court orders (to which the United Kingdom is a party), an order of the English Court will be enforced in a court of any country which is a signatory to the convention. Accordingly, in such cases, the assets are within the jurisdiction of the English Court. The circumstances of each case must come within the terms of the Convention to be effective. See *de Lavel* v. *de Lavel* [1979] E.C.R. 1055 and *Denilauler* v. *SNC Couchet Frères* [1981] E.C.R. 1553.
[80] See above, n. 69.

held it was appropriate for a worldwide order to be made subject to certain undertakings being given by the plaintiff.

The plaintiff was required to undertake to the court that no application would be made to a foreign court to enforce the order, and that no use would be made of information obtained without leave of the English Court. The court approved that provisions should be made in the Order for the protection of innocent third parties outside the jurisdiction.

In *Derby* v. *Weldon (No. 3 and 4)* [1989] 2 W.L.R. 412, the third and fourth defendants appealed against the grant of a Mareva order in which the sum claimed was about £25 million. The third and fourth defendants were, respectively, Panama and Luxembourg companies with no assets in the United Kingdom. A restraint and disclosure was made in the usual form against the fourth defendant as it was a Luxembourg company subject to the Brussel Convention, but no order was made in respect of the third defendant for there was no evidence that the order would be enforced in Panama. The fourth defendant appealed and the plaintiff cross-appealed against the refusal of the injunction in respect of the third defendant.

It was held on appeal that in an appropriate case (and this was such) the court has power to make an order concerning any foreign assets worldwide to achieve the purposes of the injunction, subject to the ordinary principles of international law. The existence of assets in the jurisdiction was not a precondition of granting a Mareva order. To safeguard the position of third parties outside the jurisdiction there was a need for a provision in the order to make it clear that the court was not seeking to exercise an exorbitant jurisdiction.

The provision reads as follows:

"Provided that insofar as this order purports to have any effect outside England and Wales, no person shall be affected by it or concerned with the terms of it until it shall have been declared enforceable or shall have been recognised or registered or enforced by a foreign Court (and then it shall only affect such declaration or . . . enforcement) unless that person is:

(a) a person to whom the order is addressed or an officer or an agent appointed by power of attorney of such person; or

(b) a person who is subject to the jurisdiction of this (in this case, English) Court and who:

(i) has been given written notice of this order at his or its residence or place of business within the jurisdiction, and

(ii) is able to prevent acts or omissions outside the jurisdiction of this court which assists in the breach of the terms of this order."

Bayer AG* v. *Winter

In *Bayer AG* v. *Winter (No. 3)*[81] the plaintiff obtained a Mareva order in England and commenced proceedings in two European courts to the same effect. The English court held that once the two European courts had issued their equivalent of a Mareva order so as to preserve the assets, providing the plaintiff

---

[81] [1986] E.C.C. 465 approved by *Babanaft International* v. *Bassatne* [1989] 2 W.L.R. 232 at p. 248.

stayed the proceedings in the two European countries the cause could proceed in England. A Mareva order will not be granted **Attempt to freeze** which attempts to freeze all the assets of the defendant whether **all assets** before or after judgment and wherever they may be situated. The reason is that such an order would involve an exorbitant assertion of jurisdiction over third parties, as well as the difficulty of enforcing the order.

The court has power to grant a worldwide Mareva order pending trial even when the relief sought is in aid of a foreign monetary claim and not a proprietary claim. Such an order is subject to the proviso protecting third parties except to the extent that the order is enforceable by the courts of the state where the defendants' assets are situated, but such proviso only extends to assets and acts done outside England and Wales.[82]

Limitation on third An order may be granted which only binds the defendant **parties** and those third parties who are within the jurisdiction.[83] This is, however, limited to Member States of the EEC and an order can be made which binds third parties in any state where the order can be enforced. In practice such an order is more likely to be granted after judgment.[84]

Position in countries outside the jurisdiction

Many countries have had a form of Mareva order for many years so that English law has been behind the international community in that respect. The international aspect of a Mareva-type order can afford opportunities for judicial trespass (which can, and does, have a serious effect on parties and their legal advisers in other jurisdictions including England and Wales). In the United **SEC v. Wang** States case of *U.S. Securities & Exchange Commission (SEC)* v. **and Lee** *Wang and Lee*,[85] SEC, the plaintiff, sued Wang and Lee, the defendants, before a district court in New York in respect of insider dealing offences. The United States system is such that, if the facts were proved against the defendants, the penalty may amount to about U.S.$57 million. The accounts of the defendants were held by the Chartered Bank, a United Kingdom bank with branches in Hong Kong as well as New York City. The accounts of the defendants were in Hong Kong and the law of Hong Kong governed the contractual position as between the defendants and the bank.

The plaintiffs obtained an order in the New York district court freezing the assets of the defendants and directing banks holding such assets to retain them. The order was directed to any bank anywhere holding accounts of the defendants. The Chartered Bank in New York was then served with an order of the New York court requiring it to pay the full amount of moneys standing to the credit of the defendants into the New York Court. The bank complied under protest and paid in about U.S.$12·5 million. The defendants, in Hong Kong through their solicitors, demanded repayment by the bank of all the moneys which had

---

[82] *Republic of Haiti* v. *Duvalier* [1989] 2 W.L.R. 261.
[83] See above, n. 69.
[84] *Babanaft International Co.* v. *Bassatne, The Times*, July 2, 1988.
[85] *The Times*, February 14, 1989.

Restraint against commencement of proceedings in other jurisdictions

been in their Hong Kong account before the New York proceedings commenced. To prevent the defendants suing in Hong Kong, the New York court issued an order to restrain the defendants from starting or continuing proceedings to reclaim the money in any jurisdiction other than that of New York.

The New York court also issued an order directed to the defendant's Hong Kong solicitors, who had a New York branch, to withdraw their demand for payment in Hong Kong. By this time, they had issued writs in Hong Kong on the bank for payment by the bank of the money paid into the New York court under protest. The defendants' solicitors withdrew the writs. New solicitors in Hong Kong were instructed for the defendants; these had no New York office and proceedings recommenced against the bank in Hong Kong. If the Chartered Bank or the Hong Kong solicitors with a New York branch had disobeyed the orders of the New York court they would have been in contempt, which, as both had business in New York, was a very serious matter.

The Hong Kong court did not regard the U.S. court order as having any validity within the jurisdiction of the Hong Kong court and ordered the bank to refrain from paying out the defendant's money under the U.S. order. The bank thus faced the prospect of being in contempt of one court or the other or in the alternative paying out the sum required into court in New York. The matter was the subject of appeal but shortly after it opened the parties settled without judgment on the appeal being given. The Chartered Bank had submitted to the Court of Appeal that:

> "the difficulties of innocent third parties might be avoided if it was accepted that no court would make orders with extra territorial effect on parties against whom no substantial relief is sought unless subject to the endorsement of the foreign court in question. In a case involving assets in the possession of an innocent third party the law of the place where the assets are located should be recognised as having precedence over the orders of any other court in the case of conflict."[86]

The problem arises because the New York court has assumed extra-territorial jurisdiction. In England, the matter should not arise in respect of a Mareva order as the plaintiff is required to indemnify any innocent third party, in the cited case, the bank.

Prevailing law

In England and countries operating the English system such as in this case, with the law of Hong Kong, the laws of the country where the assets are situated should prevail in the event of any conflict. In the cited case, this would be the law of Hong Kong which requires an innocent third party to be indemnified or protected[86a] by the plaintiff; the law of the State of New York apparently offers little protection for innocent third parties. Technically those responsible in New York for attempting to

---

[86] The Law Society's *Guardian Gazette*, February 28, 1990.
[86a] *Derby* v. *Weldon* [1989] 2 W.L.R. 412 and 276; *Babanaft International* v. *Bassatne* [1989] 2 W.L.R. 232.

Perversion of course of justice prevent the action in Hong Kong will be guilty of attempting to pervert the course of justice, and presumably could be charged with an offence if they ever visited Hong Kong. This authority should be contrasted with *MacKinnon* v. *Donaldson, Lufkin and Jenrette Securities Corp.*[87] in which Hoffman J. held that whilst in an extreme case the court could grant a *subpoena duces tecum* on the English subsidiary of a U.S. parent to enforce the parent to produce documents, this way was undesirable as application could be made to the courts where the parent was situated and in any event was a violation of the sovereignty of the courts of (in this case) New York.

Limitations on the Mareva injunction

The *MacKinnon*[88] case deals with authorities both in England and the United States on the exercise of extra-territorial jurisdiction. The order will not extend to assets outside the jurisdiction, save in the circumstance as set out, above.[89]

Ulterior purpose The Mareva injunction is solely for the purpose of preventing the defendant from dissipating in any way assets so as to defeat a claim against him. Accordingly, it is not appropriate to apply for an order if the purpose is:

    (a) to improve the plaintiff's position over other creditors of the defendant;

    (b) to prevent the defendant from paying his debts; or

    (c) to exert pressure on the defendant to settle an action.[90]

Allowable withdrawals Whilst a Mareva injunction is couched in wide terms permitting the freezing of a defendant's assets, provision must be made for the following:

    (a) the defendant must be allowed to withdraw from his account his expenses not exceeding a specified sum (these take into account the defendant's personal circumstances);

    (b) to pay for (in the circumstances of one case) nursing fees for the defendant's aged mother;[91]

    (c) to pay for other specified accounts including putting his solicitor in funds;[92]

    (d) to pay his proper business expenses.[93]

Not registrable as land charge A Mareva injunction granted before judgment can be continued after so as to facilitate execution of the judgment debt.[94] It is not, however, "made for the purpose of enforcing a judgment" even though it has that effect and thus cannot be registered as a land charge under section 6(1) of the Land Charges Act 1972.[95]

---

[87] [1986] Ch. 482.
[88] *Ibid.*
[89] See above, p. 96. See also, *Intraco* v. *Notis Shipping Corp. of Liberia*; *Bhoja Trader, The* [1981] Com.L.R. 184.
[90] See above, n. 74.
[91] *Ibid.*
[92] *Ibid.*
[93] *Iraqi Ministry of Defence* v. *Arcepey Shipping Co. S.A.* [1980] 2 W.L.R. 488.
[94] *Stewart Chartering Co.* v. *C. & O. Managements S.A.* [1980] 1 W.L.R. 460.
[95] *Stockler* v. *Fourways Estates* [1984] 1 W.L.R. 25.

Transaction in ordinary course of business

A plaintiff suing architects for professional negligence was not granted a Mareva injunction to restrain the architects from settling a claim under their professional indemnity policy insurance without the plaintiff's consent since it was a bona fide settlement of claim in a transaction in the ordinary course of business.[96]

Summary of general principles

Likelihood of judgment against defendant

1. The Mareva injunction should be granted if it appears likely that the plaintiff would recover judgment against the defendant for a certain or at least approximate sum.

Evidence of assets within jurisdiction or elsewhere

2. There are reasons for believing the defendant has assets within the jurisdiction of the English court, or in a jurisdiction where an English court order will be enforced to meet a judgment either in whole or in part or in the circumstance it is appropriate to issue a worldwide order.

Evidence of intended disposal

3. There are also reasons for believing that the defendant might deal with the assets so that they are not available or traceable when judgment is given against him.[97]

Immediate effect

4. The Mareva injunction takes effect from the moment it is granted in respect of every asset of the defendant which it covers.

Duty of persons knowing of order

5. Everyone with knowledge of the Mareva order who has possession or control of assets, the subject of the order must do what he can to preserve them. Anyone in this position disposing of or assisting in the disposal of such assets is in contempt of court, save for innocent third parties outside the jurisdiction: the order is granted in respect of assets in such jurisdiction.

Specified maximum sum

6. The Mareva injunction should extend to a specified maximum amount claimed by the plaintiff. In certain cases the maximum sum may be omitted, but if this is done, counsel will have to explain the reason for so doing, or the explanation can be in the affidavit in support of the application.

Notice to third parties

7. The Mareva injunction should be granted for a few days until the defendant can be served and the bank and other third parties given notice either by telephone, fax or similar method, providing such method of communication is followed with a copy of the order in the post or delivered by hand. In either event the order and its effect on those served must be adequately explained.

Undertakings as to damages

8. The plaintiff will normally be required to give undertakings in damages to the defendant and an undertaking to a bank or any innocent third party to pay any expenses reasonably incurred by them in complying with the order.

Disclosure of assets

9. The defendant is usually required to make disclosure of his assets, or at least of those sufficient to meet a sum the subject of

---

[96] *Norwich Housing Association* v. *Ralplus and Mansell, The Times*, November 15, 1988.

[97] *Rahman (Prince Abdul) Bin Turki Al Sudairy* v. *Abu-Taha* [1980] 1 W.L.R. 1268—but see the dictum of Ackner L.J. in *A.J. Becknor & Co.* v. *Bilton* [1981] Q.B. 923 at p. 941.

the order. The disclosure in an appropriate case can include assets outside the jurisdiction.

Draft order 10. The plaintiff should prepare a draft order, comprising the Mareva injunction which will be submitted to the judge when the application is made in accordance with the Denning Guidelines.[98]

---

[98] See above, n. 72.

9 APPLICATION FOR A MAREVA ORDER

Introduction

Procedure governed by Order 29

An application will normally be made pursuant to section 37 of the Supreme Court Act 1981, but if the circumstances of any particular case do not come within the section (though it is difficult to envisage such a situation) the application can be made as a common law right. A Mareva application is normally made in the High Court, the procedure being governed by Order 29 of the Rules of Supreme Court. The application is often made in the Chancery Division, but any division of the High Court has jurisdiction. The procedure varies according to the division in which the application is made. In general, the application for a Mareva order is similar to an application for an Anton Piller order,[1] but there are differences due to the nature of the order. Mareva orders are normally granted on the application of someone with a cause of action, but a body performing a public function which has a statutory cause of action is entitled to apply on behalf of others, even though having no interest in the funds involved.[2]

Emergency orders

Court not sitting

Appeal

Secrecy

Mareva applications often are of extreme urgency and the Court of Appeal ruling in *W.E.A. Records* v. *Visions Channel 4*[3] applies, as also the procedures pertaining when the court is not sitting.[4] Appeals in respect of Mareva orders are dealt with a little differently from those concerning Anton Piller orders. If an application for a Mareva is refused at first instance, the appeal procedure is as set out on p. 51, but the Practice Note cited only relates to Anton Piller orders, and accordingly a Mareva application will be heard on appeal *in camera*. Whether this is the intention of the Court of Appeal is not clear, for it is submitted that both Anton Piller and Mareva orders require much the same degree of secrecy if they are to be effective, though the court has recognised that one of the elements of a Mareva application is that it shall be secret.

Appeal by defendant

Ex parte

The provisions relating to the appeal procedure by a defendant whose assets are the subject of a Mareva order are similar to those for an Anton Piller order. The Mareva order is always sought by *ex parte* application. If the action which gives rise to the application has not started, the appeal is made usually by motion, with affidavits in support, accompanied by a draft order which it is hoped the court will grant, and also a draft writ for the substantive action which the plaintiff proposes to serve if

[1] See pp. 50 *et seq.*
[2] *S.I.B.* v. *Pantell* [1989] 3 W.L.R. 698.
[3] [1983] 1 W.L.R. 721.
[4] See p. 51. The authority cited there—*Refson* v. *Saggers* [1984] 1 W.L.R. 1028—is pertinent in respect of a Mareva application.

the action has not already started. If the action has commenced, the application should be *ex parte* by summons.

Order after judgment

A Mareva order can be obtained before or during the action, and after judgment in order to assist execution if there are grounds for thinking that the judgment debtors intend to dissipate assets to avoid execution.[5] It should only be applied for in cases of urgency, and is sought because there is fear of assets being dissipated, but the usual order comprises several elements including interlocutory injunctions and orders to the defendant. Further, the plaintiff is always required to give undertakings in case it is later found that the order should not have been granted.

Several elements to order

> "The injunction applied for may be granted on terms providing for the issue of the writ or summons and such other terms, if any, as the court think fit."[6]

Assets subject to a Mareva injunction

Ownership As the purpose of a Mareva injunction is to prevent the defendant's assets being moved or dealt with so as to defeat the claim of his creditors, an applicant should first consider what are the assets which may be the subject of the order. These assets should, so far as is possible, be identified before the order is sought; details should be set out in the application and an estimate of their value included. If, however, the assets cannot be identified, this will not prevent the order being granted, though it may make more difficult its implementation, for the full nature of the assets will not become known until the defendant has made his disclosure of his assets pursuant to the order.[7]

Identification of assets

Assets These include bank accounts, chattels such as motor cars, jewellery, *objets d'art*, aircraft, choses in action,[8] land and money (including foreign currency). The court has discretion whether to grant an order in respect of the bank account of a third party or a joint account, if so, provided in the draft order.[9]

Evidence for the application

Lack of direct evidence

It is seldom that there will be direct evidence that a defendant to a Mareva order will attempt to dissipate his assets so as to defeat the claims of the plaintiff. If there is such evidence, well and good, but in its absence the question arises as to what a plaintiff must bring to the court so as to initiate the order. The following are among the points which have been considered:

[5] *Orwell Steel (Erection and Fabrication)* v. *Asphalt and Tarmac (U.K.)* [1984] 1 W.L.R. 1097.
[6] O. 29, r. 1(3).
[7] For further consideration, see p. 118.
[8] *C.B.S. United Kingdom* v. *Lambert* [1983] Ch. 37; *Allen* v. *Jambo Holdings* [1980] 1 W.L.R. 1252.
[9] *Z.* v. *A-Z & AA-LL* [1982] Q.B. 558.

Risk of dissipation   (a) there is a real risk that the assets will be dissipated if the order is not granted;[10]

Inability to satisfy claim   (b) there is a real risk that if the injunction is not granted, the defendant will be unable to satisfy the plaintiff's claim;

(c) in *Dunlop Holdings and Dunlop* v. *Staravia*[11] which concerned an application for an Anton Piller order, the Court of Appeal found that it is seldom that one can get actual evidence of a threat to destroy material or

Inference of threat of destruction   documents, so it is necessary for it to be inferred from the evidence which is before the court. If it is clearly established on that evidence that the defendant is engaged in a nefarious activity which renders it likely that he is an untrustworthy person, then an Anton Piller order would be granted.

It is considered that the reasoning of the court in this particular case should apply to the grant of a Mareva order. If the

Illegal or nefarious activity   defendant is engaged in an illegal or "nefarious" activity, it is quite likely that he will do what he can to defeat creditors, and if the injunction is not granted there is a real risk that the defendant will be unable to satisfy the plaintiff's claim.[12] Likewise in such a case the balance of convenience can be in favour of granting the injunction.[13] The following are some examples which it is

Examples   submitted would be sufficient for the court to grant an order if the facts are substantiated by the affidavit evidence:

(a) a company with a small branch office or a bank account in this country but resident abroad. In the face of a Mareva order, such parties can always offer security by way of

Security by bond   bond—such as in the case with ships. While it has been suggested that there must be something disreputable about the defendant to merit the granting of an order, this has never been the practice in Admiralty law, and though in most Mareva cases there is an element of deceit or dishonesty, the test is whether the assets are likely to be lost to the plaintiff if the injunction is not granted. There is no reasoning on the line of authorities to support the view that there must be an element of sharp practice or dishonesty, though undoubtedly if there is something not to the defendant's credit, this will assist the court in making up its mind; and

(b) if the defendant is in the jurisdiction but tends to transfer

Intention of transfer to subsidiary   assets to subsidiaries or third parties so as to become depleted of assets.

As an example in one case, the defendant started to dispose of its business and assets after an action initiated by way of an Anton Piller order had been commenced against it. The method of so doing were quite legitimate but it is considered that the court would have granted a Mareva on being made aware of certain of these events. It is difficult to postulate how many of the events would need to take place before the court would act.

---

[10] See above, n. 9.
[11] [1982] Com.L.R. 3.
[12] Based on the facts of *ETS Esefka* v. *Central Bank of Nigeria* [1979] Lloyd's Rep. 445.
[13] *Barclay-Johnson* v. *Yuill* [1980] 1 W.L.R. 1259.

Evidence similar to that for Anton Piller

Though some judges seem to take the view that if the evidence is such that an Anton Piller order would be granted, then the same or similar evidence will justify the grant of a Mareva order and the two orders are commonly combined. The events included:

(a) one of the subsidiaries of the defendant increased its business so that of the defendant declined;

Sale of subsidiary

(b) the subsidiary was eventually sold to a third party and there arose a debt to the defendant;

Transfer of property

(c) a freehold property was transferred to a subsidiary and then sold to a third party;[14]

(d) the same defendant lent a very large sum to a bookmaking company owned or controlled by either the defendant or its ultimate controlling shareholder or both. The bookmaking company declared a loss slightly in excess of the debt, which was then written off in the books of the defendant. (The audited accounts of the bookmaking company later had a qualification that some of the records of the company were not available).

Debt written off by subsidiary

Effect of order

If a Mareva order had been granted it would have had the effect of either preventing such transactions taking place or to causing transfers to be set aside and the assets returned, or if the transfers were allowed, then the proceeds would be the subject of the order. The importance of the Mareva injunction is illustrated by the loan to the bookmaking company as it incurred a loss so that the monies could not be recovered. If the Mareva injunction had been in place as from the granting of the Anton Piller order, then the above events could only have taken place with the consent of the plaintiff, or if the plaintiff failed to consent, the court. The proceeds from the sales of assets would have come within the scope of the order.

Consent to transactions

Debts created by a defendant company transferring assets to another company in the same group should be considered with some suspicion, for they can easily be written off and no one will complain. The following hypothetical case is given as an example of a Mareva application in the Chancery Division. A company (the intended plaintiff) has a cause of action against another company (the intended defendant) for infringement of copyright. The damages are likely to be in excess of £500,000. The nature of the action arises because the intended defendant is alleged to deal in counterfeit video tapes in infringement of the intended plaintiff's rights. The intended plaintiff fears that the intended defendant will dissipate its assets so as to defeat any judgment it may obtain, and therefore applies for a Mareva order.

Debts between related companies

Example

---

[14] It may have been necessary to transfer the property to effect the sale because the defendant may have had difficulty in selling the freehold as any prospective purchaser having notice of the defendant's accounts could have been warned of a liability concerning an action for copyright and passing off. A transaction by way of sale would have been liable to be set aside under s. 172 of the Law of Property Act 1925 on the grounds that the sale was intended to defeat a judgment. The accounts of the subsidiary would have had no such cautionary notice.

The application

Application direct to judge

In the example given, the proceedings have not commenced and because an injunction is sought, the application is made direct to the judge.[15] The documents with the application should contain a draft order which the plaintiff hopes the court will grant.

The draft order may contain the following:

(a) a note referring to the court reading the court papers, *i.e.* the draft writ and affidavits in support;

Contents of draft order

(b) undertakings by the plaintiff;

(c) injunction against the defendant:
  (i) restraining him from removing assets from the jurisdiction or dealing with them so as to have the effect of putting them outside the court's jurisdiction;
  (ii) restraining the defendant from otherwise disposing of, or dealing with its assets within the jurisdiction of the court;

(d) there will be a provision allowing the defendant certain monies for business and if appropriate his legal expenses;

(e) provision in favour of third parties not to deprive them of pre-existing rights; and

(f) an order to the defendants concerning disclosure of assets and to verify disclosure by affidavit.

An example of a Mareva order in the Chancery Division before an action has commenced is set out below:

IN THE HIGH COURT OF JUSTICE

CHANCERY DIVISION

MR JUSTICE GRIDLEY

Example of draft order

the   day of   19

IN THE MATTER of an Intended Action

B E T W E E N

CONWAY LIMITED (Intended Plaintiffs)
and

MICAWBER LIMITED
AND GEORGE PAGNELL[16]
(Intended Defendants)

UPON MOTION made by Counsel for the Intended Plaintiff (hereinafter called the Plaintiff)

AND UPON READING the court file

AND the Plaintiff by its Counsel undertaking

---

[15] *Sony Corporation* v. *Anand* [1981] F.S.R. 398.

[16] In many cases, especially when the allegation is, in substance, counterfeiting, the defendant company will have few assets and one may cite the controlling shareholder as a defendant if one can prove, in effect that he is responsible for major decisions of importance for the company and had authorized, directed and procured the acts complained of: see *Evans (C.) & Son* v. *Spritebrand* [1985] 1 W.L.R. 317.

Plaintiff's undertakings

(1) forthwith on or before to issue a Writ of Summons claiming relief similar to or connected with that hereafter granted

(2) to make and file an affidavit verifying what was alleged by Counsel in the terms of the draft affidavit of Dorian Gray

(3) to serve upon the Intended Defendants (hereinafter called the Defendants) a copy of the said Affidavit and Notice of Motion for

(4) to pay the reasonable costs incurred by any person other than the Defendants to whom notice of this Order may be given in ascertaining whether any assets to which this Order applies are within their power possession custody or control and in complying with this Order and to indemnify any such person against all liabilities which may flow from such compliance

(5) to obey any Order this Court may make as to damages if it shall consider that the Defendants shall have sustained any damages by reason of this Order which the Plaintiff ought to pay

IT IS ORDERED

Injunction

(1) that the Defendants and each of them be restrained until after or until further Order in the meantime from doing (as regards the first Defendant whether by George Pagnell or Henry Chiltern directors or by the servants or agents or any of them or otherwise howsoever and as regards the second Defendant whether by himself or by any of his servants or agents or any of them or otherwise howsoever) the following acts or any of them that is to say removing from the jurisdiction of this Court or otherwise disposing of or dealing with its or his [respective or joint] assets within the jurisdiction of this Court including and in particular

(i) the freehold property known as Hausburg House, Ascot Road, Burford, or (if the same has been sold) the net proceeds of sale thereof after discharge of any subsisting mortgage or charge

(ii) the property and assets of the business known as "Layton Crest Videos" carried on by the Defendants from premises at 24 Thistle Road, Primrose Hill, Staines or (if and in so far as the same have been sold) the proceeds of sale thereof

(iii) any monies in [any] accounts(s)

[numbered] at the Mountview Bank Ltd., 1, The Square, Newport and without prejudice to the foregoing pledging charging or otherwise parting with title to or possession of SUCH ASSETS

Allowable disposals

(A) SAVE and in so far as the said assets of each of the Defendants exceeds £500,000.

(B) SAVE that the second Defendant is to be at liberty to expend a sum not exceeding £150 per week [per month] for ordinary living expenses

(C) AND the first Defendant a sum of £2500 for ordinary and proper business expenses

AND not otherwise in each case upon informing the Plaintiff's

Solicitors of the source or accounts from which such sums are to be drawn and

> (D) THAT the Defendants and each of them may expend a sum not exceeding £15,000 each or such reasonable sum on Legal Advice and representation as may be requisite

Right of set-off

> (E) PROVIDED nothing in this injunction shall prevent any bank from exercising any rights of set-off it may have in respect of facilities afforded by any such bank to the Defendants or any of them prior to the date of this Order

Disclosure of assets

(2)   that the Defendants and each of them do forthwith disclose the full value of its or his repective and joint assets within the jurisdiction of this Court identifying with full particularity the nature of all such assets and their whereabouts and whether the same be held in its or his or their own names or by nominees or otherwise on its or his or their behalf and the sums standing in such accounts such disclosures to be verified by affidavits to be made by the Defendants and in the case of the first Defendant by its proper officers and served on the Plaintiffs' Solicitors within days' of service of this Order or notice there being given

Delivery up

(3)   that the Defendants and each of them do forthwith upon the service of this Order deliver up or cause to be delivered up into the custody of the Plaintiffs' Solicitors the items specified in the Schedule hereto

AND   the Plaintiff   is at liberty to serve Short Notice of Motion for

AND   the Defendants or either of them are at liberty to move to discharge or vary this Order upon giving to the Plaintiff days' notice of intention so to do

The elements of the order

"And upon reading the court file"   The order sets out that the court has read the application papers such as draft writ and affidavits attached to the order. The purpose is to confirm that the court is fully aware of the plaintiff's case, as set out in the draft writ and affidavit. A draft affidavit in the example would be

Affidavit setting out case

put before the court and explained by counsel. The affidavit should be sworn if there is time and in such case, the sworn affidavit would be filed. The evidence should be such that it is plain why a Mareva order should be granted. It is on the evidence as set out in the draft or sworn affidavit and as explained by counsel and only that on which the court will judge the matter. On any review of the matter, the court may be asked by the defendant to consider evidence that the plaintiff should, in the defendants' opinion, have disclosed in his affidavits. If the court agrees with the defendants, the order may be discharged.

"And the plaintiff by its counsel undertaking to issue a writ"   The plaintiff undertakes to issue a writ forthwith on or before a stated date which will normally be within a day or so of

Form of writ   the order. The writ will be in the form of that which will be served on the defendants to commence the substantive action. This provision will not, of course, apply when the action has already commenced.

Affidavits in support   **"To make and file an affidavit"**   The court will accept draft affidavits if there has been no time to get them sworn. Counsel will, in the course of his submission, not only explain the nature of the case, but also why it has not been possible to file a sworn affidavit.

Person swearing affidavit   The affidavit must be sworn by a person or persons who have full knowledge of the matter or have access to such knowledge and are in a responsible position such as one of the plaintiff's solicitors, or an in-house legal adviser, or a senior executive. In any case, the person must have gained the knowledge personally by perusal of documents or by talking to person who are aware of the facts. If hearsay evidence is given in the affidavits, its source should be indicated. The application will not fail if some facts are not available, such as the exact details of a bank account or other property, but the affidavit should acknowledge that search has been made.[17]

In addition to the matters set out in the Denning Guidelines the affidavit in support should contain a clear and concise statement of:

Statement of facts

(a) the facts relied on as justifying the application *ex parte*, including some details of any notice given to the defendant or, if none has been given, the reasons for not so doing;

(b) any answer asserted by the defendant (or which he is thought likely to assert) either to the claim in the action or to the claim for interlocutory relief;

(c) any facts known to the applicant which might lead the court not to grant relief *ex parte*; and

(d) the precise relief sought.

Material disclosure

The ultimate test for the exercise of the court's discretion is whether, in all the circumstances, the case is one in which it appears to the court "to be just and convenient" to grant the injunction.[18] "Thus the conduct of the plaintiffs may be material" *per* Kerr L.J.[19]

Just and convenient

It should be in the forefront of an applicant's mind that the court must be fully informed of all facts that are relevant to enable the court to come to a decision as to whether or not to grant the order.[20] There are also facts which are additional to those required to prove the plaintiff's case which need to be disclosed. The following are some of the material matters:

Court informed of all facts

(a) the plaintiff has a responsibility to investigate the case as

---

[17] For further consideration of what the affidavit should disclose, see Material Disclosure, below, and Denning guidelines, p. 87.

[18] SCA 1981, s.37.

[19] *The Niedersachsen* 2 Lloyd's Rep. 600 at p. 620.

[20] Browne-Wilkinson J. in *Thermax* v. *Schott Industrial Glass* [1981] F.S.R. 289.

Results of plaintiff's investigations

Particulars about the defendant

Plaintiff's financial position

fully as possible before applying for the order, and the results of the investigation should be reflected in the affidavits;[21]

(b) there should be included in the affidavits facts about the defendants, the nature of their trade, how long they have been in business, the facts and reasoning that leads one to conclude that they may dispose of assets, including copies of their recent accounts if available. If the allegation against the defendants is such that the defendants are shown to be likely to be dishonourable or likely to engage in a nefarious activity, the evidence to justify this allegation should be included;[22]

(c) evidence of the plaintiff's financial position . The most recent accounts should be sufficient to show the plaintiff good for any award against it, if called upon to honour its indemnity which it undertakes as one of the conditions for the granting of the order. If the plaintiff is unlikely to be able to pay any award this also should be made clear.[23]

Service of affidavit

Additional facts in sworn affidavit

Serve upon the intended defendants a copy of the said affidavit and notice of motion If the plaintiff applies to the court armed only with a draft affidavit (the matter being too urgent to allow time for the affidavit to be sworn) the affidavit should be sworn and filed with the documents as soon as possible after the application; in practice this must mean immediately. The sworn affidavit should be served on the defendants, and should contain all information in the draft affidavit and also any submissions of counsel which are relevant, *i.e.* not argument, but if perhaps the court has asked counsel to enlarge on matters, then the explanation, if it contains facts, should be in the sworn affidavit. The defendant is thus in the position of being informed of all the evidence which was before the court. The plaintiff's legal advisers have a responsibility to see that this is done.

Notice of Motion

Lapse

The defendants must also be served with the Notice of Motion whereby the matter comes *inter partes*. The injunction in the order is given for a short period of time and will lapse unless renewed, either by consent of the parties or by order of the court. This gives the defendant the opportunity to come before the court to apply to have it discharged.

Return date

Notification

Priority of notification

The *ex parte* injunction will continue until the return date, which should be the earliest possible convenient date. The plaintiff will give notice to the bank and others of the existence of the order by phone, telex or fax, but this should immediately be confirmed in writing and the letter should be delivered by hand or sooner. Fax is not suitable as confirmation as the documents can fade. The notice to third parties should set out the terms of the injunction. It is the practice to advise banks and third parties of the situation prior to informing the defendant so as to allow the order to become effective, before the defendant knows. The return date may, in certain circumstances[24] be quite a long period

---

[21] *Rogers (Jeffrey) Knitwear Productions* v. *Vinola (Knitwear) Manufacturing Co.* [1985] J.P.L. 184 and *Practice Note* (1983) 1 All E.R. 1119.

[22] *Dunlop Holdings and Dunlop* v. *Staravia*, see above, n. 11.

[23] *Allen* v. *Jambo Holdings*, see above, n. 8.

[24] *E.g.* because it is difficult to make the search for assets in due time, or the defendant is out of the jurisdiction.

ahead, seven days or more. By the return date, the Mareva order should have been executed.

To pay the reasonable costs incurred by any person and indemnify any such person against all liabilities   Whilst a Mareva injunction is *in personam*, it operates *in rem* and consequently anyone becoming aware of its existence and being

Third parties bound by order affected thereby is bound by its terms, such as a bank holding an account or title deeds of the defendant. Copies of the order will normally be served on those who may have possession, custody or control of any of the defendant's assets to which the injunction applies.

Third party's expenses In order to comply with the order, a holder of any of the assets named, such as a bank, will be put to some expense, such as regulating the defendant's accounts so as to put a "stop" on the defendant's use of them. If the matter goes further, the bank must look into its records, and in putting the "stop" on the accounts, the bank might become liable to an innocent third party who has a charge over the assets prior to that of the plaintiff.

Undertaking to pay costs The plaintiff is required to undertake to pay the bank's reasonable costs in carrying out its work, and also must indemnify it against any liability to an innocent third party. This undertaking by the plaintiff is not limited to a bank but applies to any person other than the defendant who has possession, custody or control of any of the assets.[25]

To obey any order that the court may make as to damages   An undertaking by the plaintiff to pay damages ought to be given on every interlocutory injunction (save when the order is a final one).[26] If, however, a plaintiff has not the means to pay it does

No means of payment not follow that an interlocutory injunction will be refused as questions of his financial position should not effect the essential justice of the case.[27] The position should, however, be made

Application by the Crown plain to the court. If the Crown applies for an interlocutory injunction, it will ordinarily be required to give an undertaking as to damages[28] but not where the Crown is enforcing the law.

The order on the plaintiff to pay damages is to take account of those cases when the application is misconceived and should not have been granted, in which case the applicant for the order will have to make such payments as the court deems appropriate.

The form of the order

General restraint This is in a form whereby the defendant, until after a given date (the return date) is restrained from removing from the jurisdiction of the court, or disposing or dealing with, assets within the jurisdiction of the court in accordance with the order. This is a general restraint on all assets.[29] A joint account has also

---

[25] *Searose* v. *Seatrain U.K.* [1981] 1 W.L.R. 894.

[26] *Fenner* v. *Wilsone* [1893] 2 Ch. 656.

[27] *Allen* v. *Jambo Holdings* (see above, n. 8) in which the plaintiff was legally aided. See also *D.P.R. Futures, Re* [1989] 1 W.L.R. 778.

[28] *Hoffman-La Roche & Co. A.G.* v. *Secretary of State for Trade and Industry* [1975] A.C. 295 at p. 318.

[29] *C.B.S. United Kingdom* v. *Lambert*, see above, n. 8.

been the subject of a Mareva injunction.[30] An order in respect of a joint account must make it clear to the bank that it applies to such an account. If the other holders of the account are not parties to the action, the order should include a reference to the joint account and a copy of the order served on the other holders. The Mareva order will provide a given date or further order; the "further order" is most likely to arise in those cases when the defendant applies before the return date to have the order set aside or varied. On the return date, the matter becomes *inter partes* and before the court.

Particular assets   The injunction may also contain a restraint on particular assets which should be listed.[31] Since a plaintiff has no real prospect in a claim to money held to the defendant's account in his solicitor's client account, and over which the solicitor has a lien for unpaid costs, such should not be included in the ambit of an injunction restraining the defendant from dealing with his assets.[32] Assets outside the jurisdiction may, in certain circumstances, be listed.[33] Jurisdiction can have a wider meaning than England.[34] If one of the assets is a yacht or ship, such a **Arrest of ship** vessel may be arrested under the Admiralty procedure. It may be more convenient if a Mareva injunction is sought to include any vessel within the assets of the Mareva order rather than to start a separate Admiralty action, but whether an Admiralty action can be commenced giving rise to arrest of a ship will depend on the nature of the action.

Any particular property should be clearly identified, so far as **Identification or** is possible, but if this cannot be given with certainty the best **property** information should be given, *e.g.* "the leasehold flat at Brenda Buildings, Scratchwood, Middlesex." It will be noted that the assets in the precedent include a freehold property: this could be the business premises of the first defendant or a dwelling-house of the second. The assets also include the property and assets of the defendants' business: this could include any leaseholds. If any of the assets have been sold, then the order extends to the proceeds of sale. Also identified, if known, are bank accounts of the defendants or either of them. If it transpires that the defendant has made loans, these could be the subject of a supplementary order.

In most cases, it is desirable to set out the maximum sum **Maximum amount** which the plaintiff considers he can recover in his action. A bank will not know how far the defendant has assets outside the bank and whether or not they are the subject of the order. The injunction can be to restrain the defendant from disposing of any sums to its credit below the maximum, or to restrain it from disposing of any specific security lodged with the bank.

The general principal is that the bank or other innocent

---

[30] *Z Ltd.* v. *A-Z* [1982] 2 W.L.R. 288. The procedure if a joint account is the subject of the order must be followed.
[31] Note that the list given in the precedent above is not comprehensive and any particular assets may be listed.
[32] *Prekookeanska Plovidba* v. *LNT Lines* [1989] 1 W.L.R. 753; [1988] 3 All E.R. 897.
[33] But see "International aspects" p. 96, and *Derby & Co.* v. *Weldon*, [1989] 2 W.L.R. 412, setting out the circumstances when this may be done.
[34] See Chap. 8, n. 79.

Clear instructions to third party third party must know exactly what it should or should not do. The order may be so drawn that any third party on whom it is served is only obliged to freeze assets up to the maximum sum specified in the order. If this involves duplication because of different banks holding several accounts the defendant can apply for adjustment, but the third parties in receipt of the order must know what they should do.

Exceptions There may be exceptional cases when it is inappropriate to specify a maximum sum on account of the difficulties this may cause. In the event that the assets are insufficient to meet the claim, or the defendant is neither resident nor carrying on business in the jurisdiction, then the injunction will be in respect of all assets and the defendant can apply to have any excess released.

Calculation of maximum amount The maximum amount is a sum which must be inserted in the order, and assets in excess of that value cannot be frozen. It is equal to the amount of the plaintiff's claim with costs, as estimated at the time of the application. It might later prove to be greater or less, and if less, the amount which is the subject of the order should be amended in line with the claim.

Living expenses A sum is given for ordinary living expenses. The court will not deprive a defendant of the use of all his assets so that he has no money for living expenses. He should be able to incur and discharge the ordinary expenses of everyday life, including the operation of his business. The living circumstances **Each case considered** of the defendant are considered in each case. In *PCW (Underwriting Agencies) Ltd.* v. *Dixon*[35] the reasonable living expenses were allowed so as not to exceed £1,000 per week, and the defendant was allowed to pay his outstanding accounts totalling £27,000. The provision for ordinary living expenses is particularly important if the defendant's assets are less than the maximum amount in value that can be frozen, as he may need to draw on such assets or their income for living expenses. An injunction which makes no provision for the defendants' living expenses or payment of ordinary debts will be set aside.[36]

Business expenses In the course of legitimate business, assets are used to pay debts and this continues to be allowed even if the contract which gives rise to the debt may be illegal.[37] It is, of course, to the plaintiff's advantage, as well as the defendants, that the latter remains in business, but extravagant business expenses will not be allowed.[38]

Legal advice A specific sum is permitted for the defendant to engage professional advisers to represent him in defending the action which has given rise to the Mareva injunction, as well as disputing the Mareva itself. In *PCW (Underwriting Agencies)* v. **Reasonable sum on facts of case** *Dixon*,[39] the court allowed the defendant to pay his solicitor £50,000 in addition to £20,000 already paid. What is reasonable will depend on the facts of each case; thus in matrimonial

[35] [1983] 2 All E.R. 697.
[36] *Law Society* v. *Shanks, The Times,* October 19, 1987.
[37] *Iraqi Ministry of Defence* v. *Arcepey Shipping Co. S.A.* [1981] Q.B. 65.
[38] *T.D.K. Tape Distributors (U.K.)* v. *Videochoice* [1986] 1 W.L.R. 141.
[39] See above, n. 35.

matters, the sum will be modest compared with a commercial action of complexity.

Banks The order specifically provides that the bank holding accounts of the defendants may exercise any rights of set off which it may have as a result of granting the defendant loan
Right of set-off facilities. However, once a bank has been notified of the order it may not deal with any of the defendant's assets save for the right of set-off. All cheques are "stopped" but certain credit cards, bills of exchange or letters of credit will be honoured. A Mareva injunction can be granted against the holder of the proceeds of a bill of exchange as this is one of his assets, but not in respect of
Proviso as to the bill itself.[40] A Mareva application should contain a provision
exercise of rights for the bank to exercise its rights in respect of an account, so as to avoid the necessity of the bank having to go to the court to vary the order.[41]

Disclose the full value of his assets within the jurisdiction The defendant is required to list all his assets with their value or what
Verification of he estimates to be their value. The disclosure must be verified by
disclosure affidavit and served on the plaintiff's solicitor.

To some extent, the matter depends on what is claimed and the amount available; thus if the claim is for £100,000 and the defendant discloses an unencumbered freehold worth £200,000, this should be sufficient. There are cases when the assets within
Insufficient assets the jurisdiction are insufficient to support the plaintiff's claim. Normally a Mareva order will not extend to overseas assets because it is difficult for an English court to control the enforcement of proceedings in other jurisdictions, and it is oppressive for overseas assets to be frozen other than by the law of the place where the assets are situated.[42] However, there are
Extension to other situations when the order will extend to other jurisdictions.[43] The
jurisdictions development of the Mareva order is such that following *Derby & Co.* v. *Weldon* a worldwide restraint and disclosure order has to be granted in an appropriate case but subject to the proviso in respect of innocent parties.

Verified by affidavit The defendant is required to make an affidavit which will verify the disclosures of his assets. It is usual for the disclosure and affidavit to be in the same document. If the defendant fails to make a true affidavit (that is, the disclosure of assets is not complete or is false) proceedings can be commenced against the defendant for contempt. This would be the case if there was failure to disclose as required by the order. A failure to
Failure to disclose disclose includes the making of a false statement, or a material concealment or misleading statement. The defendant's affidavit should be served on the plaintiff's solicitor within a given number

---

[40] *Montecchi* v. *Shimco (U.K.) Ltd.*; *Navone* v. *Same* [1979] 1 W.L.R. 1180.
[41] *Oceanica Castelana Armadora S.A.* v. *Mineralimportexport (Barclays Bank International Intervening); Theotokos, The* [1983] 1 W.L.R. 1302. For further consideration of the position of banks and others holding pledged securities, see below under "Secured Assets", p. 118, and for unsecured assets, see p. 119.
[42] *Ashtiani* v. *Kashi* [1987] Q.B. 888.
[43] See "International Aspects" p. 96 and *Derby* v. *Weldon*, above n. 33 which concerned assets outside the jurisdiction of the English Court.

of days. The time required will depend on the complexity of the matter. If the time given is too short, the defendant can ask the court for an extension of time.

Discovery and interrogatories

Purpose of discovery

One of the elements of the order included in a Mareva injunction can be an order for discovery of documents. The purpose behind such an order is to make the injunction effective, for example to ascertain the whereabouts of property which the plaintiff claims belongs to him in equity and which he was seeking to recover in a tracing action.[44] In addition, the court may order

Cross-examination

cross-examination of a defendant on any affidavits filed by him in purported compliance with a discovery order made ancillary to a Mareva order.[45]

Deficiencies in affidavit

Application can also be made for the defendant being required to answer interrogatories; these would normally arise out of what would be considered deficiencies in the defendant's affidavit. There would appear to be no reason why, in a suitable case, a plaintiff should not also be the subject of interrogatories or cross-examined on his affidavit too. The court will not make discovery or interrogatories orders if the effect would be undesirable in its consequence and unnecessary for the operation of a Mareva injunction.[46]

Delivery up

Circumstances in which ordered

If delivery up of chattels is required, this will be specified in the schedule to the order. It is unusual to order delivery up, but this will be done if there is clear evidence that the defendant is likely to dispose of the chattels with a view to depriving the plaintiff of the fruits of a judgment. Delivery up may well be given if there is evidence that the property was wrongfully acquired by the defendant. In practice, many items are in effect delivered up in so far as the defendant's bank may hold substantial assets in addition to the defendants accounts; this may be evidenced by share certificates, bills of exchange and the like. In *C.B.S. United Kingdom* v. *Lambert*[47] the court ordered delivery up of motor vehicles in the defendant's possession which were required to be kept at a garage chosen by the plaintiff's solicitor.

Short Notice

A Mareva order being of an emergency nature, there may not be time for the plaintiff to serve on the defendant the Notice of Motion for the matter to become *inter partes* giving two clear days.[48] In such event, the plaintiff may seek, when applying for the order, leave to serve Short Notice on the defendant.

---

[44] *A.* v. *C.* (Note) [1981] Q.B. 956; *Campbell Mussells* v. *Thompson* (1984) 81 L.S.Gaz. 2140, C.A.
[45] *House of Spring Gardens* v. *Waite* [1985] 129 S.J. 64.
[46] *A.J. Beckhor & Co.* v. *Bilton* [1981] 2 W.L.R. 601.
[47] [1983] Ch. 37.
[48] O. 8, r. 2(2).

Items which may be the subject of an order

Secured, unsecured and intangible assets

Reputed ownership

Assets must be owned by the defendant whether legally or beneficially but being reputed to own them is not sufficient.[49] The assets must be available if required to satisfy a judgment debt.

Future interest

Many assets are easy to identify such as property, real or personal, but difficulties can arise with other interests. The Mareva order can embrace assets which will come into the ownership of the defendant in the future, or in which he will acquire an interest.[50] If the assets are legally owned by the defendant as trustee for an innocent party they cannot be the subject of an order.[51]

Secured assets

If the defendant has pledged assets such as a house by way of mortgage, or a charge on any property or lodging of shares as security, the position of a plaintiff obtaining a Mareva injunction is no better than if he had obtained a judgment debt and then levied execution. Thus the holder of the security does not have his position altered, but, as a result of the Mareva proceedings, it may well be that the security has to be realised in order to satisfy the injunction. If there is a claim for £1 million and a bond of the defendant to the value of £2 million charged to a bank to secure a loan to the defendant, it may be necessary to sell the bond, discharge the loan and the balance of the proceeds becomes the subject of the injunction. The realisation of the security is not generally within the scope of the Mareva injunction, which provides that the assets will not be the subject of disposition or pledge. The object of the order is to preserve the assets against a possible judgment debt. If, however, the assets are realised such as an insurance policy becoming unencumbered to a third party, then the policy or its proceeds come within the scope of the order.[52]

Cretanor Maritime Co. v. Irish Marine Management

Complications can arise as to what assets are the subject of a Mareva order as is shown by *Cretanor Maritime Co Ltd.* v. *Irish Marine Management Ltd.*[53] In this case, shipowners executed a floating charge by way of debenture over all their assets in favour of a bank outside the jurisdiction to secure a loan to them. The debenture included the power for the bank to appoint a receiver in the event of default on the loan. In addition, the debenture was guaranteed by a third party. The shipowners chartered their ship.

Facts of Cretanor Maritime

Disputes then arose under the charterparty and the matter was referred to arbitration, but before the hearing, the shipowners obtained a Mareva injunction over the assets of the

---

[49] See above, n. 41.
[50] *Cybil Inc. of Panama* v. *Timpuship* [1978] C.A. Transcript 478; *T.D.K. Tape Distributors (U.K.)* v. *Videochoice* [1986] 1 W.L.R. 141. The proceeds of an insurance policy: this authority should also be studied as it deals with the position when a solicitors fails to ensure that his client complies with a Mareva injunction and the consequences. See further p. 158.
[51] *Roberts* v. *Death* 8 [1881] Q.B.D. 319. In this case, the defendant was in the position of garnishee but the principle is of general application.
[52] *TDK Tape Distributor (UK) Ltd.* v. *Video choice Ltd* [1986] 1 W.L.R. 141.
[53] [1978] 1 W.L.R. 966.

charterer. The arbitration was settled (though the Mareva order continued) by a requirement for the charterer to pay sums to the owners in instalments, but after a while payment stopped. The owners did not, in consequence, have the means to service their bank loan. The bank called upon the third party guarantor to honour his guarantee, which he did. By operation of a foreign law to which the shipowner and third party were subject, the third party became the debenture holder in place of the bank, and the third party appointed a receiver.

Effect of appointment of receiver   The appointment of the receiver in respect of the debenture crystallised the floating charge over the assets of the shipowner. Part of the assets were the charterparty and the arbitration action previously brought by the shipowner against the charterer, whose own assets were the subject of the Mareva injunction frozen in order to satisfy the judgment debt arising out of the arbitration. The charterer's assets were not sufficient to satisfy the debenture holder and the arbitration debt in favour of the shipowner. By reason of the Mareva order, the charterer's assets could not be moved from the jurisdiction so the receiver applied to have the Mareva injunction discharged so this could be done.

Right of receiver to deal with assets   The Court of Appeal, in confirming the judge at first instance, Donaldson J, held that the appointment of the receiver under the debenture, by crystallising the floating charge, gave the receiver an immediate right to deal with all the assets of the shipowner. These included rights arising out of the arbitration which included access to the frozen assets of the charterer, of which the debenture holder became equitable assignee. It followed that the receiver could apply to have the Mareva injunction set aside so as to move the funds from the jurisdiction, in favour of the debenture holder.

Unsecured debts

The Mareva order makes provision for the payment of ordinary proper business and living expenses, and fixes sums to effect this. The intention is to allow the defendant to carry on with his normal everyday business. A bank holding an account of a defendant may exercise its right of set off against sums due to it in the ordinary course of banking. The sum for business purposes **Provision for business expenses**   is fixed in the order, but the position must be considered if a greater sum is required so as to allow the performance of a contract between the defendant and a third party, relating to the assets which are the subject of the order. Thus the defendant might be required under a contract to pay for goods and has not the means to do so, owing to the effect of the order; or there may be a requirement by contract to deliver an asset to a third party. If the contract was made prior to the date of the Mareva order, it will generally be the case that the rights of the third party will prevail over the plaintiff's desire to secure the defendant's assets for himself "against the day of judgment."[54]

This principle was carried somewhat further in *Iraqi Ministry of Defence* v. *Arcepey Shipping Co. S.A.*[55] In this case the

[54] *Per* Kerr L.J. in *Galaxia Maritime S.A.* v. *Mineral Importexport* [1982] 1 W.L.R. 539 at p. 542.
[55] [1981] Q.B. 65.

Repayment of loan

defendants, the subject of a Mareva order, had, prior to the injunction, contracted a loan. The lender intervened in the proceedings with a view to enabling the defendant to be in a position to repay the loan by lifting the injunction from certain assets. The plaintiffs objected on the grounds that the loan was illegal as a money-lending transaction and the lender was not licensed. Robert Goff J. held that a reputable businessman who has received a loan from another person is likely to regard it as dishonourable if not dishonest to avoid repayment of a loan by virtue of a legal technicality. He held that "the intervener asked not that the defendants should repay the loan but that they should be free to do so if they thought it right"[56] and allowed the injunction to be varied so that the defendant could pay his debts from his assets and satisfy debts as they fell due. This judgment has the effect that any creditors in the ordinary course of business do not have to sue on the debt to obtain satisfaction which could cause unnecessary loss of reputation.

Position of creditors

The authorities have to be studied with care, but generally the principle is that a plaintiff with a Mareva order is in no better a position *vis-a-vis* other creditors than he would have been if he had pursued the case in the ordinary course. It is the underlying intention behind a Mareva order to prevent the defendant from dissipating assets to defeat a creditor; it is not intended to prevent ordinary everyday legitimate business.

Money obtained from an illegal activity

C.B.S.* v. *Lambert

In *C.B.S. United Kingdom* v. *Lambert*[57] there was evidence that the defendant had used money obtained from a copyright infringement to purchase removable and disposable chattels. The court granted a Mareva injunction in respect of such chattels and also ordered the defendant to disclose the value, nature and whereabouts of these assets as well as its bank and other accounts. Pending trial, motor vehicles of the defendant were required to be delivered up to a garage chosen by the plaintiff's solicitor where they were stored.

---

[56] [1981] Q.B. 65. at p. 73.
[57] [1983] Ch. 37.

10 FURTHER DEVELOPMENTS

Since these orders became part of the established law, there have been developments to meet particular circumstances. In a recent case a plaintiff's solicitor and party attended on premises, and at the invitation of the occupier commenced to execute an Anton Piller order. During the course of the operation, the solicitor wished to relieve himself, and asked for the lavatory. The defendant said there was no order to invite the solicitor into that part of the premises and declined to allow the solicitor to visit it. The solicitor left the premises and on his return the occupier refused admission on the basis that he had carried out the order of the court by inviting the solicitor in and there was no requirement to do so again. It is considered that in this case the occupier was in contempt of court but to show this it required the plaintiff to return to the court, thus frustrating the object of the Anton Piller order. Accordingly there may be inserted, in a draft order: "That the defendant shall permit the plaintiff's solicitor and those named in the order the use of such washing and toilet facilities as they find necessary." It is submitted that such provision is not necessary but it removes an obstruction which otherwise might be erected.

Anton Piller orders leading to Mareva application It is common for a Mareva application to follow an Anton Piller order, the evidence obtained as a result of its execution showing that the defendant, as in the example, has been making or having made counterfeits of the plaintiff's parts and from the evidence seized the total claim in damages is likely to be a significant sum. It may also be the case that one can adduce from the evidence that the defendant is likely to dissipate his assets.

Combined order

It has now become commonplace for both orders to be the subject of one application, an example being as follows:

IN THE HIGH COURT OF JUSTICE

CHANCERY DIVISION

Example of combined order MR JUSTICE NICKLEBY (sitting in camera)

IN THE MATTER of an Intended Action

BETWEEN

CONWAY LIMITED (Intended Plaintiffs)
and
JUPITOR LIMITED (Intended Defendants)

UPON MOTION this day made unto this Court by Counsel for the Intended Plaintiffs (hereinafter called the Plaintiffs)

AND UPON READING a draft Writ of Summons and the Affidavits referred to in the Schedule hereto all file this day and the exhibits therein respectively referred to

AND the Plaintiffs by [his/her/its or their] Counsel undertaking

(1)   forthwith on or before   to issue a Writ of Summons claiming relief similar to or connected with that hereafter granted

(2)   to make and file an Affidavit [verifying what was alleged by Counsel] [in the terms of the draft Affidavit of

Plaintiff's undertakings

(3)   to serve upon the Intended Defendants(s) (hereinafter called the Defendant(s)) by a Solicitor of the Supreme Court of Judicature a copy of the said Affidavit and the copiable Exhibits thereto and Notice of Motion for

(4)   to obey any Order his Court may make as to damages if it shall consider that the Defendant(s) shall have sustained any damages by reason of this Order which the Plaintiff(s) ought to pay

[(5)   to obey any Order this Court may make as to damages if it shall consider that any innocent parties other than the Defendant(s) shall have sustained any damages by reason of this Order which the Plaintiff(s) ought to pay]

(6)   to pay the reasonable costs incurred by any person other than the Defendants to whom notice of this Order may be given in ascertaining whether any assets to which this Order applies are within their power possession custody or control and in complying with this Order and to indemnify any such person against all liabilities which may flow from such compliance

(7)   to obey any Order this Court may make as to damages if it shall consider that the Defendant(s) shall have sustained any damages by reason of this Order which the Plaintiff(s) ought to pay

AND the Solicitors for the Plaintiff(s) by Counsel for the Plaintiff(s) being their Counsel for this purpose undertaking

Solicitors' undertakings

(1)   to offer to explain to the person or persons served with this Order its meaning and effect fairly in every day language and to advise the person on whom the same is served of his right to obtain legal advice before complying with this Order provided that such advice is obtained forthwith.

(2)   to retain in their safe custody until further order all articles and documents taken or delivered to them pursuant to this Order

(3)   to answer forthwith any query made to the Defendant(s) as to whether any particular [document/article] is within the scope of this Order

(4)   to make a list of all articles and documents obtained as a

result of this Order prior to removal of any such articles or documents into their safe custody and to provide to the Defendant or the person served with this Order a copy thereof prior to such removal

(5)   to return the originals of all documents obtained as a result of this Order within two working days of removal of the same

(6)   where ownership of any article obtained as a result of this Order is disputed to deliver up any such article to the custody of solicitors acting on behalf of the Defendant within two working days of receipt of an undertaking in writing from the Defendant's solicitors to retain the same in safe custody and production if required to the Court

IT IS ORDERED

Anton Piller order   (1)   that the Defendant(s) [and each of them] be restrained until after   or until further Order in the meantime from doing (as regards the   Defendant(s) whether by   directors or   servants or agents or any of them or otherwise howsoever and as regards the Defendant(s) whether by   or by servants or agents or any of them or otherwise howsoever) are following acts or any of them that is to say
(a)   specify the particular acts[1]
(b)   directly or indirectly informing or notifying any persons company or firm of the existence of these proceedings or of the provisions of this Order of the Plaintiffs interest in these proceedings or otherwise warning any person company or firm that proceedings may be brought against [him/her/it/them] by the Plaintiffs otherwise than for the purpose of seeking legal advice from [its/his/her/their] lawyers

(2)   that the Defendant(s) do disclose forthwith to the person
Disclosure   serving this Order upon [him/her/it/them]
   (a)   the whereabouts of all
      which
      are in [his/her/its/their] possession custody power or control
   (b)   to the best of the Defendant's knowledge and belief
      (A)   the names and addresses of all persons who have supplied or offered to supply [him/her/its/them] with
      (B)   the names and addresses of all persons to whom [he/she/it/them] has/have supplied or offered to supply any
      (C)   full details of the dates and quantities each offer to supply and supply referred to in (A) and (B) hereof

(3)   that the Defendant(s) do deliver forthwith to the Plaintiff's

---

[1] See Chap. 6, p. 58 "Injunction against the defendant" for examples of details.

Production of documents and materials

Solicitor all . . .[2] which are in [his/her/its/their] possession custody or power and if any such item exists in computer readable form only the Defendant(s) shall cause it forthwith to be printed out and deliver the printout to the Plaintiff's Solicitors (or failing a printer) to be displayed in a readable form

Search and seizure

(4)   that the Defendant(s) and each of them whether by [himself/herself/itself/themselves] or by any person appearing to be in control of the premises hereafter mentioned to permit the person serving this Order upon them and such other persons duly authorised by the Plaintiffs (such persons not to exceed [four] in number altogether) to enter forthwith at any time between o'clock in the morning and   o'clock in the evening the premises known as   [and any other premises or vehicles to the extent that any of the said vehicles or premises are in the power possession occupation or control of the Defendant(s)] for the purpose of looking for inspecting photographing and taking into the custody of the Plaintiffs' Solicitors all items and materials referred to in paragraph above or which appear to the Plaintiffs' Solicitors to be such items or materials

Service of affidavit

(5)   that within seven days after service of this Order the Defendant(s) do make and serve on the Plaintiffs' Solicitors an Affidavit or affidavits setting out all of the information to be disclosed pursuant to this Order and exhibiting thereto all relevant documents

(6)   that the Defendant(s) [and each of them] be restrained until after   or until further Order in the meantime from doing (as regards the   Defendant(s) whether by   directors or by   servants or agents or any of them or otherwise howsoever and as regards the Defendant(s) whether   by   or by   servants or agents or any of them or otherwise howsoever) the following acts or any of them that is to say removing from the   jurisdiction of this Court or otherwise disposing of or dealing with his/her/its or their [respective or joint] assets within the jurisdiction of this Court including and in particular

Property

(i)   the freehold property known as   or (if the same has been sold) the net proceeds of sale thereof after discharge of any subsisting mortgage of charge
(ii) the property and assets of the business known as carried on by the Defendant(s) from premises at   or (if and in so far as the same have been sold) the proceeds of sale thereof

Money

(iii) any monies in [any] account(s) [numbered   ] at   and without prejudice to the foregoing pledging charging or otherwise parting with title to or possession of SUCH ASSETS

[2] See Chap. 7, p. 72.

(A) SAVE and insofar as the said assets of [each of] the
Defendant(s) exceeds L

(B) SAVE that the Defendant(s) [and each of them] is/are to be
at liberty to expend a sum not exceeding L [each] per
week/month for ordinary living expenses

(C) AND a sum of £   for ordinary and proper business
expenses

Informing plaintiff's solicitor AND not otherwise in each case upon informing the Plaintiff's
Solicitors of the source or accounts from which such sums are to
be drawn and

Payment for legal advice

(D) THAT the Defendant(s) [and each of them] may expend [a
sum not exceeding £   [each]] [such reasonable sum]
on legal advice and representation as may be requisite

Rights of bank in set-off

(E) PROVIDED nothing in this injunction shall prevent any
bank from exercising any rights of set off it may have in
respect of facilities afforded by any such bank to the
Defendant(s) or any of them prior to the date of this Order

Disclosure by the defendant

(7) that the Defendant(s) [and each of them] do forthwith
disclose the full value of his/her/its/their [respective and joint]
assets within the jurisdiction of this Court identifying with full
particularity the nature of all such assets and their whereabouts
and whether the same be held in his/her/its their own names or by
nominees or otherwise on his/her/its/their behalf and the sums
Defendant's affidavit standing in such accounts such disclosures to be verified by
affidavit(s) to be made by the Defendant(s) [and in the case of
Defendants by its/their proper officer] and served on the
Plaintiffs' Solicitors within   days of service of this Order
or notice thereof being given

Delivery up

(8) that the Defendant(s) [and each of them] do forthwith upon
the service of this Order deliver up or cause to be delivered up
into the custody of the Plaintiffs' Solicitors the   specified
in the Schedule hereto
AND the Plaintiff(s)   is/are at liberty to serve Short Notice
of Motion for   AND the Plaintiff(s) is/are at liberty to move
to discharge or vary this Order upon giving to the Plaintiff
days Notice of intention so to do.

Service of the combined order

The principle for carrying out an Anton Piller and Mareva order
combined are exactly the same as if carried out under separate
orders. The "search and seizure" part of the order might well
reveal details of the defendant's bank accounts and other assets.
Distinction between different elements of order These should be noted, and while (unless the Mareva part of the
order so permits) it is not permitted to seize assets, bank
statements, cheque books and so forth, photocopies of some of
these may be taken in order to identify assets, but a clear
distinction must be maintained between what is permitted under
the Anton Piller order and what should be done under the
Mareva. A failure to preserve the distinction could cause both
orders to be discharged.

Use of information obtained by a Mareva injunction

As with Anton Piller orders, the question arises as to how far one can make use of information obtained arising out of a Mareva order. The general principle is that the information should only be for the purpose of the order. If a plaintiff wishes to use the information for some other purpose, he should generally apply to the court for leave to do so to the extent of obtaining Mareva-type orders in other jurisdictions.

Ashtiani v. *Kashi*

In *Ashtiani* v. *Kashi*[3] the defendants, after receiving a Mareva order, disclosed that they had one substantial asset in the jurisdiction, namely a leasehold property, but the affidavit also disclosed substantial assets in overseas countries. The effect of the disclosure in the affidavits enabled the plaintiff to bring Mareva-type proceedings in those overseas countries in respect of the disclosed assets. The defendants applied to the judge at first instance to discharge the order, on an undertaking by the defendant not to dispose of the English asset, for otherwise the effect of the order would be to bring about attachment of the foreign assets. The judge granted the application stating that, as the defendant had given an undertaking concerning the English asset, it was no longer right to continue the Mareva injunction.

Disclosure of foreign assets

On appeal, the Court of Appeal held that a Mareva order should not usually require defendants to disclose foreign assets, but if, in the circumstances of a particular case, the defendant was required to disclose such assets (because for example it is suggested the English assets were insufficient) the information should not be used without leave of the court or consent of the defendant.

Freezing of overseas assets

The underlying principle for the decision was that it is oppressive for an English order to freeze foreign assets, as these are in effect, outside the jurisdiction of the English Court and one judicial authority should not, in general, trespass on the jurisdiction of another. An English court could not enforce the freezing of the overseas assets, and a Mareva order should not have the effect of giving greater security than the injunction over the defendant's English asset.

This authority needs to be read in the light of *Derby & Co.* v. *Weldon (No. 3)*[4] in which the English court granted a Mareva order in respect of assets worldwide subject to protective rights for third parties[5] As, however, the overseas assets in *Ashtiani* v. *Kashi*[6] were in Brussels Convention countries, the two authorities are not entirely in conformity with each other but this arises owing to the development of the Order to meet circumstances of the cases before the Court.

Circumstances in which foreign assets could be disclosed

If a Mareva injunction is granted which shows there are insufficient assets in the jurisdiction, there is no reason why the defendant should not be required to disclose foreign assets. If a foreign court is prepared to freeze these assets that is a matter for the foreign court. If foreign courts are willing to make orders

---

[3] [1987] Q.B. 888.
[4] [1989] 2 W.L.R. 412.
[5] See p. 97 for full details of this case.
[6] See above, n. 3.

similar to Marevas, it would be pointless insularity for an English court to put obstacles in the way of a plaintiff who wished the aid of the foreign courts to enforce an English judgment against a defendant's assets wherever they might be.[7]

Distinction between disclosure and restraint against disposal

The legal position is unclear as there appear to be conflicting decisions but the Court of Appeal in *Ashtiani* v. *Kashi*[8] do not appear to have addressed their minds to the distinction between ordering a defendant to disclose his foreign assets as opposed to restraining him from disposing of them. Plaintiffs are advised when applying for a Mareva order, to obtain such an order which will bring about disclosure of assets in England and, if not sufficient, also abroad. Following disclosure, if assets are disclosed in a Brussels Convention Court, a freezing order should be sought from the English court, which can be enforced by the Court of the Convention Courts. If not a Convention court, then the plaintiff must pursue what remedy he can with the information disclosed, *i.e.* if the foreign jurisdiction will grant a Mareva-type order but subject to the proviso set out on p. 96.

Right of arrest

Order *ne exeat regno*

It is sometimes the case that a defendant is likely to remove not only his assets from the jurisdiction, but also himself in order to defeat the claims of a plaintiff. To prevent this occurring there has been brought into use the right of arrest known as a writ *ne exeat regno*, which is brought into operation after the issue of a writ but before a judgment. This is a very old form of order which permitted the arrest of anyone thought to be about to leave the jurisdiction when a plaintiff has a good case of action against him which is quantifiable.

Statutory provision

The common law was embodied in section 6 of the Debtors Act 1869 and provision made for the application for an order under the rules of court. The rules of the Supreme Court which provided the procedure for making an application under the Debtors Act were repealed and not replaced, as it was considered that the procedure had fallen into disuse. But section 6 of the Debtors Act 1869 is still in force and may be used to aid an arrest to prevent a defendant leaving the jurisdiction.

Section 6 provides, *inter alia*:

Debtors Act 1869, s.6

Defendant about to quit the country

"Where the plaintiff in any action in any of Her Majesty's superior courts of law at Westminster in which, if brought before the commencement of this Act, the defendant would have been liable to arrest, proves at any time before final judgment by evidence on oath, to the satisfaction of a judge of one of those courts, that the plaintiff has good cause of action against the defendant to the amount of £50 or upwards, and that there is probable cause for believing that the defendant is about to quit England unless he be apprehended, and that the absence of the defendant from England will materially prejudice the plaintiff in the prosecution of his action, such judge may in the prescribed

---

[7] Hoffman J. in *Bayer AG* v. *Winter (No. 3)* [1986] E.C.C. 465 at p. 467.
[8] See above, n. 3.

manner order such defendant to be arrested and imprisoned for a period not exceeding six months, unless and until he has sooner given the prescribed security, not exceeding the amount claimed in the action, that he will not go out of England without the leave of the Court . . . "

In *Felton* v. *Callis*[9] Megarry J. found that, while the provision is still on the statute book, the order is so drastic (in that it causes the arrest of a person, bringing him before the court, so he cannot leave the jurisdiction) that it will only be operable if certain conditions are satisfied:

Conditions to be met

Arrest under common law

(a) The action is one under which the defendant would have been liable to arrest under the common law.[10]

(b) A very strong cause of action is established to the extent that the defendant is liable to the plaintiff for at least £50. The standard of proof is higher than is customary in civil proceedings.[11]

Strong cause of action

Defendant absconding

(c) There is probable cause for believing that the defendant is likely to leave England unless he is arrested.

Plaintiff prejudiced

(d) His absence from England will materially prejudice the plaintiff in the prosecution of his action. Even if these conditions are met the matter is still within the Judge's discretion.

Before final judgment by evidence on oath

The proceedings must have commenced and, as in the case with a Mareva injunction, the evidence on oath is provided by affidavit.

Cause for believing that the defendant is about to quit England   It is considered that it will be necessary to show that **Proof required**   the defendant is likely to leave the jurisdiction with a similar degree of proof to that which relates to the likelihood of him disposing of his assets.

Materially prejudice the plaintiff   The degree of proof is the same as with that relating to the grant of a Mareva injunction. As it is most unusual for civil proceedings to allow for the arrest of a **High standard of** person (save in contempt proceedings) the standard of proof **proof** required is high as to all the elements, but nevertheless, even if all conditions are fulfilled, the decision whether or not a writ *ne exeat regno* shall be issued is at the discretion of the court,[12] *Felton* v. *Callis*[13] is worthy of study as in it Megarry J. examines all the authorities relating to this aspect of the law.

In recent times the writ has been issued to secure the **Attendance for** attendance of the defendant for cross-examination on his **cross-examination** affidavit on the hearing of a motion before the court;[14] but in this case, the judge declined to extend the writ beyond the date specified upon the defendant agreeing to deposit his passport. The writ was issued to restrain the defendant from leaving the

[9] [1969] 1 Q.B. 200.
[10] *i.e.* prior to the coming into force of s. 6 of the Debtors Act.
[11] *In re Underwood* (1903) 51 W.R. 335.
[12] *Hasluck* v. *Lehman* [1890] 6 T.L.R. 435.
[13] See above, n. 10.
[14] *Chalvey* v. *Baldwin* (unrep.) February 10, 1983.

Securing full disclosure

jurisdiction in order to assist the plaintiff in obtaining judgment and not in executing it. It may be issued in an action to recover money and to secure a full disclosure from the defendant as to what has happened to the money he is alleged to have converted to his own benefit and also to aid in bringing about a full enquiry into his accounts.[15]

A writ *ne exeat regno* cannot be issued for the purpose of enforcing a Mareva order, for such a writ to be issued it must be shown that the absence of the defendant from the jurisdiction will materially prejudice the plaintiff in the prosecution of the action. A Mareva order is in aid of execution not part of the prosecution of the claim.[16]

Writ directed to tipstaff

The writ may be issued to support a Mareva order but should be directed to the tipstaff rather than the sheriff with the direction to bring the defendant concerned before the judge as soon as possible.[17]

The form of writ used in *Al Nahkel for Contracting and Trading Ltd.* v. *Lowe*[18] was as follows:—

To: George Baber Esq. Tipstaff attending Her Majesty's Supreme Court of Judicature, and his Deputy and all constables and other Peace Officers, Greeting: WHEREAS it is represented unto us, in our High Court of Justice, on the part of [   ], Plaintiff, against [   ], Defendant, amongst other things, that he the said Defendant is greatly indebted to the said Plaintiff and designs quickly to go into parts beyond the seas as by oath made in that behalf appears which tends to the great prejudice and damage of the said Plaintiff: Therefore, in order to prevent this injustice, we do hereby command you, that in the event that the said [defendant] should seek or attempt to depart from the jurisdiction of the said court without having paid to the Plaintiff or to their order the sum of [   ] you should arrest him the said [defendant], and unless he gives you security for the sum of [   ] then you are to bring him, the said [defendant], before a Judge of our said Court forthwith or as soon as reasonably practicable.

Witness QUINTIN MCGAREL BARON HAILSHAM OF ST MARYLEBONE (Lord High Chancellor of Great Britain) the [   ] day of 198–.

This writ was issued by [of   ], Solicitor for the Plaintiff, The Defendant's address is [   ].

Application for a writ ne exeat regno

Application for an order under section 6 of the Debtors Act 1869 is made to a judge in Chambers. It may be made *ex parte* at any time after the issue of the writ in the substantive action and before final judgment. It must be supported by affidavit evidence establishing the necessary conditions.[19] The order is operative until the defendant is brought before the court, and, in practice,

---

[15] *Lipkin Gorman (a firm)* v. *Cass, The Times*, May 29, 1985.
[16] *Allied Arab Bank* v. *Hajjar* [1988] Q.B. 787; [1988] 2 W.L.R. 942.
[17] *Al Nahkel for Contracting and Trading Ltd.* v. *Lowe* [1986] Q.B. 235.
[18] *Ibid.*
[19] See above.

once he lodges his passport, the defendant can usually go free, it being in the judge's discretion.

Development of the writ *ne exeat regno*

Though the court in *Felton* v. *Callis*[20] seemed to limit the scope of the writ, in recent times it has in practice been extended. In certain cases, the conditions for the issue of a writ *ne exeat regno* may not, or cannot, be fulfilled. The court, within its inherent jurisdiction has power to grant an *ex parte* injunction to restrain a defendant from leaving the jurisdiction. Such an order will also **Delivery of** contain a requirement that the defendant delivers his passport to **passport** the person serving the order on him. The order may be necessary to protect the plaintiff's rights pending the hearing of the action and to obtain information ordered to be disclosed under an Anton Piller order or Mareva injunction.

The courts have been anxious to ensure that plaintiffs do not use the writ *ne exeat regno* as an engine of oppression just as with Anton Piller and Mareva orders. In this respect *Allied Arab Bank* v. *Hajjar*[21] is worthy of study. In this case the judge seems to have taken the view that the plaintiffs were behaving improperly (though he does not find this as a fact) and this caused an order for damages to be made against them. As the judge found that the defendant in the case should never have gone to prison at all, in some ways the findings of the court seem moderate.

In *Bayer* v. *Winter*[22] the plaintiff applied for both Anton Piller and Mareva orders in a counterfeiting case. The plaintiff further sought an order to restrain the defendant from leaving England. The conditions for issuing a writ *ne exeat regno* could **Bayer A.G.** v. not be fulfilled but the court held that it had power, sitting *in* **Winter** *camera*, to grant an *ex parte* injunction to restrain the defendant from leaving England and to deliver his passport to the person seeking the order as it appeared just and convenient to do so. The order was also granted as it was held necessary to protect the plaintiff's right pending hearing of the substantive action, and also to obtain an information order to be disclosed in Anton Piller and Mareva forms. The injunction, and thus the impounding of the passport, ran only so long as it was necessary to give effect to such orders.

In *Bayer A.G.* v. *Winter (No. 2)*[23] the plaintiffs applied to have the order restraining the defendant leaving the jurisdiction extended and also sought an order for cross examination of the first defendant. This was refused by Scott J. on the grounds that the proper function of the court in civil litigation is to decide issues between the parties and not to preside over interrogatories. It would be an improper use of the court's power to order cross examination in advance of the service of Statement of Claim, or of any opportunity to deal with the plaintiff's evidence which has been put before the court of an *ex parte* application.

---

[20] See above, n. 10.
[21] See above, n. 16.
[22] [1986] 1 W.L.R. 497.
[23] [1986] 1 W.L.R. 540.

Order to restrain a party leaving the jurisdiction

The court has wide power under section 37 of the Supreme Court Act 1981 to ensure that its orders are complied with. In the *Oriental Credit*[24] case a director and shareholder of a company about to go into liquidation left the jurisdiction shortly before that event occurred. Attempts by the Liquidator to communicate with him failed. An order was made for the private examination of this person and thereafter the Liquidator obtained an *ex parte* order restraining him from leaving the jurisdiction until completion of the examination. On arrival in England the director was served with the order and applied to have it set aside on the grounds that there was no jurisdiction to make the order.

Harman J. discharged the application on the basis that whilst the court had wide powers under section 37 to grant the order, in the circumstances of this case where there was risk that the applicant's undertaking to attend for examination was inadequate, the order was, however, varied to the extent that the undertaking of the applicant to return for private examination on condition that the undertaking was supported by a Bond or similar obligation in the sum of £250,000, otherwise the applicant was liable to forfeiture on failure to comply with the undertaking. The report does not show how the order restraining the applicant from leaving the country would be enforced in the absence of the Bond, there is no suggestion that the applicant would be committed to jail until the Bond was lodged.

Disputes as to ownership

SCF Finance v. Masri

In *SCF Finance Co.* v. *Masri*[25] a dispute arose following the grant of a Mareva injunction as to whether assets belonged to the defendant or another. The court laid down guidelines as follows:

Guidelines

(a) if the assets appear to belong to a third party they should not be included in the injunction without evidence that they actually belong to the defendants. Thus if a third party is legal owner but it can be shown that he holds them on trust for the defendant, then they can be included;

(b) if a defendant asserts a third party owns the assets, this declaration, even if made on affidavit, need not be accepted without further inquiry;

(c) if a third party intervenes to seek a variation of the order on the grounds that certain assets are his as opposed to the defendants, then this need not be accepted without further inquiry;

(d) the court may direct issues as to ownership to be tried at any time before or after the substantive action which gives rise to the Mareva injunction;

(e) the court is obliged to take into account at any time the

---

[24] *In re Oriental Credit Ltd.* [1988] 2 W.L.R. 172.
[25] [1985] 1 W.L.R. 876.

various facts and do what appears to be just as between all the parties concerned.[26]

Rights of third parties

Payment of costs

Third parties cannot be present at the *ex parte* hearing in which a Mareva order is sought. The court takes account so far as it can of such persons' rights. A plaintiff has been required to undertake to pay income lost and administration costs incurred by Port Authorities as a result of the injunction.[27]

Interference with business of third party

If the grant of a Mareva order is likely to interfere substantially with the business of an innocent third party then the application will be refused. A Mareva injunction was refused in respect of a cargo belonging to the defendant which was loaded on a vessel of a third party. The injunction, if granted, would have prevented the vessel trading at least until the cargo was discharged. Even the offer of an indemnity by the plaintiff was not sufficient, because as the vessel would not have been able to trade for a period, its timetable for visiting ports would have been disrupted, and this would be an unwarrantable interference with a third party's business.[28]

Right to variation

An innocent third party has also the right to seek variation of a Mareva order against a defendant if the order affects him adversely.[29] Thus an application to set off a sum of money standing in credit at one of the defendant's accounts at a branch of the intervener has been permitted. In such a case, the plaintiff must pay all reasonable expenses and costs of the intervener, *i.e.* the person seeking the variation of the order under Order 29, rules 1–3 on an indemnity basis, save that the intervener must establish that the amounts claimed are both reasonably incurred and reasonable in amount.

Costs reasonably incurred

Right of set-off

A bank which holds an account of a defendant against which there is a Mareva order is entitled to variations of the injunction so as to enable it to exercise its right of set-off which would normally exist in a bank's dealings with its customers. Thus, if there is an overdraft secured, the bank is entitled to realise a security so as to satisfy the overdraft. This right extends to interest which will arise in future as well as that which has already accrued.[30] The principle is that the bank should be allowed to exercise any right, as against the defendant's account, which existed immediately before the bank received notice of the Mareva injunction. As a plaintiff cannot be expected to know the detailed personal circumstances of a defendant, once a Mareva order is served it is for the defendant to apply to the court to vary it and he must show what circumstances there are so as to be in a position to pay his way.

Responsibility of defendant to apply

[26] [1985] 1 W.L.R. 876 *per* Lloyd L.J. at p. 884.
[27] *Clipper Maritime Co. of Monrovia* v. *Mineralimportexport* [1981] 1 W.L.R. 1262.
[28] *Galaxia Maritima S.A.* v. *Mineral Importexport; Eleftherios, The* [1982] 1 W.L.R. 539.
[29] *Oceanica Castelana Armadora S.A.* v. *Mineralimportexport (Barclays Bank International Intervening); Theotokos, The* [1983] 1 W.L.R. 1302.
[30] See above, n. 29.

APPENDIX: CASE HISTORIES

A. *v.* C. [1982] R.P.C. 509; [1981] 2 W.L.R. 629

Facts: The plaintiff applied for an injunction restraining the first five defendants from removing or disposing of their assets, including moneys in the name of W.L. at the sixth defendant's bank, save in so far as the sum exceeded £1.5 million; and the first six defendants from disposing in any way of the sum of £383,872.44, or any lesser sum standing to the credit of the first five defendants or W.L. at the sixth defendant's bank.

The defendants resisted an order to disclose to the plaintiff details of the sums at present standing in the names of any of the first five defendants or W.L. at the sixth defendant's bank and an order disclosing all facts known regarding the whereabouts of the £383,872.44.

Held: The order against the sixth defendant (an innocent bank) was limited to discovery of documents. As against the other defendants, the order for disclosure stood and the court had the power, if necessary, to order interrogatories as well as discovery.

Allen *v.* Jambo Holdings [1980] 1 W.L.R. 1252

Facts: On January 27, 1979, at an aerodrome near Watford, the plaintiff's husband was struck by an aircraft propeller and killed. The aircraft belonged to a Nigerian company, Jambo Ltd. After an inquest held on March 1, 1979, the solicitor for the widow (who had a cause of action against the pilot and aircraft owner arising out of the death of her husband) was told by the pilot that he intended to fly the aircraft to Nigeria almost immediately.

The next day, counsel was instructed and he telephoned Drake J. and explained the circumstances to him. The judge granted a Mareva injunction to restrain the pilot and the owner from removing the aircraft from the jurisdiction on the basis that the Nigerian owners had no other assets in the jurisdiction, and if the plaintiff was successful in her proposed action arising out of the death of her husband, there were no other assets within the jurisdiction to meet a judgment debt and it would be very difficult to enforce the judgment in Nigeria. After some months, the injunction being continued by consent, the defendants applied to have the injunction discharged which was granted at first instance.

Held: On appeal there was no difference in seeking to protect assets for a commerical action or for an action in tort. The fact that the plaintiff was legally aided and therefore probably unable to discharge the undertaking to pay costs and damages if the Mareva should not have been obtained, should not debar a plaintiff from obtaining an injunction because they were poor. The defendants had not offered security as a condition for release of the aircraft, which tended to indicate that they could not obtain such security.

Allied Arab Bank Ltd. *v.* Hajjar [1988] 1 Q.B. 787

Facts: The plaintiffs lent vast sums to Murray Clayton Ltd., which loan was guaranteed by the first defendant, a Jordanian, normally resident outside the U.K., and certain of his associates. Murray Clayton went into liquidation and in December 1986 the Arab Bank Ltd. (unconnected with the plaintiffs) obtained a summary judgment against the first defendant and others. The plaintiffs had a claim against the first defendant on his guarantee, but they also alleged that the first defendant and his associates dishonestly procured a number of companies to dissipate the funds borrowed, so as to render the amount due unrecoverable. The plaintiffs admitted that they could obtain a summary judgment against the defendant on the guarantee, but deliberately refrained from so doing in order to take advantage of interlocutory procedures which they did not believe would be available against them as a judgment debtor.

The first defendant came to England for a short visit and the plaintiffs obtained a writ *ne exeat regno*, served it on him on January 13, 1987 at 9.00 p.m. The writ was marked with a request for the sum of £36 million or the defendant lodge such sum by way of bail or security to avoid arrest. Being unable to pay the required sum or lodge security, he was lodged in Kingston jail and the next day was taken before Hirst J. (who had issued the writ) and certain undertakings were exacted from him as the price of release from prison.

The undertakings in brief were to comply with the discovery order which the judge had made relating to the first defendant's own assets, to assets of the other defendants and inter-company dealings. He also undertook not to leave the jurisdiction without the consent of the court or plaintiff's solicitor; forthwith to deliver up his passport; to swear an affidavit that he had no other passport; not to apply for any other travel documents during the currency of the undertaking relating to discovery; to accept service of the proceedings and to lodge a bond for $250,000.

Thereafter a Mareva order was issued restraining the first defendant from dealing with or disposing of his assets until two weeks after the trial of the action. The court also ordered discovery of all the defendant's assets within the jurisdiction. There were particular orders on the first defendant relating to disclosure and whereabouts of his and the other defendant's assets within the jurisdiction.

On January 28, 1987 the first defendant applied for the

following: for discharge of the writ on the grounds that it should never have been made; for an enquiry as to damages suffered by him by reason of the issue of the writ; to be released from his undertakings; for the return of his passport; and for an order that the order relating to discovery be set aside or varied.

The plaintiff applied for an order to the effect that assets outside the jurisdiction should be disclosed as well as those within, for disclosure of a transcript of the first defendant's examination as a judgment debtor between the Arab Bank Ltd. (as plaintiff) and the first defendant and others. The plaintiff also applied for an order that the first defendant attend for cross examination on certain of his affidavits (made pursuant to the action) and to disclose full details of cheques in a list prepared by the plaintiffs.

Held: Leggat J. considered the four conditions required to be met. (See *Felton* v. *Callis* [1969]) 1 QB 200.

Firstly, was the defendant liable to arrest under the old law? Under the old law a debtor was only liable for arrest on failure to pay a defined amount. As the claim in this case was not for debt or in so far as it was, it was not for the purpose of prosecuting that part of the law that the writ was sought, the defendant was not liable to arrest under the old law.

Conditions 2 and 3 were satisfied but with regard to condition 4. As the case of action on the guarantee was not one whereby the prosecution of which required the presence of the first defendant in England, neither would his absence materially prejudice the plaintiffs.

As the necessary conditions had not been met, the writ should never have been granted in the first place. The defendant's bond and passport were returned to him and he was released from undertakings not to leave the jurisdiction, those relating to travel documents and execution of an affidavit relating to a second passport.

The court held that discovery should be limited to the first defendant's assets within the jurisdiction. The application for cross examination, the order for discovery of the transcript of the first defendant's examination in the action between the Arab Bank Ltd. and the first defendant and others, and the application for discovery of the cheques, which was for the purpose of tracing monies were refused, as there was at the time no claim for a tracing order.

The Judge ordered an enquiry as to damages by reason of the wrongful issue of the writ *ne exeat regno*.

Al Nahkel for Contracting and Trading *v.* Lowe [1986] Q.B. 235; [1986] 2 W.L.R. 317

Facts: The defendant was employed by the plaintiffs in Saudi Arabia as a sales manager and was suspected of corruption. Knowing of these suspicions he flew from Jeddah to Mecca and collected large sums of money belonging to his employers and then flew to Gatwick Airport, London, arriving on December 5, 1985 in possession of the money. He was met by the police and representatives of his employer who had been alerted to his pending arrival. He handed over three cheques payable to his employers but said that the remainder of the cash in Saudi Arabia and U.S. currency was his savings. As the alleged theft was outside the jurisdiction, he was not detained but told the police he would be flying to Manila on December 6.

That evening an emergency application was made to the judge for a Mareva order forbidding the defendant from dissipating up to £14,000, this being the approximate value of the money thought to have been stolen by him from his employers. Information was also put before the court that the defendants was likely to leave the jurisdiction the next day and that the Mareva order, if granted, would be likely to be frustrated as the defendant would most probably take the allegedly stolen money with him unless a writ *ne exeat regno* was granted.

Held: The judge, Tudor Price J., received the information orally on counsel's undertaking to have affidavits sworn as soon as possible and ordered the issue of writ *ne exeat regno* and granted the Mareva order.

Procedure: Solicitors for the plaintiff informed the police of the existence of the writ. The defendant was detained at Gatwick on December 6 before the Mareva order and writ was served; the tipstaff travelled to Gatwick armed with the writ and brought the defendant before the judge in the Royal Courts of Justice.

The judge considered it important that the tipstaff should carry out the arrest as opposed to the Sheriff for the latter would then have been obliged to commit the defendant to prison, which was considered undesirable, whilst the writ instructed the tipstaff to deliver the defendant to the judge.

Anton Piller K.G. *v.* Manufacturing Processes [1976] Ch. 55; [1976] 2 W.L.R. 162

Facts: The defendants, an English company and their two directors, were the agents of the plaintiffs, a German manufacturer of computer material. The plaintiff, in an *ex parte* motion, claimed that the defendants were giving confidential information to their competitors, and sought an order to restrain the defendants from infringing copyright, publicising confidential information, manufacturing or helping others to manufacture copies of the plaintiffs' equipment and disposing of material relating to copyright, design, manufacture and supply of the plaintiffs' equipment, the plaintiffs giving undertakings to the court to issue a writ of summons against the intended defendants and in respect of other matters.

The plaintiffs also asked for further relief which at first instance was refused. This further relief being:
That the defendants do permit—persons—duly authorised by the plaintiffs and members . . . . of the plaintiffs' solicitors to enter forthwith the premises known as . . . . for the purpose of

    (a) inspecting all documents relating . . . . to the
        plaintiffs' equipment;
    (b) remaining in the plaintiffs' solicitors' custody:
         (i) all original documents relating to . . . . the
           plaintiffs' equipment which . . . . had been
           supplied by the plaintiffs to the defendants.
        (ii) all documents or articles relating to . . . .
           the plaintiffs' equipment.

The plaintiffs appealed *ex parte* against refusal of the relief set out above.

Held: Allowing the appeal, that in most exceptional circumstances where the plaintiffs had a very strong prima facie case, actual or potential damage to them was very serious, and there was clear evidence that the defendants possessed vital material which they might destroy to defeat the ends of justice before an *inter partes* application could be made; in such a case the court had an inherent jurisdiction to order the defendants to permit the plaintiffs' representative to enter the defendants' premises to inspect and remove such material. In the very exceptional circumstances, the court was justified in making the order sought on the plaintiffs' *ex parte* application.

Bankers Trust Co. *v.* Shapira [1980] 1 W.L.R. 1274

Facts: The defendants presented two cheques for payment of $1 million on the Bankers Trust in New York City. The Bankers Trust credited Discount Bank (Overseas) Ltd. in London with over $700,000 to the credit of the first defendant. About six months later, National Commercial Bank in Saudi Arabia found the two cheques to be forgeries, and Bankers Trust repaid the National Commercial Bank the $1 million and brought an action against Shapira, another and the Discount Bank. The first two defendants could not be served. The action against Discount Bank was of a tracing nature. A Mareva injunction was also obtained to prevent Discount Bank disposing of any moneys due to the other defendants. Further, the plaintiff wished to have information relating to correspondence and dealings with regard to the $1 million.

Held: At first instance, the court refused to order that the bank should give the information as the principal defendants had not been served, *i.e.* there was no action against them. On appeal, the order was granted that the Bank disclose to the plaintiffs and permit copies of the following documents to be taken:

    (a) all correspondence passing between the Discount Bank
        and the co-defendants relating to any account;
    (b) all cheques drawn on such accounts; and
    (c) all debit vouchers, transfer applications, orders and
        internal memoranda relating to any account.

    The accounts were to be in the names of the defendants and from certain dates.

The Discount Bank incurred no personal liability, their involvement being through no fault of their own in the tortious acts of the other two defendants. They were, however, under a duty to assist Bankers Trust by giving them and the court full information and disclosing the identity of the wrongdoer. The fact that the first and second defendants had not been served did not deprive the court of its power to make the order.

Barclay-Johnson v. Yuill [1980] 1 W.L.R. 1259

Facts: The question arose as to whether a Mareva order should be granted against a person normally resident in, and a citizen of the United Kingdom.

The plaintiff claimed that she was due to be paid £2,000 in respect of a transaction concerning a flat which she transferred to the defendant (though there were further proceedings whereby the plaintiff was claiming in excess of £75,000). The defendant went abroad and the plaintiff learned that the flat had been sold, the plaintiff obtained an *ex parte* Mareva injunction in respect of the proceeds which were held in the defendant's bank account. The defendant applied to the court to have the order set aside on the grounds that the defendant was not a foreigner and thus the injunction should be discontinued.

Held: That the question of whether the defendant was a foreigner or resident citizen of the United Kingdom was just one element in considering whether or not a Mareva should be granted. If there was the likelihood of the dispersal of assets to defeat a judgment, the order should be issued irrespective of residence or nationality.

British Phonographic Industry v. Cohen [1984] F.S.R. 159

This was a copyright infringement case concerning recordings. At first instance, the Lord Ordinary (Lord Mayfield) refused an application for an order in Anton Piller form and the plaintiffs appealed.

The judge at first instance sought guidance from the Court of Session—Inner House as to whether an application for an order *ex parte* could be granted; and if so what circumstances justify the order.

The court found that under section 1(1) of the Administration of Justice (Scotland) Act 1972 and pursuant to Rule 95A(c) of the Rules of Court, the court could have jurisdiction to grant an application. The Lord President held that the tests which the Outer House judges in Scotland should apply are those deriving from the principles laid down in the *Anton Piller* case, and *Universal City Studios* v. *Mukhtar* and *Yousif* v. *Salama*, but subject to refusal if the respondents would be required to incriminate thereunder in accordance with *Rank Film* v. *Video Information Centre*.

Campbell v. Tameside Metropolitan Borough Council [1982] Q.B. 1065; [1982] 3 W.L.R. 74

Facts: A schoolteacher was attacked in school by an 11-year-old pupil. She suffered severe injuries and in consequence had to take early retirement. She wished to bring proceedings against the local authority for personal injuries contending that they were negligent in allowing a child of violent disposition to attend an ordinary school. To be sure of her grounds before commencing proceedings, the teacher applied for preliminary discovery under RSC Order 24, rule 7A(1) of certain reports on the child which she contended would show that the authorities had knowledge of the violent nature of the pupil. The Education Authority resisted disclosure on the grounds that such reports were highly confidential and against the public interest and, further, if such reports were disclosed, it would in future inhibit the candour of those marking them. The Registrar upheld the objection but was overruled by the judge, on appeal by the local authority to the Court of Appeal.

Held: The courts have never ordered disclosure of reports on children by local authorities because, as a class, they should be kept confidential and also justice could be done without compelling disclosure. In the present case, having looked at the reports, the court found they could be of considerable significance. The public interest in the reports being kept confidential had to be weighed against the public interest in justice being done to the citizen and in this case it was decided that discovery of the reports should be made available.

C.B.S. United Kingdom v. Lambert [1983] Ch. 37; [1982] 3 W.L.R. 746

Facts: Allegations were made that defendants had infringed copyrights by producing and selling counterfeit records and cassettes. As a result of proceedings against a distributor and an admission to the police by the first defendant, there was clear evidence which showed the first defendant to be a record pirate. The plaintiffs applied for a combined Anton Piller/Mareva order but were refused the latter element at first instance, which included an application for delivery up of motor cars.

On appeal, the court found that the following inferences of facts were justified by the affidavit evidence put forward concerning the first defendant, who:

(a) helped by his wife—the second defendant—was engaged in counterfeiting cassettes, and it was alleged that 35,000 tapes worth £105,000 had been sold;

(b) claimed to be unemployed and improperly drew social security money;

(c) was spending money on expensive cars which could easily be hidden or disposed of so as to defeat creditors;

(d) intended to do what he thought was necessary to ensure

that if his illegal activities were discovered, the owners of the copyright would be unable to enforce judgment.

Held: The Mareva injunction was brought into use to prevent such activity. The court should grant a Mareva injunction in all cases in which it appears just and correct to do so. See section 37(1) and (3) of the Supreme Court Act 1981. In considering when should the court exercise the power to order disclosure of assets and delivery up, certain guidelines were provided as follows:

(1) There must be clear evidence that the defendant is likely, unless restricted by order, to dispose of or otherwise deal with chattels to deprive the plaintiff of the fruits of his judgment. The court will be slow to order delivery up of property unless there is evidence that it was acquired by the defendant as a result of his wrongdoings.

(2) No order should be made for delivery up of defendant's clothes, bedding, furniture, tools of his trade, farm implements, livestock or any machines (including motor vehicles) or other goods such as materials or stock in trade which are probably used for his lawful business. Furnishings may consist of *objets d'art* of great value; if the evidence is clear that such were bought for the purpose of frustrating judgment creditors, they may then be included in the order.

(3) All orders should specify as clearly as possible what chattels or classes of chattel are to be delivered up. A plaintiff's inability to identify what he wants delivered up and why is an indication that no order should be made.

(4) The plaintiff has no right to enter upon premises to seize goods, but as with the Anton Piller order, is invited into them by the defendant; otherwise, the plaintiff may face contempt of court proceedings.

(5) Delivery up should only be made to the plaintiff's solicitor or a receiver appointed by the High Court and a receiver should be appointed by the court unless the court is satisfied that the plaintiff's solicitor can arrange suitable safe custody for what is delivered to him.

(6) The court should follow the guidelines of *Z* v. *A–Z and AA–LL* in so far as they are applicable to chattels in possession, custody or control of third parties.

(7) The court ordered that the defendants:
   (a) be restrained from removing or otherwise disposing of, or dealing with their respective or joint assets, or charging any of the same;
   (b) disclose their assets with full value within the jurisdiction, identifying them and their whereabouts, and in whose names they are held, also specifying the identity of all bank accounts or other accounts held in their names or by nominees, and the sums standing to their accounts;
   (c) disclose the models and registration numbers of all motor vehicles owned by them and their whereabouts and the name and address of any person having custody and control.

(8) The above was followed by an order as to making an affidavit concerning the disclosure and an order to deliver up three identified vehicles and all other vehicles to the custody of plaintiff's solicitor together with keys and registration and other documents.

Columbia Picture Industries *v.* Robinson [1987] Ch. 38; [1986] 3 W.L.R. 542

Facts: This case is the first reported case where an action has gone to full trial following an Anton Piller order. It concerned copyright owners' action against video pirates for infringement of their copyrights in video cassettes. The case is important as it sets out the faults of the plaintiffs through their legal representatives in obtaining and executing the Anton Piller order as well as in the manner of dealing with seized material.

The judge found that the following wrongful acts had taken place in obtaining the order:

1. Failure on the part of the plaintiffs' solicitor to give due consideration as to whether an Anton Piller order should be sought against the defendant.
2. The court being misled in obtaining the order in three specific respects.
   (a) The plaintiffs' solicitor deposing that the defendant knew what he was doing was unlawful and in flagrant disregard for the rights of others. No mention was made that plaintiffs' investigator had asked the defendant to purchase on his behalf pirate video cassettes or that in the investigator's view, the defendant may have been an innocent dupe. The reason for the failure to give this information was that Hamlins (solicitors for the plaintiff), had a common form affidavit;
   (b) it was alleged that the investigator was still investigating the defendants. This was false;
   (c) it was complained, with justification, that the solicitor's affidavit gave the impression contrary to the facts that an element of secrecy was associated with part of the business premises.
3. In breach of their duty to the court, the plaintiffs through their legal advisers failed to disclose to the court material facts within their knowledge. The following was not disclosed which the court felt should have been:
   (a) the plaintiffs' investigator had entered and inspected certain of the premises, with access to all of them, and there was co-operation between the investigator and defendant;
   (b) the investigator had freely removed from the business premises certain tapes and had also returned a number of them which indicated that the defendant also had a legitimate business;
   (c) the plaintiffs' investigator had an arrangement whereby the defendant was an active informant for the investigator;

       (d) two of the plaintiffs (there were 35 altogether) had brought copyright infringement action against the defendant;

       (e) the defendant purchased pirate video tapes for the plaintiffs' investigator;

       (f) the defendant had paid a substantial sum for a certain licence to reprint video cassettes (though not from any of the plaintiffs).

4. The court also found that the plaintiffs had failed to carry out the order properly, and in particular:

       (a) material was taken that was not covered by the order and in general the behaviour of the solicitor was oppressive, and an abuse of the position of power in which they had been placed by order of the court;

       (b) there had been a failure to provide adequate receipts for material taken. In this particular case, the solicitor was not found to be at fault but in future, *i.e* after the judgment, any solicitors, if they fail to do so. will be in breach of their undertaking to the court;

       (c) material not the subject of complaint was not returned for nearly three years. This was oppressive and in flagrant disregard of the defendant's rights;

       (d) there was a failure to keep in safe custody some of the seized material as it was lost in Hamlin's offices.

The court also found that it was the intention of the plaintiffs in applying for and obtaining the Anton Piller order to close down the business being conducted from certain of the defendant's premises; such an intention was an improper one and represented an abuse of the Anton Piller procedure and had led to an oppressive execution of the order.

The defendant claimed damages against the plaintiffs for breach of their undertaking when the Anton Piller order was granted and were awarded £10,000 (in lieu of an inquiry) and in addition costs of their application of 1983 to have the Anton Piller order discharged and of all other applications coming out of the Anton Piller order. The plaintiffs, who had proved infringement of their copyright, obtained injunction and an inquiry as to damages. The senior partner of Hamlin apologised to the court for his firm's breach of their undertaking.

Cook Industries Inc. *v.* Galliher [1979] Ch. 439; [1978] 3 W.L.R. 637

Facts: The plaintiff, a United States Corporation, issued a writ claiming a declaration that Galliher, first defendant, a United States citizen, but resident for part of each year in London, held a flat and its contents in Paris as trustee for the second defendant and that the transfer of assets by the second defendant to Galliher was made so as to defeat and delay his creditors and other claims. On the same date, the plaintiff obtained *ex parte* an injunction restraining the first defendant from disposing of or removing the contents of the flat, and ordering that the first defendant should disclose full particulars of the flat, to which he claimed to be beneficially entitled. It was ordered that he should admit a named

French advocate to inspect the contents of the flat. The advocate was also apparently a member of the Bar employed in the French firm of solicitors, Clifford Turner of Paris.

Held: It was found that the court had jurisdiction to entertain the action for determination of rights to possession of immeasurable property outside the jurisdiction where there was equity between the parties (as in this case); as the first defendant was in the jurisdiction, the court granted the Anton Piller order in order to obtain inspection of the Paris flat.

Crest Homes *v.* Marks [1987] A.C. 829; [1987] 3 W.L.R. 293

Facts: The plaintiffs had commenced a copyright action in 1984 against the defendants with an Anton Piller order, following which the defendants swore an affidavit of compliance. In 1985, the plaintiffs commenced a further copyright action with an Anton Piller order and in so doing found the defendants were in breach of their undertakings in the 1984 action and had failed to comply totally therewith. The plaintiffs sought leave to use the documents of the 1984 action for the general purposes of the 1985 action and also for taking proceedings for contempt of court in respect of the 1984 order. The defendants pleaded that the use of such documents by the plaintiffs would tend to incriminate them and in view of the *Rank Films* decision to which section 72 of the Supreme Court Act 1981 did not apply, the documents should not be used.

Held: Section 72 of the Supreme Court Act had the effect in this case of granting a discretion to the court as to whether the documents should be admitted or not and in its discretion allowed them to be produced in evidence.

Customs and Excise Commissioners *v.* Hamlin (A.E.) & Co. [1984] 1 W.L.R. 509

Facts: The defendants, acting as solicitors, obtained Anton Piller orders on behalf of clients. The orders were in usual form and required that the defendants disclose to Hamlin copies of films (made in breach of copyright) and allow films and any documents relating in any way to an action for infringement of copyright to be removed. Hamlin gave an express undertaking "that all records, tapes, equipment, documentation or other articles obtained as a result of this order would be retained in their safe custody or to their order until further order."

One of the Anton Piller orders was against a Mr. Rover and the other against a Mr. Hubbard. The orders were executed and documents and materials taken into the custody of Hamlin.

At the time, the activities of the two defendants were being investigated by the authorities in relation to unpaid V.A.T. The plaintiffs (Customs and Excise) took the view that they would be unable to investigate the defendants effectively unless they had sight of the documents in Hamlin's possession. One of the defendants gave leave for certain documents to be produced by Hamlin, the other declined. The plaintiff applied to the court for Hamlin to deliver up the material which they required, as Hamlin declined to do so on the grounds that if they did, it would be in breach of their undertaking given in obtaining the Anton Piller order.

Held: Notwithstanding the wide powers granted to the plaintiffs with regard to seizure of documents under the Finance Act 1972, Hamlin were restrained from parting with any documents by reason of their undertaking to the court to preserve until further order; the further order was that of the court. In the circumstances of this case, the court permitted the plaintiffs to inspect the material and take copies.

Distributori Automatici Italia S.p.A v. Holford General Trading Co. [1985] 1 W.L.R. 1066

Facts: The plaintiffs obtained default judgments against the defendants. The second defendant (manager of the first), on examination as to means, said that he personally had no assets and that he was unaware of the first defendant's situation as the information was in an office which he could not get into as, owing to failure to pay the rent, the landlord would not permit entry.

The second defendant agreed to inform the plaintiffs' solicitors when he gained access to the office so that they could collect any documents pursuant to an order in the default judgment proceedings. Without informing the solicitors, the second defendant gained access and removed two briefcases.

The plaintiffs obtained an Anton Piller order restraining the defendants from parting with, destroying, defacing or hiding any documents relating to their assets and requiring them to disclose the whereabouts of any such documents and to permit the plaintiffs' agent to enter the second defendant's home and other premises for the purpose of carrying out the Anton Piller order.

Held: Jurisdiction to grant Anton Piller orders was founded not on the narrow ground of an internal jurisdiction to make orders in the terms of RSC Order 29, rule 2 but in the broader principle that such an order was essential so that justice could be done to both parties. The second defendant would destroy the documents or use them to dispose of any assets, and therefore it was appropriate to make an Anton Piller order.

Dunlop Holdings and Dunlop v. Staravia [1982] Com.L.R. 3, C.A.

Facts: The plaintiffs manufactured and sold under licence from the appropriate authorities, the Civil Aviation Authority and the Ministry of Defence, parts for aircraft. They applied for an

Anton Piller order against the defendants on becoming aware that they were selling copies of the plaintiffs' parts. The defendants appealed against the grant of the order on the grounds that there was no evidence that they would be likely to destroy evidence and it could be supplied in the ordinary way by discovery.

Held: It was customary to infer the probability of disappearance or destruction of evidence where it is clearly established on the evidence before the court that it is likely that the defendant is engaged in a nefarious activity, which renders it likely that he is an untrustworthy person.

Emanuel *v.* Emanuel [1982] 1 W.L.R. 669

Facts: The wife, having divorced her husband, obtained financial provision whereby the husband was required to assign two properties to the wife and make periodical payments. The husband, despite prior undertakings, (he was committed at one time to jail for six weeks for contempt arising out of the failure to comply with his undertakings and the order of the court) sold one of the properties and transferred the other to his sister. The wife made an *ex parte* application for an order permitting her solicitor to enter the premises usually occupied by another woman, to inspect and look for documents relating to the husband's means, including the sale of the two properties. A similar order was given in respect of the premises occupied by the sister who was the second respondent.

Held: As the husband was clearly ready to flout the authority of the court as well as mislead it, the order was granted as there was grave danger that evidence would be removed or destroyed. The wife had a strong prima facie case that, as the relevant documents had not been produced in the past, they would be unlikely to be so in the future without the order.

EMI *v.* Pandit [1975] 1 W.L.R. 302

Facts: The plaintiffs owned copyrights in music recordings. They were initially granted, *inter partes*, an order *inter alia* restraining the defendants from infringing the plaintiffs' intellectual property rights, and ordering delivery up of infringing material, discovery of suppliers and customers of the infringing materials, together with an order for discovery of documents. An interlocutory order was made but the defendant, in addition to failing to comply satisfactorily with the order, swore an affidavit that appeared false.

The plaintiffs applied *ex parte*, submitting evidence tending to show the falsity of the defendant's affidavit—that he had forged a document and that the probability existed that evidence vital to the plaintiffs' case was at the defendant's premises. The plaintiffs applied under RSC Order 29, rules 2(1) and (2) that persons authorised by the plaintiffs should be at liberty to enter the defendant's premises and inspect and seize relevant material.

The plaintiffs feared that if they served notice on the defendants as required by Order 29, rule 2(5) the vital material sought would be destroyed or removed, and the plaintiffs effectively barred from obtaining relief in the action.

Held: As *ex parte* orders for discovery had been granted in earlier unreported cases (see p. 40) the court had jurisdiction and would grant the order substantially in the form of that sought owing to the facts of the case. The court also followed *Hennessey* v. *Bohman, Osborne & Co.* (p. 40).

EMI Records *v.* Kudhail [1983] Com.L.R. 280; [1985] F.S.R. 36

Facts: The plaintiffs established that numerous street traders were selling recordings in breach of the plaintiffs' copyright. They were sold under the label "Oak Records" which belonged to the defendants. The plaintiffs applied for a representative order against all those selling "Oak Records" cassettes. The street traders had no trading premises, sold from suitcases and often adopted an alias.

Held: It was found that an injunction could be granted against a represented class of persons, that is traders selling cassettes under "Oak Records." The Anton Piller order was granted against certain named persons and those selling goods under the "Oak Records" label.

EMI Records *v.* Spillane [1986] 1 W.L.R. 967

Facts: Solicitors Hamlin, acting for EMI, obtained and executed an Anton Piller order and took into their possession documents and other materials in the course of the search and seizure operation. The cases were eventually settled and Hamlin undertook on May 4, 1984 to return forthwith to the defendant all goods or items of a non-illicit nature belonging to them and/or removed from the defendants' premises. Hamlin took the view that their undertaking did not extend to documents.

In 1985, the Customs and Excise Commission started to investigate the Spillane business on the grounds that they had not accounted properly for V.A.T. Customs asked Hamlin for the documents but they refused to part with them unless Spillane consented, which they did not. On December 10, Customs demanded under their statutory powers that Hamlin deliver the documents to them. Hamlin applied to the court for direction, giving Customs as the only respondent.

Held: It was found that, as from May 4, 1985, the documents ceased to have the character of documents seized under an Anton Piller order in view of the settlement and became merely documents held to the order of Spillane by Hamlin. As such, Hamlin could be required to deliver them to the Customs and

Excise Commission. If, however, the documents had still been held under the Anton Piller order, the court would have refused to release them.

> "In my judgment it would be quite wrong to authorise the use in criminal proceedings brought under fiscal laws and having no connection with the original course of action" Browne-Wilkinson V.-C. at p. 977.

Faith Panton Property Plan v. Hodgetts [1981] 1 W.L.R. 927

Facts: The plaintiff obtained judgment against the defendants for £9,679.23 but a stay of execution was granted pending determination of other proceedings. After a series of motions, costs were awarded against the defendants, which when taxed (4/5 months after the award) were likely to amount to about £12,000.

The first defendant informed the plaintiff's solicitor that he would be unable to pay the costs when taxed and that he intended to sell his business assets. The plaintiffs applied for an order restraining the defendants from assigning and dealing with certain assets relating to their business. At first instance this was refused, and the plaintiffs appealed.

Held: The first defendant had shown by his behaviour that he intended to divest himself of assets if he could, and there was a lack of frankness to the court in failing to disclose to whom he had sold some of his assets, and that accordingly the order restraining disposition of assets was granted.

Felton v. Callis [1969] 1 Q.B.D. 200

Facts: The plaintiffs and the defendant were in partnership as Chartered Accountants. The partnership was dissolved and the parties agreed that of moneys owing by the partnership to the Midland Bank the plaintiffs would jointly repay £900 (which they did and the balance (about £3000) would be repaid by the defendant, which he failed to do. The plaintiffs applied by writ to compel the defendant to pay his share and a day later, the bank claimed against the plaintiffs and the defendant for the sum thus due.

The plaintiffs then applied *ex parte* for a writ of *ne exeat regno* to restrain the defendant from leaving the jurisdiction until the court made a further order or until payment was made or security lodged.

Megarry J. reviewed the history of the writ and found it was referred to in Bearne's "A brief view of the writ *ne exeat regno*" (1812) and *Stories, Comments on Equity Jurisdiction* (3rd English Ed. 1920).

The writ dated from the thirteenth century but by the time of Elizabeth I it had begun to be used for civil purposes. It was a means of arresting a person to prevent him leaving the jurisdiction to avoid his obligations. The Debtors Act 1869 abolished such arrest but provided a closely confined alternative in section 6.

In its developed form, the writ as issued to the Sheriff commands him to cause the debtor to give security for the amount of the claim or the sum due and if this is refused the debtor is committed to prison.

The former RSC Order 69 laid down the procedure to be followed on an order to arrest under section 6 of the Debtors Act 1869. By 1969, Order 69 was repealed and not replaced and the writ of *ne exeat regno* is no longer noted.

Held: The judge found that the writ could still be issued providing the requirements of section 6 are satisfied. See p.127.

In the present case the court was unable to find any evidence to show that the defendant's absence from England would materially prejudice the plaintiffs in the prosecution of their action, though it could affect the plaintiffs in obtaining the fruit of this action. Further the sums due from the defendant were obligations at law not equity and the writ is an equitable remedy.

The court was satisfied on the evidence that the defendant having sold his house and furniture was intending to take up work in Thailand.

General Nutrition *v.* Pradip Pattni [1984] F.S.R. 403

Facts: In March 1984 the plaintiffs obtained an Anton Piller order against the defendants. Following the grant, it was executed. The plaintiffs' solicitors, having considered the seized evidence requested by Notice of Motion dated May 1984, and addressed to the defendants and their solicitors that they be permitted to make available to the police certain parts of the material which they had found when carrying out the search.

Held: The court distinguished *Customs and Excise Commissioners* v. *Hamlin (A.E.) & Co.* [1984] 1 W.L.R. 509, on its facts found that although there might be circumstances in which it would be proper for the court to permit the release to the police of documents seized under an Anton Piller order, the mere fact that such documents might show that a criminal offence had been committed did not, of itself, justify a departure from the general rule that documents seized under such an order should be used only for the purposes of the proceedings in which the order had been obtained, and so refused the order sought.

Hennessey *v.* Bohmann, Osborne & Co. [1877] W.N. 14

Facts: The defendants purchased old cases and bottles, previously used by the plaintiffs and filled them with their own inferior brandy, without removing the plaintiff's distinguishing labels. The plaintiffs sought an order for a person to be authorised to enter the defendants' premises to inspect the cases and bottles and to take samples. The motion, with affidavits in support, was made *ex parte* as the plaintiff feared that if the defendants had prior notice they would remove the evidence.

Held: Though the court would never make such an order *ex parte* save in an emergency, the circumstances of the case warranted the making of an immediate order to the defendants to permit inspection and to enable the terms of the order to be carried out.

Iraqi Ministry of Defence *v.* Arcepey Shipping Co. S.A. (Gillespie Bros. intervening) [1980] 2 W.L.R. 488

Facts: The plaintiffs owned cargo in the defendant's vessel, which sank. The plaintiffs sued for damages in respect of the lost cargo and obtained a Mareva order. The defendants had no assets within the jurisdiction but had the prospect of recovering the proceeds of a Lloyd's insurance policy.

Intervenors had lent money to the defendants to buy the lost vessel; the insurance policy in respect of the vessel had been assigned to them as security. If the intervenors were entitled first to the proceeds of the policy after they had been paid what was due, there would be little money left for the plaintiffs' claim. The defendants said they had no interest in the insurance moneys which should be paid to the intervenors, but this could not be done as there was a Mareva order in force which did not allow payment out of the money. The plaintiffs alleged that the loan by the intervenors was an illegal transaction and was void as a money-lending transaction with the intervenors being unregistered money lenders.

Held: The purpose of a Mareva injunction is not to improve the position of a claimant over another, but to prevent injustice being done by the defendants removing assets. The defendants should not be prevented from paying their debts (incurred before the action giving rise to the Mareva order) as and when they fall due. It was immaterial whether or not the loan was illegal, for the intervenor, in seeking variation of the Mareva injunction, was not seeking to enforce the loan.

Island Records, Ex p. [1978] Ch. 122; [1978] 3 W.L.R. 23

Facts: The plaintiffs were songwriters, artists and record companies to whom both classes of artist were exclusively contracted. The defendant was alleged to be making records of live performances of the artists (known as bootlegging) contrary to section 1 of the Dramatics and Musical Performances Protection Act 1958. At first instance, an Anton Piller order was refused on the grounds that although bootlegging was a criminal offence it was not a civil wrong, because there was no right in a live performance to infringe and the 1958 Act gave no right of action to performers or record companies against unauthorised performances.

Held: On appeal, the court held that an Anton Piller order may be granted where the plaintiff suffered damage as a result of the defendant committing a crime which is not a civil wrong.

I.T.C. Film Distributors *v.* Video Exchange, *The Times*, June 17, 1982, C.A.

Facts: The plaintiffs were concerned with the production and distribution of films, including film cassettes. An investigator made a trap purchase from the defendants, and also informed the police that he had reason to think that pornographic films were on the defendants' premises. An Anton Piller order was obtained largely based on the investigator's affidavit but only dealing with films in infringement of the plaintiff's copyright. At the time of the application, solicitors for the plaintiff anticipated that the police would be willing to co-operate with them in the execution of any order obtained, and that the police having obtained a search warrant for looking for obscene material, the Anton Piller order and search warrant should be carried out together.

In the application for the Anton Piller order, the only reference to the plan placed before the court was that after discussing the form of the order, counsel mentioned that the police were interested in the defendants in relation to "adult films" and that they "proposed a visitation at about the same time" as it was proposed to serve the order.

The Anton Piller order provided that it should be served by plaintiffs' solicitors accompanied by not more than three persons, and in addition another solicitor. The police decided that 11 officers were necessary for the search. The two activities were carried out simultaneously, the police knocking at the defendants' door and insisting on entry, the solicitors following. The Anton Piller order was properly explained. Application was made to discharge the order on the grounds that the judge was not informed of the simultaneous civil and police activities. The defendant was not given the opportunity of saying whether or not he would permit the solicitor and his helper into his premises. The question is as to whether, in these circumstances, the order should be discharged.

Held: Before the judge that it should be discharged but on appeal this was revised; however, the Court of Appeal considered that what had occurred was regrettable and it was undesirable that "solicitors executing an Anton Piller order should be seen to be the hangers-on of a squad of police officers executing a search warrant."

Searches, as in this case, could be carried out "more or less contemporaneously" but not contemporaneously as in this case. The court also found that it was undesirable that the defendant was not given an opportunity at "street-level" to say whether or not he would permit entry of the Anton Piller party.

Kynaston *v.* The East India Company [1819] Ch. 3 Swanston 248; (1821) 3 B.L.I. (O.S.) 153

Facts: The plaintiff claimed tithe payments in respect of property occupied by the defendant. The value of the claim could not be ascertained without the plaintiff inspecting the premises.

Held: That an order to permit inspection by the plaintiff should be granted. Lord Redesdale:

"If the East India Co. should refuse to permit inspection they will be guilty of a contempt of court, it is an order operating on the person requiring the defendant to permit inspection, not giving authority of force or to break open the door."

Loose *v.* Williamson [1978] 1 W.L.R. 639

Facts: The plaintiff claimed by writ that the defendant was not entitled to remove shellfish from a fishery leased to the plaintiff and claimed for an injunction restraining the defendant from removing shellfish from the fishery. The plaintiff, by Notice of Motion, applied for an order that the defendant should supply his solicitor *inter alia* with the names and addresses of persons aboard certain named vessels, and the name and number of a third vessel, all of which vessels were said to be improperly taking products from the plaintiff's fisheries. The writ and Notice of Motion were *ex parte* and issued the same day. The defendant's objection to supplying the identity information submitted that *Norwich Pharmacal* and *EMI* v. *Sarwar* should be distinguished as relating to different forms of property rather than relating to fisheries.

Held: The principle set forth in *Norwich Pharmacal* was the same and there was justification for making the order sought, especially as the fisheries were in imminent danger from unlawful fishing and, further, the giving of the information can do no harm to the defendants, particularly if they are innocent of the facts alleged against them. The order was granted substantially as sought.

Manor Electronics Ltd. *v.* Dickson [1988] R.P.C. 618; *The Times*, February 8, 1990

N.B. The two cited reports arise out of the same cause but the first is concerned with Anton Piller procedure and the second the subsequent events arising out of the insolvency of the plaintiffs' and their solicitor's responsibility to the defendants.

Facts: The two plaintiff companies were of the view that former employees had conspired to pass on technical secrets of the plaintiffs to Dychem International (U.K.) Ltd. (also defendants) and that they would leave the plaintiffs' employ and join Dychem.

On October 27, 1987 Lawton J. granted an Anton Piller order which contained the usual provisions but not the requirement that the defendants invite the plaintiffs' representative to "search and seize."

The *ex parte* application contained an undertaking to issue a writ forthwith and serve as soon as issued, as well as other undertakings. The affidavits in support of the application contained allegations of the conspiracies but failed to disclose details of the plaintiffs' financial position, so as to indicate that the plaintiffs were good for any damages if the order was wrongly granted. The solicitor instructed by the plaintiffs was a very close relative of the Chief Executive of the plaintiffs.

It appears that once the order was granted it was served on the defendants, but the writ though issued on October 29 was not served until November 4. In pursuance of the order the defendants produced a large number of documents, as a result the plaintiffs returned to Lawton J. and obtained a full Anton Piller, *i.e.* with the "search and seize" provision. This was in two parts, one relating to the defendant Dychem Ltd. which ordered them to permit the plaintiffs' solicitor and one other to enter the premises, and search for and remove material. The second part related to the private dwelling of one of the defendants and provided that "a solicitor accompanied by Mr B. shall be entitled to enter the dwelling house, workshop and garage . . . "

The Anton Piller order was executed, including the "search and seize" element at both the premises.

The defendants applied to the court of the discharge of the *ex parte* orders, whilst the plaintiffs requested the injunctions to be continued. The defendants' affidavits disclosed the plaintiffs' accounts for the year ending September 30, 1986 and interim accounts as at May 1987. These showed a substantial excess of liabilities over assets and a questionable balance-sheet solvency.

Held: There were defects in the form of the *ex parte* orders as put before the judge and granted in that:

(a) the court cannot bestow on one party the right to enter premises of another. The court can only order that the defendants invite the plaintiffs' representative to come in;

(b) there was a failure on the part of the solicitor to honour the undertaking to serve the writ as soon as issued, *i.e.* forthwith;

(c) the solicitor attending the execution of the order should do so in a professional capacity, *e.g.* as an Officer of the Court, and in the present case it was unwise for the solicitor who attended the execution of the order to act as such, being a very close relative of the Chief Executive of the plaintiffs;

(d) the most serious defect was a failure to disclose the full information relating to the financial position of the plaintiffs to Lawton J. when application was made for the order.

The orders were discharged because of this failure to disclose.

There was an application by the plaintiffs for an *inter partes* injunction. This was refused and the plaintiffs withdrew their notice of motion. Thus, the action was discontinued with an order on the plaintiffs to pay defendants' costs (about £25,000).

Within a year, both plaintiffs had gone into liquidation and there was no prospect of the costs being paid. The defendants, Dychem, applied for an order that the plaintiffs' solicitor should pay the costs and the damages covered by the undertaking.

Held: The writ and exhibits were not served "forthwith" as it took six days. There was a failure by the professional advisers to enquire as to the plaintiffs' financial position, and also there was a failure to take instructions on the nature of the plaintiffs' "confidential information," to ascertain whether or not it was information that could be the subject of protection.

The court held that neither procedural breach had caused any increase in costs or wasted any or caused any extreme damage to Dychem, whose claim for costs and damages was dismissed, but to signal the seriousness of the two breaches, Dychem had to pay no more than three-quarters of the plaintiffs' solicitor's costs.

Morton-Norwich Products Inc. *v.* Intercen D.C. (No. 2) [1981] F.S.R. 337

Facts: The case is noted for its costs element only, arising out of the *Norwich Pharmacal* decision, the plaintiffs being the same plaintiffs for the purpose of this action as the plaintiffs in the *Norwich Pharmacal* decision. Action for discovery was commenced against the Commission for Customs and Excise to compel them to disclose the names of persons importing "furazolidone" into the United Kingdom in infringement of the plaintiffs' patent.

At first instance, the plaintiffs were ordered to pay the Customs legal costs. In the Court of Appeal and the House of Lords there was no order as to costs. In the action against United Chemicals, the plaintiffs sought to recover their own costs and those of the Customs so far as they had to pay them.

Held: The plaintiffs were entitled to recover the costs of the discovery action, as a plaintiff was entitled to ensure, as far as he could, that his information was in order before starting the substantive action. Thus the defence that the information would have come to light in the normal course of the legal process does not avail the defendants when, as in this case, their conduct was evasive and gave good cause for suspicion of their conduct.

Norwich Pharmacal Co. *v.* Commissioners for Customs and Excise [1974] A.C. 133; [1973] 3 W.L.R. 164

Facts: The Commissioners for Customs and Excise published information that a chemical compound "furazolidone" had been

imported into the United Kingdom. Norwich Pharmacal Co.
owned a patent which claimed furazolidone as their invention.
No licences had been granted and the furazolidone reported to
have been imported was likely to infringe the patent. The
Customs authorities knew the names of the importers but refused
to disclose them to Norwich Pharmacal, claiming they were
prohibited by law and it was against the public interest. Norwich
Pharmacal sought an order for discovery of the names and
addresses of the importers.

At first instance ([1972] 1 All E.R. 972), the order was
granted, but was reversed on appeal ([1972] 3 All E.R. 813), the
court holding that an action for discovery could only succeed, if
at all, where the plaintiff has a cause of action against the
defendant (other than that for discovery). The House of Lords
allowed the appeal and the order for discovery, as sought, was
made.

Held: The action for discovery will be granted in exceptional
circumstances where, through no fault of his own, a person
becomes involved in the tortious acts of others so as to facilitate
their wrongdoings. While he may incur no personal liability, he is
under a duty to assist the person wronged by giving him full
information and disclosing the identity of the wrongdoers.

Orr *v.* Diaper [1876] 4 Ch.D. 92

Facts: Diaper, a forwarding agent, shipped goods bearing
counterfeits of the plaintiff's tickets and infringing his
trademarks. The plaintiff asked for names and addresses of
consignors which the defendant refused to give. In an action for
Discovery for the information, the defendant pleaded that
discovery was not obtainable against him, as he neither would be,
nor was intended to be, party to an action.

Held: It was ordered that the information should be given by
the defendant because the plaintiff did not know, and could not
otherwise discover, who the persons were who had invaded his
rights.

Paterson *v.* Chadwick [1974] 1 W.L.R. 890

Facts: The plaintiff alleged that she had suffered injuries as a
result of negligent dental treatment at a hospital. She instructed
solicitors to pursue her claim but they failed to institute
proceedings and the claim became statute barred. The plaintiff
then instructed other solicitors to claim against the first solicitor
for damages for breach of contract or duty. A writ was issued and
pleadings exchanged and it became necessary for the new
solicitors to discover the hospital records relating to the plaintiff's
injury. Application was made under the equivalent section 34(2)
of the SCA 1981 (section 32(1) Administration of Justice Act
1970) for an order for the hospital authorities to produce the
patient's records.

Held: Though the hospital authorities argued that they were not a party to any proceedings, and the proceedings in any event were for breach of contract against solicitors and not a claim in respect of personal injuries, the words "in respect of personal injuries" in section 34(1) conveyed some connection or relation between the plaintiff's claim and the personal injuries that she had sustained, that is, a claim against her ex-solicitors. As the plaintiff had to prove her injuries, else the claim against the ex-solicitor would fail, there was a clear and firm connection in relation to her claim against the solicitors and her personal injuries.

Piver (L.T.) Sàrl v. S. & J. Perfume Co. [1987] F.S.R. 159

Facts: When executing an Anton Piller order on behalf of one client **P**, a private investigator **L** came to the conclusion that the defendants were counterfeiting goods of another client **R**. He removed (technically improperly) an empty perfume box and later obtained a similar box by legitimate means. The court granted a second Anton Piller order in respect of **R** and the private investigator made a full declaration in his affidavit as to how he obtained the boxes. The improper method of obtaining the first was expressly emphasised to the court by **R**'s counsel. The order was granted and executed and 17,000 counterfeit units were seized.

The defendants sought an injunction to restrain the plaintiffs **R**, their solicitors, the firm of private investigators and the investigator who took the first box, from dealing in any way with the goods seized not relating to **P**'s action. If the injunction had been granted, this would have prevented **R**'s actions from proceeding.

Held: In the circumstances of the case, the injunction would be refused. The court found that the box taken by the investigator was of negligible value, but it would have been wrong if anything of value had been taken, such as a bottle of perfume, even if in infringement of **R**'s rights.

Comment: The court appeared to be influenced by the fact that the firm of investigators Carratu Ltd. are well known and of high repute and that the affidavit of the investigator made full disclosure of what happened. The judge seemed inclined to the view that if the investigator was in contempt of court (by taking the box) his act of contempt prevented the defendants engaging in a major fraud.

Rank Film Distributors v. Video Information Centre [1982] A.C. 380; [1981] 2 W.L.R. 668

Facts: The plaintiffs owned copyright in certain cinema films. They obtained an Anton Piller order in the usual form, which was granted. The defendants applied to have the order discharged or varied on the ground *inter alia* that by disclosure documents and answering the interrogations, the defendants might expose themselves to criminal proceedings.

Held: (In the House of Lords). It was found that the defendants were entitled to rely on the privilege against self-incrimination since if they complied with orders of the nature of those granted there was a real and appreciable risk of criminal proceedings. In respect of the orders requiring the defendants to allow access to premises for the purpose of search and seizure of illicit copy films and allowing them to be removed with safe custody, there was jurisdiction to make the order and the privilege against self-incrimination had no application.

N.B. The privilege allowed in this case was removed in respect of infringement of intellectual property rights or for passing off, or proceedings brought to prevent any apprehended infringement of such rights, or proceedings brought to obtain disclosure of information relating to any infringement of such rights, by the Supreme Court Act 1981, section 72.

R.C.A. Corporation *v.* Reddingtons Rare Records [1974] 1 W.L.R. 1445

Facts: The plaintiff sought by Motion an injunction to restrain infringement of copyright by the defendants who were selling pirated copies of pop music. Part of the proposed order, along with the injunction, contained a provision that the defendants should, by affidavit, set forth the names and addresses of all persons or companies responsible for supplying the defendants, and whom the defendants had supplied with infringing copies.

Held: The question was whether the order should be granted on Motion and the court answered in the affirmative.

Refson & Co. *v.* Saggers; Exclusivity Horlogere *v.* Peoples Jewellers; Whittaker *v.* Jolley [1984] 1 W.L.R. 1025

Facts: Each of the three plaintiffs applied by *ex parte* motion to be granted injunctions restraining each of the three defendants from disposing of certain moneys. Counsel gave undertakings in two cases, on behalf of the plaintiffs, to issue the writs forthwith and in the third case as soon as was reasonably practicable.

In the *Refson* case, the writ was issued 16 days after the undertaking; in *Horlogere*'s, 18 days; and in *Whittaker*'s, 19 days after the injunctions were granted as a matter of emergency. One injunction was granted on December 19 and the other two on December 22.

The court, of its own volition, noting the writs were not issued, required the several solicitors for the plaintiffs to attend with counsel and explain an apparent breach of the undertakings. The solicitors sought adjournment to file evidence which was granted and subsequently counsel addressed the court.

Held: In each case, the plaintiff personally was not to blame, they were relying on their solicitors, and in the circumstances, the court, save in one case in which the costs of the plaintiff were disallowed, warned the profession of the consequences of breaching an undertaking. (The costs issue in two cases was not relevant as the parties had settled).

The court issued directions as to the practice for the future to the effect that when an undertaking was given to issue a writ forthwith (as soon as reasonably practicable was held to mean "forthwith" and "forthwith" should be used) then it should be so issued, and failure to do so was a serious breach of the undertaking given to the court. While solicitors had a particular responsibility as officers of the court, counsel should advise them appropriately.

Rogers (Jeffrey) Knitwear Productions v. Vinola (Knitwear) Manufacturing Co. [1985] F.S.R. 184

Facts: An Anton Piller order was sought and granted in respect of infringement of copyright. The defendants applied to have the order discharged on the grounds that it should never have been made. The plaintiffs, in seeking an Anton Piller order, failed to make a full disclosure to the court on the credit rating of the defendants. Insufficient investigation was made of the Dun & Bradstreet report on the defendant, and of the likelihood that the defendants might dispose of evidence. The court was also misled as to the nature of the defendants' business, that is supplying wholesalers and not market traders.

Held: The judge found the affidavit evidence unsatisfactory, that there had not been full disclosure and that the order should never have been made. The order was discharged, the costs of the motion were costs in the cause, and the costs to discharge the Anton Piller order were payable by the plaintiffs in any event on a common fund basis. Leave was granted to proceed on an inquiry as to damages in respect of the undertaking given by the plaintiff in the event the order should not have been granted.

Salford Plastics v. Greene [1986] 11 E.I.P.R.D. 197

Facts: The plaintiffs manufactured extruded plastic products and fearing that the first defendant (a former employee) would misuse confidential information, applied for an Anton Piller order in the customary form. The order was given *inter alia* on an undertaking by the plaintiffs to file under oath their last draft and audited accounts so that the court could judge if they were in a position to pay damages if the order was wrongly granted.

The defendants applied to have the order discharged on the grounds that the accounts were not made available. There had been technical reasons why this was not possible and the court

ordered the affidavit and accounts to be served on the defendants'
solicitor within 28 days of delivery of the accounts. On May 15
the defendants obtained an order that the affidavit and accounts
should be made and filed before June 12. The plaintiffs failed to
serve the accounts and the defendants applied to discharge the
order but the accounts were delivered on July 8, the day of the
hearing.

Held: The court had a discretion to discharge the injunction
and though in this case it was deplorable that the commercial
interest had been treated as more important than compliance
with a court order, in the circumstances (the court had been
satisfied earlier that the plaintiffs were good for any damages),
the order would not be discharged but the plaintiff should pay to
the defendants costs of the motion up to July 8.

Shaw *v.* Vauxhall Motors [1974] 1 W.L.R. 1035

Facts: The plaintiff alleged that he had suffered injuries at
work through a defective truck operated by his employers. His
legal adviser took the view that, in order to assess the chances of
success in the action, it was necessary to see the employer's
records relating to the maintenance of the truck. If these showed
the truck was in good condition and properly maintained, the
legal adviser would feel unable to recommend the legal aid fund
to continue the proceedings. The employer declined to disclose
the records prior to the action being commenced. The plaintiff
applied for discovery under section 31 of the Administration of
Justice Act 1970 (now SCA 1981, section 34).

Held: The legal adviser took the view that if the records
disclosed that the truck was properly maintained and in good
condition, the claim would no longer be proceeded with, and this
would be a great saving in costs. Accordingly the order for
discovery was granted.

T.D.K. Tape Distributors (U.K.) *v.* Videochoice [1986] 1 W.L.R. 141

Facts: In 1982 the plaintiff obtained an order in the Mareva
form against the defendants, whereby *inter alia* the fourth
defendant was restrained until further order from disposing of or
dealing with any of his assets or any interest which he might have
in such assets within the jurisdiction except so far as they
exceeded the sum of £601,524.73, save for £100 per week whch
might be used for living expenses. A second order relating to the
fourth defendant's failure to comply with the first order was also
made in 1982.
    At the material time, the plaintiff owned a dwelling-house
jointly with his wife, being subject to an endowment policy

mortgage, which was assigned to the mortgagees as security for a loan which enabled the fourth defendant to purchase the dwelling-house. The plaintiff obtained a judgment in default against the fourth defendant and in enforcement of the order a charging order was made against the house.

In filing his affidavit of assets, the fourth defendant negligently failed to disclose that the house was subject to an endowment policy mortgage. Subsequently the wife died, leaving the fourth defendant as sole owner of the house. The mortgage was redeemed (the policy apparently surrendered) and a balance of £4,422 was paid under the policy to the fourth defendant's solicitors, which was paid into his solicitors' client account. The fourth defendant then agreed with the solicitor that it should be used (and it was used) to meet the costs of his defence to a criminal charge.

The plaintiff by motion sought an order that the fourth defendant be fined or such order as might be made in respect of his contempt of court in failing to comply with the order, whereby he was restrained from dealing with his assets save for £100 per week for his expenses, and also for failing to disclose his assets, *i.e.* the insurance policy. The plaintiff sought leave to serve a writ of sequestration against the fourth defendant's solicitors and, separately, the named solicitor acting for the fourth defendant with regard to their contempt in disobeying the Mareva injunction, or in aiding and abetting the fourth defendant to do so.

Held: The endowment policy was an asset that existed when the Mareva order was made and was subject to the terms of the order. It should have been disclosed in the fourth defendant's affidavit of assets. Since the expenditure of money by the fourth defendant from the realisation of the assets was not living expenses excluded from the injunction, the money had been spent contrary to the order. The fourth defendant was in contempt for failure to disclose and improper usage of the money, as also was the solicitor who advised, but no finding was made against the partners of the firm of solicitors since they had taken reasonable care to employ a competent solicitor.

The responsibility of the fourth defendant was found to be a technical fault as he was advised and acted throughout on the advice of his solicitor when dealing with the disclosure of assets and dealing with the money.

> "From the moment they received the money . . . the solicitors went seriously wrong. With any reasonable care they ought to have been put on guard by the existence of the order, which they knew about, and the receipt of a fairly substantial amount of money. The fact that (the solicitor) was dealing with the criminal matter and therefore . . . lost sight of the civil action and did not apply his mind to it is, in my judgment, no defence to this motion, although it clearly will mitigate the penalty." Shinner J. at p. 146.

The solicitor and fourth defendant were ordered to pay the costs of the plaintiff on a common fund basis and the sum of £4,422.98 was paid to the plaintiff's solicitors.

Television Broadcasts v. Mandarin Video Holdings Sdn. Bhd. [1984] F.S.R. 111

The plaintiff's Hong Kong film-producing companies and also their licensees commenced proceedings concerning video tapes and obtained an Anton Piller order in the High Court in Malaysia (Commercial Division). The defendants applied to have the order discharged on several grounds but this was refused; see the reasoned judgment of Chan J. at p. 114.

Thermax v. Schott Industrial Glass [1981] F.S.R. 289

Facts: The plaintiffs obtained an Anton Piller order in respect of alleged infringement of their rights. The defendants were a company run by three former directors of the plaintiffs, and 30 ex-employees of the plaintiffs were engaged by the defendants. There was a pending action against the former directors for *inter alia* taking with them confidential information which they were using to establish the defendants' business. There was evidence that the defendants had copied a design of the plaintiffs who had consequently lost business. There was also evidence from the plaintiffs that could lead one to suspect that the three former directors were dishonest. When the Anton Piller order was served, the defendants agreed to abide by the negative injunction but declined to allow the search and seizure operation, and said they would apply to the court to have the order discharged. The grounds for discharge were that the order had been made without full disclosure of the facts, and on the evidence given by the defendants, there was failure to disclose the following facts.

The defendants were a wholly-owned subsidiary of a company in Mainz which was part of the Carl Zeiss Foundation which had an annual turnover exceeding a billion marks. The directors of the defendants were largely German nationals. The Mainz Company had originally done business with the plaintiffs but, owing to disagreements, had set up the defendants' company, which was not just the vehicle of the former directors. Further in the course of the pending action, the plaintiffs had suggested to the defendants' solicitors that they should inspect the defendants' premises, but this the defendants had refused to allow on the grounds that it could constitute a roving commission to look into the business of the defendants.

In addition, the plaintiffs' solicitors had, in earlier correspondence, accepted that there was confidential work being carried out by the defendants at their premises.

Held: The matter as to ownership of the defendants should have been disclosed because of the presumption that a large industrial group will organise its affairs honestly and competently. Also the matter of the technology work should have been disclosed; likewise the fact that the defendants had already declined to admit the plaintiffs to their premises. The order was discharged with costs.

Universal City Studios Inc. *v.* Mukhtar & Sons [1976] 1 W.L.R. 568

Facts: T-Shirts with a "Jaws" insignia were being sold in infringement of the plaintiffs' rights. The market in these garments was transient depending on the popularity of the "Jaws" films.

The original seller, on being challenged by **A**, sold them to **B** and told the plaintiffs that they had had only a few shirts and had stopped selling them. **B** gave the same answer to the plaintiffs, having passed the shirts to **C**. The plaintiffs, in applying for an Anton Piller order, were unable to show that there was a real possibility of the defendants **C** destroying or removing the garments.

Held: In granting the order, the court took the view that there was a real possibility that the plaintiffs' fear as to destruction or removal of evidence would be realised.

Upmann *v.* Elkan [1871] 7 Ch.App. 130

Facts: Elkan, forwarding agent received cigars to distribute to named persons. The plaintiff learned the cigars were packed in boxes, the appearance of which infringed the plaintiff's trademark. In subsequent injunction proceedings, the defendant voluntarily gave the plaintiff the names and addresses of parties supplying and receiving the cigars. The court held that the defendant was not privy to the infringement, and the dispute became one of costs. To resolve this, the court had to decide the right and duties of the parties on the basis that the defendant had no knowledge of the matter until informed by the plaintiff.

Held: It was the duty of the defendant to inform the plaintiff of the identity of the persons concerned as soon as they were made aware of the infringement and information requested.

VDU Installations Ltd. *v.* Integrated Computer Systems & Cybernetics Ltd., *The Times*, August 13, 1988

The plaintiffs applied and obtained on April 28, 1988, an Anton Piller order in the conventional form. The draft affidavit in support was sworn by a Director of VDU. In the affidavit there was reference to material which it was desired to seize and search at the defendants' premises.

The solicitor responsible for execution of the order obtained a copy of it but found the draft affidavit missing. He arranged for it to be faxed to his firm's branch office on the next day when he intended to execute the order. It did not arrive and at 8.00a.m. the solicitor attended the defendants' premises and attempted to explain what he thought it contained. He said the order gave him wide power of search and he and some of the plaintiffs' employees removed material not covered by the order.

On May 17, the defendants issued a motion to have the solicitor in charge of the execution to be committed to prison for contempt and that the assets of the plaintiffs and the solicitor be sequestrated. The grounds for contempt were:

(a) the execution of the order was in breach of the undertakings given by the plaintiffs' solicitor to explain the order properly, and also for removing items not covered by it;
(b) failure to issue the writ until May 4; and
(c) alleged improper use of information obtained.

Held: The solicitor was guilty of contempt, the judge observing that the solicitor preferred the urgency of his client's business to his duty to the court which was to explain the Anton Piller order to the defendants' representative in a fair and accurate manner and to see they were not misled. Knox J., held that the conduct of the solicitor amounted to negligence. His action allowed the plaintiffs' employees to see papers of the defendants which were not covered by the order.

The report does not give the court's finding on the delayed issue of the writ (but see *Manor Electronics* v. *Dickson*). The misuse of the information by the plaintiffs, whilst serious, was not considered to be of the gravest nature.

The plaintiffs were ordered to pay the costs of the defendants on an indemnity basis, but no financial penalty was imposed on the solicitor or the plaintiffs. It is probable that the solicitor reimbursed the plaintiffs.

W.E.A. Records *v.* Visions Channel 4 [1983] 1 W.L.R. 721

Facts: The plaintiffs marketed video cassettes of popular films of which they owned or were licensees of the copyright. They found that counterfeit products in infringement of their rights were being sold. As the matter was urgent, an Anton Piller order was applied for by counsel armed with only a draft writ and instructions as to the nature and results of plaintiffs' inquiries. No affidavit evidence was produced and counsel did not have a draft but an unsworn affidavit. Counsel informed the judge of matters which were thought to be so confidential that it was felt that they could not be revealed to the defendants. The order was granted in the usual form but subject to the affidavits being filed within 48 hours. The defendants, on receipt of the order, complied with it.

Later, the defendants moved to discharge the order and the judge suggested that a transcript of counsel's statement in the *ex parte* proceedings be made available to defence counsel alone. The matter came before another judge and the defendants' solicitor and counsel were allowed a transcript of the first proceedings. Before completing his submission, counsel for both parties indicated that whatever the court decided, there would be an appeal. The judge made no order but gave leave to appeal. The defendants appealed against the original order in the Court of Appeal.

Held: Since the original Anton Piller order had been executed and no judge had made a definitive order on a review of the provisional *ex parte* order, it was inappropriate for the Court of Appeal to entertain an appeal from the provisional order. Information should not be given to a judge on an *ex parte* application which cannot later be revealed to the party affected by the application. It was held that if defendants against whom an Anton Piller order is made *ex parte* refuse immediate compliance they do so at their peril, and that solicitors, as officers of the court, are to be treated in the same way as counsel.

If, following the grant of an Anton Piller order, the evidence shows that the grant was justified, the fact that the evidence on the *ex parte* application was not as strong as it ultimately becomes does not, in the absence of *mala fides* or of some material non-disclosure, provide a ground for challenging the order.

Yousif *v.* Salama [1980] 1 W.L.R. 1540

Facts: The plaintiff had a claim for breach of contract against the defendant and sought an Anton Piller order with respect to two files and a desk diary which the plaintiff suspected might be destroyed prior to the trial of his contractual claim. The only evidence of intention to destroy the documents was the alleged forgery of a cheque by the defendant.

Held: (Court of Appeal, Donaldson L.J. dissenting). The court granted the order but on the basis that as the defendant would have to produce them in due course in any event it did no harm to grant the Anton Piller order.

Z. *v.* A–Z and AA–LL [1982] Q.B. 558; [1982] 2 W.L.R. 288

Facts: The parties to the case were concealed by letters of the alphabet. Lord Denning M.R. in his judgment uses the imaginary country of Ruritania to set out the facts, which are summarised below.

A large company had a head office in Ruritania, a main bank account in Hentzau, Ruritania and a London office. Conspirators decided to defraud the Ruritania company, and telex and cables purporting to come from the company's head office to its bank in Hentzau were sent authorising the transfer of funds to London, to be paid to suppliers of goods. The telex and cables were forged, no goods were supplied and the company was defrauded of about £2,000,000. When the fraud was discovered, the Ruritania company took steps to trace the bank accounts to which the money had gone and to stop any dealings before the conspirators knew the fraud had been discovered. The matter was so urgent that the plaintiffs applied to the commercial judge before issuing a writ seeking orders against any who might be a party to the fraud, as well as those innocently mixed up in the transaction, such as estate agents, banks or solicitors.

The plaintiffs did not know who the defendants should be,

so named 36 who were required by the order at first instance to stop dealing in certain assets purporting to be of or derived from the defendants. The plaintiffs, following the grant of an Anton Piller/Mareva order, issued a writ against the 36; against numbers 1 to 17 there was an allegation of conspiracy to defraud, and against numbers 18 to 36 there was sought an order for specific discovery and interrogatories. Injunctions were served on all 36 to preserve the subject-matter of the action, *i.e.* the action to recover the £2,000,000.

By reason of the combined orders, the Ruritania company recovered about £1,000,000 and, following a settlement, a good deal of the balance. Five clearing banks kept the action alive by appealing against the orders on them as they wished to know the position of innocent third parties like themselves when served with notice of a Mareva-type injunction. It was not a true Mareva, as in the case the banks were named as defendants, whereas in the usual type of Mareva order they would be named, if known, as holders of accounts of the defendants.

Lord Denning in his judgment set out the problems facing third parties, especially banks. A plaintiff obtains a Mareva injunction and notifies the bank holding the defendant's account that it must not dispose of the defendant's assets, and the account is frozen. The question arises as to what principle suggests that the bank, not being a party to the action, is justified in freezing the account?

Held: As soon as the order is made it operates *in rem* on anyone having notice of it—as with a ship arrested under the Admiralty procedure. If the bank or a third party knowing of the order disposes of any assets identified in the order, such party would be in contempt of court. If the bank was sued by the customer for dishonouring a cheque, their defence would be that to honour it would be an illegal action.

INDEX